CM

International Political Risk Management

Exploring New Frontiers

D1563581

International Political Risk Management

Exploring New Frontiers

Theodore H. Moran, Editor

The World Bank
Washington, D.C.

Cover design by Ultra Designs, Inc.

Library of Congress Cataloging-in-Publication Data has been applied for.

Contents

Part Five   Cooperation, Competition, and the "Science of Pricing" in the Political Risk Insurance Marketplace

Appendixes

Preface

This "Working Papers" volume originated in a symposium on International Political Risk Management held on April 11, 2000, under the joint auspices of the Multilateral Investment Guarantee Agency of the World Bank Group and the Karl F. Landegger Program in International Business Diplomacy at the School of Foreign Service, Georgetown University.

The objective of the Multilateral Investment Guarantee Agency (MIGA) is to facilitate the flow of foreign direct investment to developing and transition countries by alleviating investors' concerns about non-commercial risks. MIGA has always pursued this objective in multiple ways. In addition to providing political risk insurance to investors and offering assistance in investment promotion to host countries, MIGA has selectively sponsored research on and analysis of the problems and challenges in managing political risk. This "Working Papers" volume is a part of these larger endeavors.

The Karl F. Landegger Program in International Business Diplomacy sponsors teaching and research at the intersection of international corporate strategy, public policy, and the conduct of business-government relations. The examination of tools and techniques for investors to manage international political risk and of associated impacts on the development prospects for host countries, ranks high on the agenda of the Landegger Program.

The purpose of this volume is to present the ideas and experiences of some of the most distinguished practitioners from the investor, financial, and investment insurance communities in the world today. As the reader will see, many of the issues that arise are controversial and do not lend themselves to a single set of conclusions. This has been entitled a "Working Papers" volume precisely because of the desire to provoke debate and discussion without waiting for a firm consensus to emerge.

To assist the reader, the editor of this volume, Dr. Theodore H. Moran, has provided a brief overview to introduce each of the separate topics, without passing judgment on the merits of the various positions that emerge in the course of the discussion.

This is the second symposium sponsored under the auspices of the Multilateral Investment Guarantee Agency and the Karl F. Landegger Program. Information about the book that resulted from the first symposium, in 1998, is provided in an appendix to this volume.

Our shared objective is to promote productive foreign direct investment in ways that enhance the growth and welfare of developing countries. Our common hope is that this volume contributes to that objective.

Gerald T. West
Multilateral Investment
Guarantee Agency
The World Bank Group

Theodore H. Moran
School of Foreign Service
Georgetown University

BK Title: NIA

Introduction

Motomichi Ikawa
Executive Vice President
Multilateral Investment Guarantee Agency

It is my great pleasure to introduce this *Working Paper* volume on "International Political Risk Management: Exploring New Frontiers." The papers and commentary grow out of the 2000 MIGA–Georgetown University Symposium on International Political Risk Management, held at the World Bank on April 11, 2000, to address important pending issues that come to light at the intersection where insurers, investors, and financiers meet.

It is particularly important to point out that the original session, upon which this volume is based, was a symposium and not a conference. As many readers will be aware, the word "symposium" is Greek in origin. It referred to a friendly gathering of people coming together to discuss a topic of mutual interest. Our goal is to report on a discussion and dialogue among some of the most important and respected people in the political risk management field.

With the global financial crisis largely behind us, foreign direct investment flows to developing countries have begun to pick up. In this environment, demand for political risk insurance has been increasing rapidly, and is likely to continue to grow further in the coming years. Faced with the possibility or the prospect of sudden, recurring financial crises, many investors and lenders will continue to actively seek political risk insurance for their long-term investments. According to an anonymous survey of 152 investors conducted recently by MIGA, approximately 50 percent expressed the view that political risk is *more* of a concern today than five years ago, while one-third of them indicated no change. Indeed, despite a

spectacular growth of 30 to 40 percent per annum in the private
political risk insurance market in the past two years (to the extent
that private insurers now have more than 50 percent of the political
risk investment insurance market), only a small percentage of foreign direct investment is covered by political risk insurance from
any source. This is partly because some investors choose to use alternative risk mitigation instruments. Overall, considerable unmet
demand still exists for projects in such countries as Brazil, Turkey,
and Russia; for complex projects in the infrastructure sector; and
for projects in the poorest countries. MIGA, by filling a portion of
this unmet demand, strives to cooperate with, and complement,
national and private insurers.

In pursuit of our mandate, we also seek to give access to those
investors who often have the greatest difficulty obtaining political
risk insurance. These include small and medium-size enterprises
and investors from developing countries who usually lack access to
the national insurance providers available in most Organization for
Economic Co-operation and Development (OECD) countries. As a
developmental agency within the World Bank Group, MIGA makes
its best efforts to reduce poverty by contributing to enlarging and
deepening the political risk insurance market on a global level.

For the last decade, some traditional forms of political risk have
seemed to be on the wane; the threat of nationalization and expropriation has declined. However, currency transfer and war and civil
disturbance remain, while risks of intervention by governments in
the operation of private investments in the infrastructure sector and
concerns about breach of contractual obligations have increased.
Privatization and extensive involvement of the private sector in infrastructure projects have created new challenges for political risk
managers. These are some of the central topics of today's symposium.

At MIGA, the proportion of the infrastructure sector in the guarantee portfolio has increased from 3 percent in fiscal 1993 to about
25 percent in fiscal 2000. The risks for MIGA have also increased.
The first claim in MIGA's 10-plus years of operations was filed in
the power sector. So far, apart from a dozen cases of mediation activities in which MIGA's guarantee was not involved, MIGA has
dealt with five investment disputes that would have developed into
a claim situation without some claim-avoidance activities. All five
cases were projects in the infrastructure sector.

Despite this, in response to the growing market demand for coverage of specific contractual obligations by the host government in

a more complex infrastructure sector, MIGA has recently resumed offering breach of contract coverage under certain conditions. As more infrastructure projects involve sub-sovereign entities as parties to contractual obligations, it has become harder for political risk insurers and investors to reach an agreement on who should bear which risks. MIGA has recently offered breach of contract coverage that involved a subsovereign entity, but it was a painful internal process to reach a final decision.

Given the rapid growth of the political risk insurance market, driven by private insurers and the changing needs of investors, MIGA is trying to redefine its unique and distinctive role as a multilateral insurer in the political risk investment insurance market. In our current review of the next five years, we are working to establish a multi-niche strategy.

MIGA tries to be at the innovative edge in finding ways to mitigate political risk. A prime example of MIGA's approach is our issuance of coverage to BCP (owned by BellSouth and the Safra Group) in Brazil last month, which involves our cooperative underwriting program (CUP), that is equivalent to the International Finance Corporation's (IFC's) B-loan program. In this $230 million exposure — MIGA's largest to date — $175 million was placed under the CUP program, with five different Lloyds' syndicates (Brockbank, ACE Global Markets, SJ Catlin, H. H. Hayward, and Cox Insurance Holdings) and two private insurers (Unistrat and Chubb & Sons). We are particularly pleased that this involves the addition of four new private insurers to the CUP: Catlin, Cox, Hayward, and Unistrat. Additionally, the deal involved coinsurance with another private insurer (AIG) and two national insurers [the Overseas Private Investment Corporation (OPIC) and the Export Development Corporation (EDC)]. This project vividly illustrates how different insurers can cooperate, leveraging their respective comparative advantages, to meet an investor's need for coverage on a large, complex project in a high-demand market. This year should see the CUP start to move gradually into the mainstream of MIGA's activities, and it will be used selectively for projects in countries where capacity in the political risk insurance market is limited or in countries where mobilization of private capacity would be difficult without the involvement of a multilateral insurer.

Another example of our innovative approach is multicountry coverage. The growing interconnectedness of the world economy has led to a steadily increasing number of multicountry projects, be it in Africa, the Caspian region, or South America, especially in the energy sector. These projects often involve large amounts of capital and are particularly sensitive, politically and environmentally, and pose a new challenge for political risk insurers. In fiscal 1999, MIGA signed guarantee contracts for two gas pipeline projects in Latin America with multicountry coverage.

I have highlighted only a few of the issues that are included in this volume. The goal here is to present a broad agenda of topics that are vital in determining how political risks should be managed in the future. They are important for all of us, whether private or public insurers, brokers, or managers of political risk.

PART ONE

The Multiple Pledge-of-Shares Problem: Overview

Theodore H. Moran, Editor

Political risk insurers, both public and private, provide expro-priation coverage to investors on the assumption that if the insurers are required to pay compensation, they will then have a legal basis to pursue recovery against the host government. To provide such a legal basis, the insurers typically require that the equity investor turn over its shares, free and clear of liens, as a condition of receiving compensation. The insurers are thus in a position to make a claim against the host. Multi-lateral and national political risk insurers usually have formal agreements with developing countries that the latter will honor claims of this kind.

Lenders that provide project finance support to these same investors generally require, at the same time, that all assets associated with a given project, including equity shares, be pledged as collateral for the loans. Possession of the shares may enable the lenders to make their own claim against the host, or they may be sold as part of liquidating the project company's assets.

With the growing use of project finance to raise capital for major private investments in the developing countries, this leads to a dilemma: both insurers and lenders would like to require that the shares of the project be pledged to them in the event of an expropriation.

This has generated repeated tugs of war, according to **Kenneth Hansen of Chadbourne & Parke, LLP**, on a deal-by-deal basis, between project lenders and political risk insurers. Despite much time and effort, no easy way out of this dilemma has emerged. The result is that some projects have had to proceed without the benefits of political risk insurance and (while no exact data are available) other projects have doubtlessly been delayed or cancelled.

In March 2000, however, two major contenders, the U.S. Export-Import Bank (Ex-Im) and the U.S. Overseas Private Investment Corporation (OPIC), both of which are U.S. government agencies, reached a "Joint Claims Agreement" that represents what Hansen calls "a little progress." It is not entirely clear, however, to what extent the approach embodied in this Agreement may help point the way to other parties to this dilemma.

The Ex-Im/OPIC Agreement was fashioned around the principle that, in the event of an expropriation, the two agencies would cooperate to maximize their joint recovery, with pro rata sharing of the proceeds of any settlement in proportion to the relative exposure of each. The Agreement includes additional understandings about how to perfect the insurance claim, how to allocate expenses, and other matters.

While this may offer some insights for other lenders and insurers, there are numerous complications and difficulties, according to Hansen, that may prevent smooth progress in the same direction. Ex-Im and OPIC are part of the same fiscal family, for example, whereas most major infrastructure projects involve multiple commercial and official lenders and political risk insurers. This complicates formulation of a common approach for recovery and division of potential proceeds. Even the principal of joining forces to optimize recovery may founder on the objection that equity claims be subordinated to the debt claims. At the same time, however, the adoption of a cooperative approach between project lenders and political risk insurers would provide relief to some of the major up-front disputes that impede project financings and speed the process of bringing the projects to fruition.

In dealing with the multiple pledge-of-shares problem, **OPIC**, according to **Julie Martin**, has worked out solutions on a case-by-case basis, both with multilateral lending agencies such as the International Finance Corporation (IFC) of the World Bank Group and the European Bank for Reconstruction and Development (EBRD) and with bilateral export finance agencies such as Ex-Im and the Nederlandsche Ciediet-verzekering Maatschappij (NCM). From this process come several observations.

First, it is more efficient to try to agree on general principles rather than work out all the details in advance. When this is successful, the agreements have been as short as a page and a half. The temptation to explore every possibility has led, by contrast, to documents of 30 pages.

Second, to be successful, all parties must want to reach a solution and be willing to compromise toward this objective. In particular, the sponsors themselves must be involved in this process, rather than leaving the outcome to the interaction between the lenders and the insurers.

Third, in OPIC's view, a narrow focus on pledge of shares has given way to a broader discussion of the assignment of rights to anything representing a portion of the economic value of the project. This might include a pro rata portion of an arbitral award rather than shares per se.

Fourth, in addition to agreeing that the parties will work together to maximize recoveries, they should also agree that they will not compromise each other's interests in holding the host government responsible for violation of international law with respect to both equity and debt.

Some proposals for practical solutions in recent years have included the following examples. Commercial lenders can obtain political risk insurance themselves so that they do not have to rely on pledged shares for recovery. Alternatively, lenders might agree to release their lien on shares in return for an increase in the pricing to the borrower. Also, lenders could be willing to release shares pledged to them in return for a portion of any insurance proceeds from a claim. Lenders might agree to observe a "standstill period" or to "suspend" their lien on shares while insurers pursue resolution, perhaps requiring the latter to deposit the proceeds in escrow pending a decision whether to pursue a parallel claim. Finally, multilateral lenders might release their liens on the shares, allowing official insurers to pay claims to insured equity investors. The official insurers and the multilateral lenders could then make simultaneous claims on the host government, contractually agreeing to share whatever compensation they obtained on a pro rata basis. The presentation of case studies from OPIC's experience helps illustrate some of the strengths and weaknesses in each approach.

Anne Predieri of Banc of America Securities endorses the proposition that the challenge in the multiple pledge-of-share issue is to identify practical business solutions to otherwise seemingly intractable problems. In some cases, she notes, uncovered commercial lenders have been willing to release a proportionate number of shares to effect a claim by covered lenders. In other cases, commercial lenders have been willing to release shares to perfect an equity claim. In both cases, they have determined that they have the best chance to maximize recovery by cooperating with a multilateral agency charged with seeking remedy.

When recovery is sought through restructuring the project rather than through demanding a separate payment, moreover, the project's debt (including uncovered commercial debt) must still be serviced by the operating company, even if an insurer has taken over ownership of the company. Government off-take contracts, Predieri points out, may more likely involve renegotiation rather than a traditional expropriation and confiscation.

To arrive at a "practical" resolution, it is probably advantageous, Predieri suggests, for investors and lenders to discuss the possible remedy scenarios at the outset, including the advisability of expropriation insurance coverage, to arrive at a predetermined allocation of risks prior to the moment when lawyers for all parties are sitting at a table trying to draw up all the documents.

The Multiple Pledge-of-Shares Problem: Report of a Little Progress

Kenneth Hansen
Partner
Chadbourne & Parke, LLP

Among the more intractable challenges in structuring and closing infrastructure project financings in emerging markets has been the tug-of-war between project lenders and political risk insurers (of equity) for control of project shares in the event of an expropriation. After years of protracted deal-by-deal negotiations, the Export-Import Bank of the United States (Ex-Im) and the Overseas Private Investment Corporation (OPIC), two U.S. government agencies that have been principal supporters of U.S. businesses active in emerging market infrastructure projects, reached an accord with respect to this issue. The programmatic clash over rights to project company shares continues, however, among other bilateral and multilateral agencies, commercial lenders, and insurers and even with OPIC or Ex-Im when other lenders or insurers are involved in a financing.

The Problem

The last decade has seen explosive growth of private business participation in the development and operation of infrastructure in emerging markets. A project developer typically seeks to leverage its equity investment with significant project debt to be provided on a limited recourse basis, a so-called "project financing." A core piece of the collateral package required by project lenders to secure project debt is often a lien on the shares of stock that represent the developer's equity investment.

In the challenging emerging markets where many of these projects have been undertaken, many project sponsors seek political risk insurance on their equity investments. Under the terms of typical expropriation coverage, the insured investor must assign to the insurer its *unencumbered* shares in the expropriated company in order to receive compensation. This traditional provision obviously conflicts with the now prevalent practice of securing project debt with a first priority lien on the shares that represent the sponsors' equity interest in the project. If an expropriation were to occur while the debt remains outstanding, the project sponsors would be unable to collect from their insurer, unless the lenders were at that point to agree to release their lien on the shares.

This development has led political risk insurers of equity to ask project lenders to agree, in the event of an expropriation, to release their share pledge. The typical insurer asserts that (a) it needs unencumbered shares in order to have adequate salvage; (b) it is not feasible to price to the enhanced risk of accepting pledged shares as salvage; and (c) any sharing of claims proceeds with the lender needs to be subject to the lender's proof of a valid international law claim against the expropriating government, a hurdle of uncertain height given that the actual circumstances of a particular expropriation cannot be known in advance.

Project lenders maintain, on the other hand, that (a) neither the sponsors nor the equity insurers should expect the collateral package supporting project debt to be undermined in order to facilitate equity insurance; (b) it is not feasible to price the enhanced risk associated with promising to release the lien on pledged shares in the event of an expropriation; and (c) to the extent of any uncertainty as to the legal standing of the debt claim following an expropriation, it is all the more critical to have the right to foreclose on the shares and thus to stand in the shoes of the equity.

These positions have, in many projects, led to a costly standoff, one particularly ironic for the bilateral and multilateral development institutions that have joined in the fray. By structuring conventional collateral packages that seem appropriate for the risks associated with the emerging market projects that they have agreed to support, the development lenders, by refusing to release their lien on shares in the event of an expropriation, make it impossible for equity investors to mitigate a key set of risks associated with emerging market investment, that is, political risks. Their best intentions to structure appropriate collateral packages discourage developers from allocating their efforts to emerging market projects.

The irony is compounded by the decision of a number of governments to offer political risk insurance as an instrument to encourage foreign direct investment in emerging markets. That mechanism is rendered ineffective by financing programs that deprive the investor of the benefit of such insurance. This has been particularly awkward when the clash of programs has arisen between agencies within the same government, such as between OPIC and Ex-Im, or between otherwise related organizations, such as between MIGA and the IFC within the World Bank Group.

Although data is scanty, my informal review of roughly two dozen project financings that have faced this issue suggests that the most common outcome has been for equity investors to forego, one way or another, the economic benefit of political risk insurance. In some cases, the equity has ultimately decided to invest without such insurance. In others, the lenders have agreed to release the pledge of shares, but only upon assignment of the proceeds of any expropriation claim, once again depriving the equity of the economic benefit of the insurance. In still others, developers have decided to go forward with both insurance and pledged shares, keeping their fingers crossed that, if expropriation ever happens, either it happens after the debt has been repaid or some deal will be struck with the lenders at that time so that some benefit of the insurance may be realized notwithstanding the pledge. What is not at all clear is how many projects have not gone forward at all because of the practical unavailability of meaningful political risk insurance.

The OPIC/Ex-Im Solution

Several years of interagency discussions on this issue were characterized by efforts to elaborate an extensive variety of possible expropriation scenarios and to attempt to agree on a specific way of handling each of them. The "Joint Claims Agreement" signed by OPIC and Ex-Im on March 18, 1999 (the "Agreement") was finally reached by abandoning this approach. Instead, the agencies first agreed on a principle, namely, that, if an expropriation occurs, each agency would cooperate with the other to maximize their total joint recovery from the expropriating government. The details of what that would require are left to be determined if and when an expropriation actually occurs.

The Agreement also provides that the proceeds of any settlement will be shared between the agencies pro rata in proportion to their respective exposures to the expropriated project. This reflects their agreement that each investor's claims, both those of the lenders and those of the equity investors, should be treated as equally valid and deserving of compensation by the expropriating government.

The Agreement provides further parameters for post-expropriation cooperation: (a) a stay of execution of the share pledge once OPIC notifies Ex-Im that an expropriation has occurred; (b) a waiver of any share retention obligations that could impede the assignment of insured shares to OPIC to perfect an insurance claim; (c) a two-year window within which Ex-Im may choose to accept the credit of the post-expropriation entity and opt out of pressing a joint claim with OPIC, although Ex-Im would still, if necessary in order to recover salvage from the expropriating government, release its share pledge; and (d) a provision regarding the allocation of expenses. Most fundamentally, however, the Agreement commits each agency to endeavor to achieve maximum post-expropriation recovery, with the particular steps required to achieve that goal being left to be determined if and when a project supported jointly by OPIC and Ex-Im is expropriated. The most important immediate consequence of the Agreement is that prospective equity investors in emerging markets can seek Ex-Im project financing without foregoing the comfort afforded by OPIC insurance—and without having to await the outcome of protracted, case-by-case interagency renegotiations of the pledged share conflict.

The Way Forward

Although OPIC and Ex-Im have now reached agreement, most major infrastructure projects involve multiple commercial and official lenders and political risk insurers. Where lenders or political risk insurers other than OPIC and Ex-Im are at the table, the share pledge problem remains a hurdle to be cleared deal-by-deal, posing the continued likelihood of lost time and legal fees as the pledged share battle is continuously refought. Developers must also deal with the very real prospect that political risk insurance may not, as a practical matter, be available to support their equity investment if, at the same time, they intend to raise project debt.

Consequently, an important open question is whether other lenders and political risk insurers will be willing to go along with this—or some other—model to resolve the pledged share conflict. A prevalent view among those involved in negotiating the Agreement was that the accord made sense (only) because the two agencies were part of the same fiscal family so that the taxpayers' sole interest is in maximizing the post-expropriation recovery. The interagency allocation of those proceeds was of no importance to the federal budget. If, however, insurers and lenders lacked some common institutional bond, there was a presumption that the pledged share conflict would continue. Most lenders and insurers have, however, no such familial ties. So, if such ties prove to be critical for a once-and-for-all, conventional solution to the pledged share problem to emerge, then the prospects for such a general solution are exceedingly dim.

On the other hand, the principle of maximizing the total — in contrast to permitting an expropriating government to play competing claimants off against each other during settlement negotiations — makes good sense for investors to a project, whether or not they share any affiliation other than their respective exposures to the expropriated project.

If agreement to act jointly is to be reached, however, the question of how to allocate settlement proceeds needs, as in the OPIC/Ex-Im Agreement, to be confronted. Lenders may continue to insist that satisfaction of equity claims against the expropriating government must be subordinated to prior payment in full of their debt claims. Equity insurers may continue to insist on (at least) pro rata allocation and even to hesitate to commit in advance to join forces in pressing joint claims with lenders. If so, the pledged share standoff may continue to plague international project financings in emerging markets.

Alternatively, each side may conclude, as did OPIC and Ex-Im, that the details of the post-settlement sharing formula are of less importance than the certain benefits to be achieved by cooperating to maximize joint recoveries and by removing this conflict from the agenda of issues needing to be negotiated up front. Such an outcome would guarantee a reduction in the up-front costs of bringing many emerging market project financings to closure.

Comment on the Multiple Pledge-of-Shares Problem Between Lenders and Insurers

Julie A. Martin
Vice President for Insurance
Overseas Private Investment Corporation

As project financing has become a major source of funding for large projects in emerging economies, the Overseas Private Investment Corporation (OPIC), other official investment insurers, and private market insurers have found themselves involved as insurers of equity in increasingly complex transactions with one or more lenders to a project company. These lenders often include bilateral and multilateral international financial institutions (IFIs) as well as commercial banks and bond investors. A recurrent issue in many of these transactions concerns the differing, and sometimes conflicting, requirements of insurers and lenders if the project company is expropriated.

The Insurers' Perspective

Some official and private market insurers provide expropriation insurance based on the risk underwriting assumption that, when the insurer pays compensation for expropriation, it will receive in return the legal basis on which to assert a valid claim for compensation from the host government. This claim will generally be based on principles of international law that require governments to pay compensation for expropriation of foreign investors. The insurer succeeds to this claim against the host government by requiring, as a condition to payment of compensation for expropriation, that the insured equity investor deliver its shares or other evidence of its interest in the project company to the insurer, together with any right to compensation for expropriation from the host government, free and clear of liens. The result of this requirement is that, when an insurer pays compensation for expropriation, it effectively buys the expropriated investor's claim for compensation against the host government (a "Host Government Claim"), which puts the insurer in a position to approach the host government for payment. Some official insurers also benefit from agreements with the host government that facilitate their assertion of claims of this kind. For example, OPIC has agreements with approximately 140 developing countries and emerging markets requiring that the expropriating government negotiate and if necessary submit to ad hoc international arbitration with OPIC to resolve such claims.

The risk underwriting model used by insurers that provide expropriation insurance on this basis presumes that recoveries from host governments, and not just insurance premiums and investment income, will be an important source of funds to cover the cost of expropriation claims. (In this respect, expropriation insurance differs from more commonly known forms of insurance, such as property and casualty insurance or life insurance, where premiums plus investment income are generally adequate to cover the cost of claims.) The risk underwriting model based on the ability to assert a claim against the host government has been the foundation of expropriation insurance provided by the United States Government since the Marshall Plan, and 50 years of experience have validated its underlying assumptions.

The Lenders' Perspective

Project finance lenders have their own risk underwriting assumptions. Generally, these include an assumption that virtually all assets related to the project being financed, including the shares held by any equity investors in the project and related rights to compensation for expropriation, will be pledged to the lenders as collateral for the loans. There are several reasons why lenders particularly want the pledge of shares: (a) shares may be easier to sell than hard assets and offer an alternative means of liquidating the project company assets, particularly in countries where systems for pledging and executing on collateral security are new or uncertain; (b) the shares represent voting control of the project company; and (c) in the event of an expropriation, the shares offer an additional basis for a lender to make its Host Government Claim.

Many lenders are reluctant to release their liens on shares to permit the insured equity investor to make an insurance claim in the event of expropriation because doing so would allow the insured equity investor to recover its investment before the project company's debt is paid and deprive the lender of the benefit of its security interest.

The Unfortunate End Result

Some equity investors are unwilling to make direct investments in developing countries without political risk insurance. Consequently, if the insurers and lenders cannot resolve their conflicting requirements regarding the pledged shares, these equity investors will not invest. The unfortunate end result, of course, will be less foreign direct investment in developing countries. It is particularly important for the official insurers and IFIs to remember their mandates. They were established to aid and encourage private investment in developing countries by offering the means to mitigate some of the inherent political risks that private equity investors and commercial lenders otherwise would face. Therefore, these organizations have a particularly strong duty to resolve this issue.

Summary of Theoretical and Actual Solutions

As much as we would like to develop a single model applicable to most cases, we have been unable to do so. Over the last several years, OPIC has worked out solutions with a range of institutions including both multilaterals (IFC and EBRD) and bilaterals (Ex-Im and NCM). None of these has been easy, but we have learned several lessons.

First, in my view, it is best to agree on general concepts rather than try to account for every possibility in the agreement. We have agreements that range in length from one and a half to 30 pages. I would argue that an agreement on general principles is the most efficient use of everyone's time, although most of us find it hard to resist trying to nail down every item.

Second, the parties need to be willing to compromise and must want to reach a solution. Occasionally, sponsors have argued that this is an issue solely between the lenders and the insurers. On the contrary, this is an issue of the sponsor's making if the sponsor has already pledged the shares or the interest to more than one party, and it is in the sponsor's interest to bring pressure to bear to reach a resolution. In several instances, agreements would not have been reached without the active involvement of the sponsors.

Third, with our increased experience, our original view that this issue was limited to the pledge of the shares has changed. In essence, what we are looking for now is an assignment of rights to whatever represents the economic value of the project, in a form that cannot be compromised away by other parties. This may be shares, but it might also be a pro rata portion of an arbitral award under a power purchase agreement or a termination payment. We have found that this may further complicate the negotiations. As you will note in our comments on breach of contract, we now require that the "net litigation payment" be assigned to us because it may represent the true economic value of the company.

Fourth, I believe that the fundamental principle of any such agreement should be that the parties should work together to maximize recoveries from the host government and that they should not be allowed unilaterally to compromise each other's interest when the basis for the claim is a violation of international law under which the host government should be held responsible for its actions with respect to both the equity and the debt.

The following list represents a variety of theoretical solutions that have been proposed by parties over the last several years. As noted, OPIC has reached agreements with lenders involving various combinations of these solutions.

1. *Insurance for Lenders*: The easiest solution is for commercial lenders to obtain political risk insurance themselves so that they do not have to rely on pledged shares for their recoveries in the event of expropriatory action. This solution has been employed by many commercial lenders, particularly after the Asian and Russian crises. However, project limits for insurance and cost considerations mean that this solution is not always possible. In addition, the IFI lenders are not inclined to utilize this solution as they do not want to purchase — or be seen as needing to purchase — political risk insurance.

2. *Increased Returns to Lenders*: A lender could increase its pricing to the borrower in exchange for an agreement to release its lien on the shares. From the lender's point of view, the increased pricing

would reflect the reduction in the value of its collateral package in the event of an expropriation.

Case Study

Several years ago, OPIC was involved as an insurer in a power transaction in Asia with an IFI lender. In this transaction, the borrower agreed to pay an increased fee to the IFI lender, in exchange for an up-front agreement that the IFI would release the shares to OPIC in the event of an expropriation claim. OPIC and the IFI then negotiated a cooperation agreement that included the following elements: (a) the parties would cooperate in making a claim to the host government; (b) no settlement with the host government could be reached without the consent of both parties; and (c) any compensation received from the host government would be shared between the parties.

3. *Assignment of Insurance Claim Proceeds*: Lenders may agree with the equity sponsor to release shares pledged to them in exchange for an assignment of a portion, or the entire amount, of the proceeds of the equity sponsor's insurance claim payment. This approach has been effectively used by some smaller companies to facilitate financing when they were borrowing at the corporate level rather than at the project level.

This approach works well for commercial lenders who cannot otherwise obtain political risk insurance. However, OPIC and other official insurers generally do not support this approach as it deprives the equity investors of the full benefit of their insurance.

4. *Encumbered Shares/Suspended Liens Approach*: Under this approach, lenders would agree to deliver encumbered shares to insurers, but the operation of the lien on those shares would be "suspended." In other words, the lenders would not attempt to claim either a portion of the equity investor's insurance claim proceeds or any Host Government Claim payment made to the official insurer. In addition, lenders would agree to observe various "standstill periods" in relation to execution on their liens on the pledged shares to permit the insurers to make their various claims.

5. *Escrowing Insurance Claim Proceeds until Lenders Are Paid*: Under this approach a lender could agree to release its lien on the shares so that the insured equity investor could make an insurance claim and receive payment from an insurer, provided that the insured

equity investor then deposits the proceeds in escrow until the maturity of the loan or earlier payment in full to the lenders. Like Solution 3 on the previous page, this approach has limited appeal for insured equity investors since it is uncertain whether they will obtain any benefit themselves from the insurance.

Case Study

OPIC has reached an agreement with other multilateral lenders and insurers that combined elements of Solutions 4 and 5 listed on the previous page.

In this large mining project in the Newly Independent States (NIS), the official insurers and IFIs reached a cooperation agreement after intensive negotiations. In the agreement, the lenders agreed to postpone taking action against their collateral ("standstill periods"), with periods varying based upon the political risk event, so as not to prejudice the insurers' ability to make claims against the host government. In addition, the parties agreed to consult and cooperate in making a Host Government Claim, with the goal of maximizing recoveries for all parties. The lenders also agreed to release encumbered shares to the insurers, if the insurers were able to receive an acknowledgment from the host government regarding the outstanding loans. If the host government would not agree to this, then the parties could proceed to make parallel claims, or joint host government Claims. Finally, if the host government made an unfair/inequitable claim payment, then the parties agreed to negotiate in good faith regarding sharing, or to use an escrow account to hold the claim payment until they reached a decision.

6. *Full Sharing of Host Government Claim Compensation between IFI Lenders and Official Insurers*: Under this approach, IFI lenders would release their liens on the shares and official insurers would pay claims to the insured equity investors. Then the official insurers would make a Host Government Claim for compensation with respect to the insured equity, while IFI lenders would make a Host Government Claim for debt. IFI lenders and official insurers would contractually agree to share whatever compensation they received from the host government on a pro rata basis.

Case Study

In a power generation project in Eurasia, OPIC insured equity, debt was provided by an IFI lender and a commercial lender, and an official insurer insured the commercial lender. In this transaction, OPIC reached agreement with the other parties on the following points: (a) OPIC and the IFI lender agreed to share pro rata any compensation received by either party from the host government with respect to the events that gave rise to a claim of either party against the host government, pursuant to formulas included in the agreement setting out the basis for determining the pro rata share of OPIC and the IFI lender; and (b) in the event of an expropriation claim, OPIC and the IFI lender agreed to postpone any enforcement actions under the financing agreements (with certain exceptions) until OPIC and the IFI lender had made a claim against the host government, or a period of 270 days has elapsed, whichever was earlier.

Comment on the Multiple Pledge-of-Shares Problem Between Lenders and Insurers

Anne Predieri
Senior Vice President
Banc of America Securities

Ken Hansen deserves much praise for his success in obtaining a most welcome agreement between the Overseas Private Investment Corporation (OPIC) and the Export-Import Bank of the United States (Ex-Im) on this long-standing issue, and I certainly look forward to witnessing its implementation. Ken's approach to "managing the forest rather than getting lost in the trees" strikes me as a terribly appropriate way to begin a discussion of political risk insurance issues. Our hosts gave us an equally appropriate assignment of identifying practical business solutions to some of these seemingly intractable problems. The growth of the private sector in the political risk insurance industry should help in this quest as commercial insurers are often willing to make business decisions regarding risk allocation, even if it involves setting a new precedent. Policy decisions can get bogged down in analysis at times, and public sector "mistakes" can be harder to accept, but the political risk insurance industry is now evolving much faster, and a practical approach will be necessary for players to thrive, if not survive.

As Ken describes, the pledge-of-shares issue has been most vigorously debated in an interagency context. The issue is a real one, however, not just between private investors historically seeking political risk insurance for equity and official lenders insisting on retaining senior secured interests regardless of equity's status, but also between covered and uncovered lenders, including lenders under multilateral development bank "B-Loans." In some cases, uncovered commercial lenders have been willing to release a proportionate number of shares to effect a claim by covered lenders. In others, commercial lenders have even been willing to release the shares to perfect an equity claim, believing, just as Ken describes, that they are likely to maximize recoveries by cooperating with an official insurer who can negotiate indirectly on their behalf through bilateral government treaties. To the extent that recoveries are offered through a restructuring of the project rather than through a separate payment, uncovered commercial or official debt must still be serviced by an operating company, even if it is owned by an insurer.

In most infrastructure projects and in most multilateral development bank loan scenarios, renegotiation of government off-take contracts may be more likely than a traditional expropriation through confiscation where a separate payment may be considered by a future government with no ongoing project involvement. It may still be more difficult to obtain lender consent to release shares for payment of a claim when B-Loans are involved, given the different inter-creditor rights of B-Loan Participants. One of the advantages of the B-Loan is the avoidance of separate political risk insurance premium costs, but those premiums may be well spent if expropriation is a concern. If all investors, equity and debt, are covered, the pledge-of-shares issue is solved. If an equity investor has saved those premiums, lenders may not feel as compelled to share expropriation proceeds as the investor would like.

Ex-Im and OPIC have made beneficial progress in addressing this issue within the U.S. government, but like every situation where investor interests are not aligned, the repercussions of the diverging interests must be considered when developing a financing plan. The practical business question can be posed at the outset without incurring any legal fees during documentation: Is expropriation coverage required as a condition of making the investment? If not, can the investor forego the benefits of any future claim proceeds accordingly, or at a minimum agree to release collateral on the principle of maximizing the total recoveries available to all parties? Some investors will have an easier time agreeing to a predetermined allocation of risks than others (i.e., if the question is posed as a policy decision for an official lender rather than a business decision about commercial creditors taking "reasonable risks"). The stakes, and related costs, are greatly increased when the discussion takes place during the documentation phase and becomes an exercise of asserting relative positions of strength at the negotiating table. It may be helpful to bear in mind that no amount of negotiation will change the limited scope of possible outcomes!

PART TWO

Preferred Creditor Status: Overview

Theodore H. Moran, Editor

Multilateral lending agencies, including the World Bank Group, claim preferred creditor status, or the right to be paid first, when developing country governments prove unable or unwilling to service all of their obligations. As part of their effort to facilitate flows of private capital to emerging markets, multilateral lending agencies are spreading the "umbrellas" of their preferred status over other parties who participate with them in supporting infrastructure and other private investment projects, presumably protecting these parties from reschedulings or default as well.

Where is the proper place to draw a line between preferred status and nonpreferred status?, asks **Mac Johnston of FMJ International Risk Services**. And at what point might the "umbrella" of protection against default, rescheduling, or other unfavorable treatment be overextended?

The preeminent institution to claim preferred creditor status in its relations with sovereign borrowers, Johnston points out, is the World Bank. Since the World Bank does not reschedule debt and will not provide new funding or continuing disbursements to borrowers who are in default, virtually all governments (except for a handful of rogue states) give priority to keeping current on loans from the IBRD.

Similarly, World Bank "partial risk" and "partial credit" guarantees of government financial obligations (covering specified risks and specified maturities, respectively) usually involve counter-guarantees by host authorities and are thus transformed, upon default, into a demand obligation held by the IBRD. These guarantee arrangements would thus appear to enjoy preferred creditor status as well. Other multilateral lending agencies have developed similar guarantee programs also backed by counter-guarantees on the part of host governments, and thus endow themselves with a claim to preferred creditor status.

Even though the IFC and MIGA do not lend to governments or guarantee government borrowings, both agencies, Johnston points out, assert that they, as World Bank Group members, enjoy the same preferred status as the IBRD. Both the IFC and MIGA have programs, moreover, that extend their "umbrella" over co-participants that support private investors. The IFC sponsors a B-loan program in which the IFC acts as lender of record on behalf of a larger syndicate and agrees to collect debt service and distribute payments on a pro rata basis. MIGA operates a "Cooperative Underwriting Program" (CUP) in which the Agency agrees to pursue recovery on behalf of all participants and share proportionally in any claims losses. While it is arguable whether the term "preferred creditor status" is technically applicable to rights that are not directly backed by host government obligations, Johnston observes, the important issue is whether hosts do or do not provide preferential treatment.

Other multilateral lending agencies have been developing guarantee programs that do not necessarily require a host government counter-guarantee, so that if an action or inaction on the part of indigenous authorities leaves them liable to a claim, there is no outstanding debt obligation from the host government owed to the multilateral. Here again, they rely instead on the potential consequences of alienating an official member of the multilateral lending community as a disincentive to trigger a claim, thus providing some comfort to participants without clear legal status as preferred lenders.

Finally, there are equity investors, lenders, and insurers who participate side-by-side with multilaterals in common projects, but who are not formally part of a multilateral-fronted syndicate or co-insurance arrangement. These equity investors, lenders, and insurers frequently indulge themselves in a "perception," according to Johnston, that they are indirect beneficiaries of the "umbrella" of protection from the multilaterals even though they have no formal claim to special status.

To what extent should "preferred status" be considered a scarce resource that should be husbanded, rather than steadily proliferated?, asks Johnston. If it is a scarce resource, at what point might it be overextended? Would it not be useful to develop some method to calculate the extent of preferred exposure on a per-country, or per-sector, or per-institution basis?

Suellen Lazarus of the IFC takes issue with Mac Johnston's questioning whether the term "preferred creditor status" might be technically applicable to products like the IFC B-loans. On the contrary, states Lazarus, both A-loans and B-loans have been structured by the IFC to have identical preferred creditor status. It is important to be clear that while different parts of the World Bank Group offer different products, the preferred creditor status is the same for all of them.

In the aftermath of a financial crisis, however, when a country may not have adequate reserves to service all of its preferred creditors, a host country must make short-term decisions about how to rank who will be paid first. It may choose to do so on the basis of who might offer the country new money most quickly, or on the basis of what projects will promote exports and generate foreign exchange, or on the basis of securing a new International Monetary Fund (IMF) or regional development bank program.

Experience shows that the prioritization of allocating foreign exchange to different creditors will be determined on a case-by-case basis, according to practical considerations, but, argues Lazarus, this is temporary and the preferred creditor status of all institutions is protected.

The importance of the "preferred creditor status" issue is underscored, according to **Anne Predieri of Banc of America Securities**, by the fact that many private lenders are showing reluctance to lend new funds into countries where a relatively high percentage of all debt has some privileged status, with or without coverage. To be sure, whenever resources are limited, a queue may be inevitable. What is important, Predieri argues, is that the rules establishing priorities need to be transparent and consistently applied.

Nevertheless, Predieri contends, some export credit agencies (ECAs) have begun to argue that the practice of granting preferences among *pari passu* creditors is probably not tenable; those parties that are "nonprivileged" cannot easily be expected to accept relegation to a subordinated status in comparison to other parties in a private transaction that are otherwise equally secured. Moreover, as the volume of private capital increasingly dwarfs flows from official agencies, the entire debate about who should enjoy preferred status may shift.

022 H54
G22

Preferred Creditor Status:
Husbanding a Valuable Asset

Felton (Mac) Johnston
President
FMJ International Risk Services, LLC

The "preferred creditor status" enjoyed by multilateral agencies plays a vital role in maintaining the flow of financing to emerging markets. Public agencies claiming some form of preferred status not only expect special protection for their own exposures in emerging markets, but increasingly are casting the "umbrella" of their status over other parties who participate with them in supporting emerging market projects. This paper briefly examines the special privileges enjoyed or expected by certain public agencies, and how they are being conveyed to other parties. Also, the paper discusses the implications of the increasing deployment of preferred status on the agencies, on the beneficiaries of their umbrellas, and on lenders and investors involved in emerging markets.

I. Preferred Creditor Status and Its Deployment

A. *Obligations to the World Bank and Other Multilateral Lenders.* The institution generally deemed to have a paramount claim to preferred creditor status (PCS) is the World Bank. Simply stated, in its dealings with sovereign borrowers, the Bank gets paid even when others don't. Except for certain rogue governments that effectively have opted out of the traditional international financial system, governments that are unable to meet their financial obligations will default on (or more decorously, reschedule) virtually any creditor but a multilateral lender, and least of all the

World Bank. Quite apart from whatever de jure status the multilaterals enjoy, they, and especially the World Bank, are seen as the lenders of last resort to whom official borrowers may turn when other sources are closed, and whose terms are most favorable. The Bank does not reschedule debt and will not lend anew, nor disburse on outstanding commitments, to defaulting borrowers. In turn, other prospective lenders, and regional multilaterals, are unlikely to lend or to reschedule if the multilateral community, especially the World Bank, is not being kept current. (This is not a matter of devotion to the well-being of the Bank. If the borrowing government is unable or unwilling to keep current with the Bank and to accept its discipline, it is hardly likely that, with the Bank's help, it is headed out of its difficulties.)

B. *Implications for Other Lenders.* The reciprocal of the Bank's and other multilaterals' privileged status is that other official or private lenders to governments in financial difficulties are obliged to negotiate a new schedule of payment. Exceptions are made for short-term creditors and historically for bondholders. The latter owed their exemption to a quantitative insignificance that may no longer prevail and to the inconvenience or impossibility of negotiating with the atomized bondholder community.

C. *Other Obligations Counter-guaranteed to Multilateral Development Banks (MDBs).* When multilateral institutions issue guarantees of government financial obligations, they will typically be counter-guaranteed by the responsible governments, and thus a default on the underlying obligation will be transformed more or less immediately to a demand obligation held by the guaranteeing multilateral, and one that should enjoy PCS no less than a direct multilateral loan to the government. Accordingly, the World Bank's Partial Credit Guarantee (of specified maturities) and like programs of other multilaterals are generally deemed powerful enhancements of underlying credits. Depending on their terms, the Bank's "partial risk" guarantee and like programs of other multilaterals that involve borrower government counter-indemnification are deemed to convey similar PCS status. MDB-guaranteed loans that are not counter-guaranteed by governments are discussed below.

D. *Other Products.* The IFC and MIGA, both members of the World Bank Group, do not lend to governments, nor do they guarantee government borrowings, but they do claim to enjoy a special status vis-à-vis host governments in their activities supporting the private sector. World Bank Group officials informally assert that all World Bank Group members enjoy the same preferred status, and that when an exchange crisis arises they will cooperate to ensure that each member continues to enjoy preferred status. Thus, although it is arguable whether the term "preferred creditor status" is technically applicable to rights that are not directly tied to host government obligations, the important point is whether the governments accord preferential treatment during an exchange crisis to remittances backed by multilateral institutions. The IFC, in addition to providing debt and equity project financing, operates the premier "B-loan" program, replicated by other regional multilaterals, that syndicates private lending to private projects. In its own words, the IFC, acting as lender of record, extends its "umbrella" to participating financial institutions. Under its participation agreement with private lenders, the IFC agrees to collect debt service and distribute payments pro rata among loan participants and itself. The IFC notes that "Bank regulatory authorities of many capital-exporting countries enhance IFC's ability to raise financing for companies in emerging markets by exempting IFC loan participations from country risk provisioning." The IFC reported a $9 billion B-loan portfolio in 1998, an amount that surpassed the IFC's own loan portfolio.

What is the nature of the "umbrella" that so impresses regulators? IFC publications refer to the comfort participants derive "from IFC's multilateral ownership and special status in terms of the treatment given by host governments to IFC-financed projects." This status might forestall a broad range of government-associated difficulties, but the IFC notes in particular that "no IFC loan, including the portion taken by participants, has to date ever been included in the general rescheduling or restructuring of a country's foreign debt made necessary by a shortage of foreign exchange." [1]

The favorable treatment that the IFC has enjoyed derives partly from its own importance as a source of support for private sector investment, but also from the potential consequences of alienating a member agency of the World Bank Group and the multilateral development community.

MIGA also claims to enjoy and offers to share through its "Cooperative Underwriting Program" (CUP) with private co-insurers its "special status as a multilateral entity and as a member of the World Bank Group." The CUP program is a political risk insurance variant

on the IFC A-/B-loan structure, in which MIGA "fronts" for participating private insurers whose claims liability is separate from
MIGA's, but who share proportionally in claims losses and recoveries associated with a cooperatively insured project. MIGA refers to
its "unique subrogation rights as an international institution" and
notes that "MIGA concludes agreements with each host country
member government on legal protection of MIGA-insured investments and the use of local currency derived from such investments."
Like the IFC's, though, MIGA's involvement is generally deemed
to provide an element of deterrence against sovereign risks generally, not just against convertibility/transfer risk.[2]

Although MIGA's "umbrella" has roots in special agreements
with host governments, like the IFC, its affiliation with the World
Bank and the multilateral community and the value of its continuing contribution to encouraging investment flows alone provide a
basis for favorable treatment.

Other regional MDBs have, or are developing, "partial credit"
and "partial risk" guarantee programs, the former being all-risk
guarantees of loans to private sector projects that, like the World
Bank's partial credit guarantee program, are counter-guaranteed by
the host government and thus arguably enjoy a preferred status similar to that of the World Bank's partial credit guarantees. The same
may be said of "partial risk" guarantees covering currency convertibility and loan defaults attributable to government nonperformance
of obligations to private projects offered by the World Bank and
regional multilaterals, if there is a government counter-guarantee
to the multilateral institution.

But unlike the World Bank, other multilaterals do not necessarily
require a government counter-guarantee for their partial risk guarantees. Their situation and their product are then much more like a
guarantee/insurance product from MIGA.[3] If government action
or inaction falling within the scope of their guarantee causes them
to pay a claim, there is no directly resulting debt obligation of the
host government that must promptly be repaid to the multilateral.[4]
Instead, the disincentive to take the covered action, or the incentive
promptly to reverse it, arises out of whatever agreements may exist
about such matters, the multilateral's status as such, and its role as
a source of investment encouragement.

The Overseas Private Investment Corporation (OPIC) presents a
more ambiguous case because it is a bilateral U.S. government
agency that combines the functions of an IFC (lending to private
projects) and a MIGA (political risk insurance). OPIC is not a multilateral agency, but its all-risk guaranteed loans and loans it insures

against political risks have historically been exempted from reschedulings and the agency has agreements with host governments that OPIC can argue give it rights to special status.

II. If Not Umbrellas, Perhaps Some Shade?

Multilaterals' preferred status may be conveyed beyond the community of guaranteed or insured lenders, B-loan participants, and insurers participating with a fronting multilateral agency. There is a common perception that you are better off participating in a project that has multilateral involvement (as a lender, equity holder, insurer, etc.) than in one that does not, even if you are not formally "protected." The perception is that association of these agencies with a project may result in greater protection from reschedulings than can be expected by ECAs and by most private parties having no special claim to exemption. And it may also provide a degree of deterrence against both currency blockage and expropriatory behavior toward sponsored projects, and failing that, the likelihood of obtaining prompt compensation. To the extent these perceptions are borne out in practice, the benefit conferred ultimately represents a potential claim against host government resources that is superior to others.

Into this category of indirect beneficiaries fall so-called "C-loan" participants who lend side-by-side with but not as coparticipants in a multilateral-fronted syndicate, co-insurers with multilateral agencies covering lenders under their own separate policies but to the same borrower/project, and possibly any lender/investor to a project in which there is substantial multilateral involvement. One gets the sense that multilaterals do not object to the perception that they cast such beneficial protection on project bystanders, but that does not mean that they would be under any obligation or necessarily have the inclination to attempt to protect such parties during an exchange crisis or an expropriation.

Even bilateral agencies are presumed to offer a measure of protection from adverse host government action against the projects they support, although exclusion from general debt reschedulings is not one of the benefits they are likely to confer.

III. If Preferred Status Is Not a Limitless Resource, What Will Happen If It Is Stretched Too Far?

The major premise of preferred status is that those who enjoy it—or have a claim to participate in it—will receive timely payment during an exchange crisis, while others may not. The presumption is that the resources of the government involved will always suffice to cover obligations to all of the preferred parties. [5] But suppose it does not? We do not know how any particular government will address the problem. Perhaps they would give priority to direct or directly guaranteed obligations, at the expense of at least some obligations for which they are responsible only by nature of understandings, relationships, or even some general agreement. Or possibly the government would give priority to its own public sector obligations over those arising from private sector transactions, even if they were transformed into public sector debts. Another approach might be to decide which multilateral lenders were more critical to maintain unblemished relations with. That some governments — not just the rogue and marginal states — will simply challenge the notion that you do not reschedule multilateral debt, is unimaginable only if you imagine that such governments will never become so overextended that they will be unable to satisfy all preferred and privileged creditors.

The unattractiveness of such choices demonstrates the desirability for all parties to avoid the necessity of imposing them on any government.

A related question is whether the apparent proliferation of institutions and programs claiming and sharing some form of preferred status is appropriate, and indeed whether the concept of granting preferences among *pari passu* lenders should continue. As more of a country's debt is preferred and more applicants for foreign exchange seek preference, will lenders be willing to come forward in an effectively subordinated position, and will exchange crises prove increasingly difficult for countries to manage?

IV. Husbanding the Asset

In the mechanics of international finance, the preferred creditor status of multilateral institutions has played a critical role in maintaining the flow of finance to emerging markets, in good times and bad. It is not clear how international financial markets would be coaxed toward an orderly reconstruction of financial support for emerging nations in financial crisis, if multilateral lenders lacked preferred status and therefore declined to maintain or increase their support. Nor is it apparent how, in the absence of privileges enjoyed by leading public agencies, cautious private lenders would be encouraged to continue their prevailing level of support — especially now "umbrellaed" support—for those markets. But it is also difficult to see how, if a country in crisis simply could not meet its obligations to all of the multilateral claims to preference, the multilaterals could simply refuse to reschedule and to provide continued support. For just these reasons, moderation in the use of preferred and privileged status is essential to preserving the value and effectiveness of this asset.

How do we know whether a problem of overuse might exist? Overuse is a matter of judgment about facts. At some point, in some country, privileged obligations could rise to some level, and conform to some maturity pattern, in relation to other obligations, that passed an unknown threshold beyond which there would be too great a danger that such privileged obligations could not all be met. Overuse could also mean that some threshold was reached beyond which lenders not sharing in the privileged status would become reluctant to continue bearing risk in a secondary position.

No one knows where these thresholds are, and upon examination we may find that in most cases we are a long way from reaching them. A way to begin to address the question would be the development of an accounting of the dimensions of preferred exposures on a per-country basis. It should be valuable for the institutions that enjoy and dispense privileged status to be able to gauge how great a burden privileged obligations may become in relation to the benefits they bring. It should be comforting to the private lending community to be assured that multilaterals and other institutions even had such a grasp of the situation in each country; were monitoring it as they operated their loan, guarantee, and insurance programs; and perhaps even coordinated among themselves to maximize the benefits and minimize the associated risks of their privileged positions.

Notes

1. Participants in IFC loans also share in the IFC's tax benefits in the host country, including exemption from withholding taxes on loan interest.

2. Private insurers who reinsure MIGA or other agencies effectively benefit from their "umbrellas" as much as private insurer participants in "CUP" programs. The use by public agencies of private political risk reinsurance to augment capacity to manage exposures is increasingly widespread.

3. "Guarantees" issued by MIGA and partial risk guarantees issued by the World Bank and others are essentially indistinguishable from similar "insurance" products offered by OPIC and private insurers.

4. If a public agency pays a claim based on a government's breach of an obligation to a borrower whose loan is under the agency's insurance/ guarantee protection, the agency may end up being subrogated to an asset in the form of a government. Whether that obligation is then excluded from reschedulings — and what becomes of other nonprivileged parties who may share an interest in that subrogated asset — is not clear.

5. When a government grants to a project and its creditors the right to capture export proceeds offshore, it is granting preferred access to scarce foreign exchange that contributes further to the pool of "privileged" creditors. Combining privileged public agencies, short-term lenders, (so far) exempted bondholders, and lenders having these offshore capture arrangement can result in a very large proportion of obligations that theoretically are immune to rescheduling.

522

H54 G22

Comment on Preferred Creditor Status

Suellen Lazarus
**Director, Syndications & International
Securities Department
International Finance Corporation**

My comments spring from my experience in being responsible for syndications in the International Finance Corporation (IFC). The issue of the preferred creditor status and how it relates to B-loans and to Intercreditor Agreements is a vital one for us and we have, of course, been dealing with it quite regularly. The issue of preferred creditor status has become particularly heated as a result of events in the past few years in Russia and Pakistan and with the Asian crisis.

In his discussion of preferred creditor status, Mac Johnston asserted that B-loans do not really have preferred creditor status, but instead have some kind of preferential status. I need to put on the table that we would strongly disagree with that. Our B-loan program has been structured to ensure that the preferred creditor status for both the IFC A-loans and B-loans is identical. Based on the structure, there is no distinction between the A-loans and the B-loans. They are one and the same loan and are embodied in the same loan document. The status that applies to them is the same.

Then the issue of ranking of preferred creditor status was also raised and whose preferred creditor status is bigger than whose and which institution would rank superior? It is a worthy question. One of the things that is very important to note is that within the World Bank Group, we make the statement very clearly that our preferred creditor status is all the same. Mac Johnston mentions this in his paper. We each have different products, but the fact that the products are different has nothing to do with the status.

The question of ranking of the preferred creditor status has to do with the following: when a foreign exchange crisis occurs in a country, and there must be the allocation of scarce foreign exchange, are we treated as preferred creditors or not? And we would say that regardless of whether a World Bank Group project has sub-sovereign guarantees or sovereign guarantees, or no guarantees, the status remains the same. In other words, when there is an obligation to the IFC or the World Bank or MIGA, that obligation ranks preferred to other obligations. And that is a fundamental point. With MIGA, because of its different range of products and because equity coverage is involved as well as debt, it becomes a little bit more complicated, and there probably needs to be more discussion on that issue.

But in terms of the principle of which institution within the Bank Group ranks higher than another, we do not rank one another. That is an ex-ante discussion. We are saying that theoretically we are all the same. Ex post, when a foreign exchange crisis occurs in a country, when there is a preferred creditor event, a country is going to do different things depending on its circumstances. Hopefully, the country has adequate reserves to service all of its preferred creditors. But as we saw in Pakistan, there was a situation where they had very limited reserves and had to do some temporary ranking.

How a country makes this short-term decision, of course, may have to do with who is going to give it new money most quickly. But it may also have to do with allocating funds to investments that promote exports and generate foreign exchange. So governments make different choices depending on their current circumstances. They may be in active negotiations with the IMF for a new program; therefore, with only a very limited foreign exchange available, they choose to service the IMF first in the short term.

Alternatively, a government may choose that because they are in active negotiations with the Asian Development Bank for a program, today they are servicing the Asian Development Bank. They may decide that because of an upcoming transaction with the IFC that is strategically very important, perhaps a major exporting project, they have to service the IFC to get that project going because otherwise they know that the IFC would not be able to proceed with the project and with disbursements. Each country is in a different situation and the ex-post outcome in the short term will be on a case-by-case basis. The experience throughout the 1980s and 1990s has demonstrated that it is very much on a case-by-case basis. Governments, faced with extreme foreign exchange shortages, will prioritize allocating that foreign exchange in different ways depending on the circumstances. But these are short-term, practical decisions that must be made. The crucial point is that when such allocations are made among preferred creditors, they are temporary and that ultimately the preferred creditor status of all the institutions is protected.

It is vital to note that we always insist to governments that all the institutions in the World Bank Group are preferred creditors. They should be treated equally, and we work together to make sure that the status of each institution in the World Bank Group is protected.

Comment on Preferred Creditor Status

Anne Predieri
Senior Vice President
Banc of America Securities

I fully concur with Mac Johnston's premise that "Preferred Creditor Status" is an asset that needs to be husbanded. Having spent a lot of time in recent months discussing this issue with a number of entities with different interests in the outcome, I fear that managing the total "Preferred Creditor Status" exposure may be the only element on which all parties can agree. I would add only that many private or commercial creditors are loathe to lend new money with or without coverage into countries where a relatively high percentage of overall debt is preferred, further underscoring the incentive for all parties to manage this resource carefully.

As Mac Johnston's paper posits, everybody cannot be preferred, but I would respond that it is not only possible but indeed the norm for some to be preferred. Realistically, if resources are limited, a queue may be inevitable. The rules establishing priorities need to be transparent and consistently applied, just as they are in every other class of capital where different rights accrue to different categories of debt and various classes of equity. These distinctions are commonly accepted — indeed, one could argue that this is the crux of the pledge-of-shares issue, which arises expressly because lenders assert their "preferred" status over equity.

Having said that, as Mac notes, many of the benefits of the multilaterals' preferred status may be more firmly rooted in perception and precedent than in a defined legal status as is the case with other classes of capital. Those precedents have proven to be quite strong when the multilateral is in a position to continue to contribute to the development of a country and can be a part of the solution, thereby providing a basis for favorable treatment that ultimately benefits all parties. As Mac also notes, the existence of a government counter-guarantee to the multilateral can contribute to the justification for a preferred status.

As capital flows shift from sovereign lending to private sector borrowing, especially for infrastructure projects, and as the total volume of private capital flows begins to dwarf flows from official sources, it is nevertheless appropriate to take a step back. The reversal of these two trends results in a significant change in the overall context of the preferred creditor status debate and may harbor an equally significant change in the final analysis of a government being forced to choose among its "preferred" creditors. It is conceivable that a growing reliance on private creditors could affect the perceived importance of the traditional preferred creditors. Mac's paper includes a very important footnote on this point: the current lack of clarity on what becomes of other nonprivileged parties who may share an interest in the subrogated private sector asset after a multilateral pays an insurance or guarantee claim.

As infrastructure financing has shifted from multilateral credits with government borrowers to the private sector, multilaterals can no longer provide all of the financing. Multilateral private sector programs are indeed designed to catalyze private capital. Just as with the pledge-of-shares issue, when multiple sources of financing are involved, it is important to evaluate the long-term alignment of interests to ensure the long-term success of the investment. The only time all project creditors' interests are truly aligned appears to be when the multilateral is the only source of credit to the project, typically through an A-/B-loan. Not only do infrastructure project financing requirements often exceed the capacity of multilaterals, but multinational sponsors increasingly procure capital goods from a variety of sources to minimize project costs in order to win competitive bids. Multilaterals are now, therefore, often no more than a component of the overall financing. Further, the tools available to mitigate country risk have evolved significantly over the past several years, which is only likely to accelerate this trend.

As a number of ECAs have recently argued, the concept of granting preferences among *pari passu* creditors is probably not a tenable one. "Nonprivileged" parties cannot necessarily be expected to accept an effectively subordinated position to counterparts in a private transaction that are otherwise equally secured. Recent experience and the rising decibels of the background noise on this issue are also starting to challenge the perception that association with these agencies may result in greater protection ("win-win") and have begun to raise the prospect of a "win-lose" scenario where there is room for one or the other entity but not both, and borrowers are forced to choose between ECAs and multilaterals. It behooves all of us to correct the direction of this debate.

Multilaterals are understandably loath to waive any potential privileges in the context of a single transaction given the importance of precedence in the overall status. On the other hand, multilaterals are intended to serve as a catalyst to private investors and to cooperate, rather than compete, with private investors. The intercreditor relationship, which is analogous to the claims cooperation debate with MIGA, is fundamental to the willingness of private, as well as many bilateral, entities to co-finance or co-insure with the multilaterals. MIGA recently considered a constructive approach to this issue by focusing the exercise of any preferential rights outside the contractual arrangements of a private transaction rather than asserting priority among parties that are equally secured under private contracts. This approach is consistent with the premise that the preferred status is conferred by the government and remains completely separate from the private transaction. I remain hopeful that a cooperative solution can be documented, in keeping with MIGA's mandate not to displace private parties otherwise interested in supporting an investment. Long-term alignment of interests is a fundamental element of successful project financings and sustainable development. It is healthy to keep up the dialogue to avoid misinterpretations and to encourage informed decisions.

PART THREE

Breach of Contract Coverage: Overview

Theodore H. Moran, Editor

Projects with large fixed costs are particularly vulnerable to problems related to slowdowns or interruptions in production or payment for production. This is especially true if those projects must service sizable amounts of debt from the proceeds of their operations. As infrastructure investment has grown in importance alongside traditional mining and petroleum investment—all of which have large fixed costs mainly financed via debt—vulnerability to host government actions or inactions that might disrupt production or delay payment has become a major concern.

In the case of foreign participation in infrastructure privatization, the vulnerability is compounded by having parastatal agencies such as local utilities writing take-or-pay contracts for most of their output and by having subnational regulatory agencies supervise their operations.

Investors and lenders in infrastructure, as well as petroleum and mining, have increasingly looked to political risk insurance for "breach of contract" coverage to try to mitigate their vulnerability. Breach of contract coverage is triggered when host authorities fail to honor the original investment or offtake agreements, or subject those agreements to unilateral revision, often with forced slowdowns of operations to compel acceptance of the new terms.

Breach of contract coverage, as **Rick Jenney of Morrison & Foerster, LLP,** points out, usually requires investors to exhaust local remedies (including appeals), go to arbitration, win a judgment, and attempt to enforce the judgment, without success, before seeking compensation from the insurer. The length of time required for this process may push the project company into bankruptcy before the process is complete.

How might breach of contract coverage be restructured to fit the needs of infrastructure investors more closely?

Jenney begins by making a distinction between "disputes coverage" and "breach coverage." Just because an investor has a dispute with a host government about an off-take contract, for example, this does not elevate the host country actions to the political level associated with expropriation without compensation; only host government refusal to honor an independent arbitral award generated by a dispute resolution procedure to which the government had expressly agreed would do that. For this reason, "disputes coverage" requires that all the steps, from arbitration and appeal through attempts at enforcement, be deliberately thwarted before a claim can be paid.

Breach coverage that does not require prior exhaustion of all remedies in order to make a claim, or what Jenney calls "enhanced breach coverage," might be a help in such situations. It could be structured as a kind of catastrophe payment to make up for the cancellation of an off-take contract, without any violation of international law necessarily being involved. "Enhanced breach coverage" would provide a lump-sum payment of the accelerated loan amount to lenders, for which the lenders would surrender their rights to pursue the dispute resolution procedures to the political risk insurer.

But this would be a lump-sum payment "with a string on it," a provisional payment. If the dispute resolution procedures yield an award to the project company and its insurer that is at least equal to the provisional payment, the latter would become final. If the offtaker or the host government prevailed in the dispute resolution procedures so that the project company and its insurer were entitled to an aggregate amount less than the provisional payment, then the lender would have to repay that portion of the provisional payment, with interest.

This enhanced breach coverage, argues Jenney, might be a useful tool for many types of projects (including infrastructure, oil, gas, and mining projects), but it has "some wrinkles remaining." Its "catastrophic" nature does not cover variations in periodic payments or other kinds of contractual adjustments at the margin that the project investor considers "creeping expropriation." The coverage provides protection only to lenders, not to equity holders. And the price for such coverage might be quite high.

In **OPIC's Case Study** of the first claim settlement based on its infrastructure coverage—**MidAmerican's Dieng and Patuha Projects in Indonesia**—**Julie Martin of OPIC** points out that under OPIC coverage the investor must first seek recourse against the host government through the dispute resolution mechanism applicable to the project agreement, and that the government must fail to honor a favorable award or judgment. There must be a violation of international law. Total expropriation is required. And the investor must transfer all its rights, title, and interest to OPIC free and clear.

In the case examined here, MidAmerican Energy Holdings operated geothermal power projects in India, on the basis of a take-or-pay power purchase agreement with Perusahaan Listrik Negara (PLN), the state-owned utility. The Indonesian Ministry of Finance provided a support letter, pledging that it would cause the state-owned oil and gas corporation (Pertamina) and PLN to honor and perform their obligations under the project agreements.

After the onset of the Asian financial crisis in 1997, PLN failed to make all the payments required, and MidAmerican filed for arbitration. In 1999, two successive arbitration panels found PLN in breach of contract, whereupon MidAmerican filed claims with OPIC and private market insurers and received full payment of the political risk insurance claims totaling $290 million.

Given the concern about the duration of time required to go through arbitration to resolve a case involving breach of contract coverage, including arbitration and appeal, OPIC provides a precise time-line for the MidAmerican case study.

In contrast to the arbitration approach taken by MidAmerican, certain other international power investors looked to negotiation with PLN and the Government of Indonesia to address their difficulties. This raises the issue of moral hazard, according to OPIC, leading to questions about whether the existence of OPIC coverage causes investors to act differently than they might have in the absence of OPIC coverage.

Anne Predieri of Banc of America Securities argues that breach of contract is (along with devaluation) the primary concern of investors and lenders in the contemporary era. The innovative thrust of Jenney's proposal, according to Predieri, is that it is not structured as a form of expropriation coverage and therefore is not tied to a violation of international law. As Jenney points out, lenders may not have been at the table when the decision to accept imperfect dispute resolution procedures in an off-take contract was made, and may not be willing to commit their capital without adequate coverage.

There may be a problem, however, with formulating the enhanced breach coverage as catastrophic coverage, designed for cases where the host government has offered a guarantee of termination payments, Predieri points out, since this kind of guarantee is not always provided.

Moreover, even though political risk insurers have long maintained that commercial risk is commercial and political risk is political, and never the twain shall meet, "the reality is that commercial and political risks are increasingly blurred." In most infrastructure projects, for example, the viability of the investment depends upon a mechanism for raising rates to pass through increased costs. This tariff mechanism may be a commercial agreement, but the regulator's willingness to implement it as the years go by may often be a political decision.

Breach of Contract Coverage in Infrastructure Projects: Can Investors Afford to Wait for Arbitration?

Frederick E. Jenney
Partner
Morrison & Foerster, LLP

One of the greatest dangers faced by investors in projects with large fixed assets is that they will find the terms of their initial investment or offtake agreement subjected to breach or unilateral revision, often with forced slowdowns of operations to encourage them to accept new terms. What is often referred to as "breach of contract" coverage typically requires investors to exhaust local remedies, including appeals, and go to arbitration, before seeking compensation from a political risk insurer. In the meantime, the losses from operating at less than full capacity may threaten to bankrupt the project company.

As a result, most investors view this type of coverage as inadequate protection against the real risks they face in contracting with host government parties. On the other hand, the risks that investors want covered have long been viewed by political risk insurers as uninsurable commercial risks.

This paper outlines (a) some of the common misunderstandings about this type of coverage, (b) some of the reasons that political risk insurers are reluctant to expand this type of coverage, and (c) notwithstanding that reluctance, how this type of coverage can be made more useful for investors.

One model now being developed, referred to in this paper as "Enhanced Breach Coverage," creates a form of coverage for lenders to projects where the project company (i.e., the borrower) depends on a stream of payments from a foreign governmental party.

In essence, Enhanced Breach Coverage is protection against the borrower's nonpayment to the lenders of amounts due on the loan (including accelerated principal amounts) because of the offtaker's nonpayment to the borrower of amounts due under an offtake contract such as a power purchase agreement (including termination amounts).

But with respect to Enhanced Breach Coverage, as always, the devil is in the details.

Misunderstandings about Breach Coverage

A Typical Case

Consider the following typical case: A U.S. investor (the "Investor") wants to buy political risk insurance for its investment in a local company (the "Project Company") that is developing a power project (the "Project") in Country X (the "Host Country").

The Project Company enters into a power purchase agreement (the "Offtake Contract") under which a purchaser (the "Offtaker") that is wholly owned by the government of the Host Country (the "Host Government") agrees to buy power at a specified price on specified terms.

Since the Offtaker is not creditworthy, or at least not creditworthy independently from the Host Government, the Offtaker's obligations under the Offtake Contract are guaranteed or otherwise supported by the Host Government (the "Host Government Guarantee").

The Investor correctly determines that the Offtake Contract, together with the Host Government Guarantee, are the key elements in the Project, and that the key risk in the Project is nonpayment by the Host Government on the Host Government Guarantee.

Having just laboriously negotiated the Offtake Contract through political twists and turns in the Host Country, and having just gauged the political will of the Offtaker and the Host Government to make payments over the term of the Offtake Contract and the Host Government Guarantee, the Investor goes to its favorite political risk insurer (the "Political Risk Insurer") for coverage.

Much to the Investor's surprise, the Political Risk Insurer explains that nonpayment by the Host Government on the Host Government Guarantee is not considered a political risk! How can this be?

A Common Misunderstanding About Political Risk Insurance

Users of political risk insurance often mistakenly assume that the breach by a governmental party of its payment obligations under an Offtake Contract, such as a power purchase agreement, is (or should be) a covered expropriation under their political risk insurance policy. That is, many Investors assume that political risk insurance coverage for expropriation covers *all* wrongful acts of the Host Government.

However, most political risk insurance policies distinguish actions by the Host Government as a government (which may be covered if they otherwise meet the tests for expropriation), and actions by the Host Government as a commercial party (which generally are not covered).

For example, most expropriation policies expressly exclude from the scope of coverage any failure of the foreign governing authority, the Offtaker, or other relevant agencies to honor their obligations under any purchase agreement or support document in favor of the Project Company.

Confusion Between Disputes Coverage and Breach of Contract Coverage

This also raises an important distinction between Disputes Coverage and Breach Coverage.

Political risk insurance protection against wrongful failure by a Host Government party to pay an award following an agreed-upon arbitration or other dispute resolution procedure is referred to in this paper as "Disputes Coverage."

Political risk insurance protection against failure by a Host Government party to pay an amount—particularly a lump-sum termination amount—due under an Offtake Contract, such as a power purchase agreement, without first resorting to international arbitration or another dispute resolution procedure specified by the parties (the "Dispute Resolution Procedure") is referred to in this paper as "Breach Coverage."

The key distinction is exhaustion of remedies. Upon breach by the Offtaker of its payment obligation under an Offtake Contract, Disputes Coverage requires systematic compliance with an often lengthy dispute resolution procedure and the granting of a final and binding arbitral award. Breach Coverage offers a political risk insurance claim payment immediately upon the mere breach by the

Offtaker of its payment obligation. No wonder Investors would prefer Breach Coverage to Disputes Coverage.

Only Political Risks Are Covered, Not Commercial Risks

Many risks that Investors would like to see addressed by political risk insurance coverage (in an ideal form of Breach Coverage, for instance) have long been viewed by Political Risk Insurers as uninsurable commercial risks.

Political Risk Insurers—as distinct from all-risk Guarantors, for example—are required to draw the line between commercial and political risks. Just because a dispute is with the Host Government, they note, does not make it a political dispute. In other words, governmental disputes may be commercial or political or (more often) a mix of both.

The implicit idea is that when a Host Government is in a commercial dispute, its actions are not necessarily political, and its refusal to pay is certainly not expropriatory. However, when a Host Government refuses to honor an independent arbitral award resulting from a dispute resolution procedure to which it has expressly agreed, its actions are more akin to the high-handedness normally associated with an expropriation without compensation.

Don't Make a Bad Deal Better

Insurers also frequently chant the political risk insurance mantra "don't make a bad deal better." That is, if the Investor has agreed to a Dispute Resolution Procedure in the underlying Offtake Contract, if there is a payment dispute it should be an expected precondition to payment that the Investor go through with the agreed-upon procedure. To do otherwise would put the Investor in a better position than it bargained for—it might make a bad deal better.

Particularly in Offtake Contracts where there might be legitimate issues of nonperformance by the Project Company, it would be imprudent for a Political Risk Insurer to agree to pay an amount before it has been finally determined to be due to the Project Company.

In short, Political Risk Insurers have long maintained that commercial risk is commercial and political risk is political, and never the twain shall meet.

Investors, on the other hand, recognize breach of contract risk as a risk they cannot adequately manage or mitigate. Until recently, however, all that has been available to Investors is Disputes Coverage.

Overview of Disputes Coverage

There are several reasons why most Investors view Disputes Coverage as inadequate protection against the real risks they face in contracting with Host Government parties.

Dissatisfaction with Host Country Courts and Other Local Dispute Resolution Procedures

To begin with, many Investors are fundamentally dissatisfied with the local dispute resolution procedures available with respect to international investment.

For example, the Host Government might suggest to a foreign Investor that any disputes between the Host Government and the Investor in a Concession Agreement for a mining project be resolved by the Minister of Mines—a suggestion that is summarily rejected by even the most unseasoned international Investors.

A second alternative is local adjudication in the Host Country, but Investors are appropriately wary of resolving a dispute under a contract with a Host Government party by resorting to local courts that are agencies of the same Host Government.

For this reason, foreign Investors often refuse to submit to the jurisdiction of local courts in Host Countries where the judicial system is not seen as independent enough from the executive branch of the Host Government that is party to the contract. Similarly, Host Governments often for various reasons refuse to submit to the jurisdiction of the Investor's home country. This creates a stand-off as to the Dispute Resolution Procedure.

Resort to International Arbitration

Therefore, the dispute resolution mechanism of choice for contracts with Offtakers and other Host Government parties is arbitration under the rules of one of many international arbitration regimes (such as the American Arbitration Association (AAA), the United Nations Commission on International Trade Law (UNCITRAL), and the International Chamber of Commerce (ICC)) at a neutral international site (such as Stockholm, Singapore, or another arbitration haven) before disinterested arbitrators selected by some method perceived as being free from bias.

Today, virtually all contracts of any type requiring significant payments by a Host Government or its agencies contain international arbitration as the stipulated Dispute Resolution Procedure.

What Disputes Coverage Requires

As noted above, Disputes Coverage has been available for years in various forms from most public and private Political Risk Insurers. It is designed to preserve for the Investor the benefits of a Dispute Resolution Procedure such as international arbitration.

Several common elements are present in disputes coverage offered. Typically, these elements fall into two categories: (a) steps involved in the normal exercise of the Dispute Resolution Procedure to yield a final determination, and (b) events that signal that the Dispute Resolution Procedure has gone seriously awry and will not yield a meaningful determination.

The normal steps for Disputes Coverage are as follows:

Resort to Arbitration. A dispute between the Investor or the Project Company, as the case may be, and the Host Government is submitted to an international arbitration procedure (or similar Dispute Resolution Procedure) contained in the Offtake Contract.

Final and Binding Award. The arbitral procedure yields a final and binding award, not subject to appeal, in favor of the Investor or the Project Company, as the case may be.

Enforcement Action Initiated. The Investor or the Project Company, as the case may be, has sought to enforce the arbitral award in a court of competent jurisdiction.

Enforcement Action Thwarted. The Host Government fails to pay the Investor or the Project Company, as the case may be, the amount of the arbitral award within 90 to 180 days of the date of such attempted enforcement.

Because Investors are concerned that already slow Dispute Resolution Procedures might come to a complete halt because of foot-dragging by the Host Government, Political Risk Insurers have traditionally agreed to cover events that signal unambiguously that the Dispute Resolution Procedure will not yield a meaningful determination.

For example, basic Disputes Coverage usually is expanded to cover the following situations:

Resort to Preliminary Dispute Procedure. A dispute has been resolved in favor of the Project Company through a preliminary or special Dispute Resolution Procedure contained in the underlying contract (such as the decision of a project engineer or technical panel), the dispute is not further subject to the overall dispute resolution procedure (such as arbitration), and the buyer does not pay the Project Company the amount due within a specified period of time after the preliminary or special determination becomes final;

Impossibility of Dispute Procedure. Resort to arbitration has been rendered futile, impracticable, or exceptionally hazardous to the physical safety of representatives of the Project Company as a result of policies or practices of the Host Government or conditions in the Host Country not in effect as of the date of this policy and lasting a specified period of time; or

Frustration of Dispute Procedure. The Investor submits a dispute with the buyer to arbitration and uses its best efforts to cause the arbitral procedure to function but, solely due to action or inaction by the buyer lasting at least a specified period of time, the procedure is prevented from proceeding as provided by its rules and the underlying Offtake Contract.

Problems with International Arbitration Plus Disputes Coverage

Many Investors are dissatisfied with Disputes Coverage, largely because they are dissatisfied with international arbitration as a Dispute Resolution Procedure. There are a number of reasons for this.

International arbitration can be slow. The minimum period from initiation of the dispute until payment of an arbitral award is probably 6 to 18 months.

International arbitration is not self-executing. The winning party must bring a separate legal action to enforce the arbitral award in the Host Country or another jurisdiction where the Host Government has assets that are subject to attachment or other judicial processes to satisfy the arbitral award.

International arbitration is perceived as being subject to too much review after the initial determination. Appeals and annulments are not unheard of, and there always lurks the possibility that the local courts of the Host Country will try to start over and review the merits of the matters previously arbitrated, rather than honoring the arbitral award.

Since Disputes Coverage is only as prompt, efficient, and final as the underlying Dispute Resolution Procedure that it covers, for many Investors the package of international arbitration plus Disputes Coverage has its limitations.

Until recently, though, Investors have signed Offtake Contracts, entered into arbitration arrangements, bought Disputes Coverage, and hoped for the best.

Dreams of Perfect Breach Coverage

Investors Want Something Quicker Than Disputes Coverage

Exhaustion of remedies, whether under international arbitration or some judicial mechanism, takes time. Even if sometimes Disputes Coverage does not explicitly require the Investor to exhaust all remedies in order to make a claim, the practical effect is the same if the precondition to payment is a valid, binding, and final arbitral award.

So Investors, always concerned with the time value of money, want a procedure — whether a pure contractual arrangement with the Host Government or some combination with political risk insurance — that is quicker than international arbitration and Disputes Coverage.

Lenders to the Project Company also want a faster payment procedure, as they may be required by their regulators to write down nonperforming loans if interest is not paid during the pendency of the Dispute Resolution Procedure.

Because the Host Government is almost always the payor, and the Investor the payee, Investors (and their Lenders) want the process to go as fast as possible. Ideally, Investors really want a letter of credit–style mechanism, in which they are paid first and then can argue later.

Insurers' Concerns with Respect to Commercial Disputes

Insurers, on the other hand, do not want to step into the middle of a messy commercial dispute. For this reason, most political risk insurance policies that have attempted to address Breach Coverage include requirements (often in the form of exclusions from coverage) that, for example, (a) neither the Investor nor the Project Company has materially breached the Offtake Contract, or (b) the Offtaker could reasonably have been expected to perform its obligations under the Offtake Contract.

But these exclusions go to the heart of the matter: if the Project Company has materially breached the Offtake Contract, then the Offtaker could reasonably be expected *not* to pay under the Offtake Contract, and in that case neither should the Political Risk Insurer be obligated to pay a claim.

Industries For Which True Breach Cover Would Be Particularly Valuable

Some industries cry out for Breach Coverage. For power and similar projects that depend on Offtake Contracts, nonpayment by the Host Government of the Offtaker's obligations is the essential risk.

An even more pressing case can be made for oil and gas, mining, and similar projects that depend on concession contracts or production sharing agreements. For these projects the key risk, more than either nonpayment or nonperformance by the Host Government, is affirmative Host Government action to interfere with rights previously awarded. Coverage against these risks for these projects, coupled with some protection against tax and tariff increases, would certainly make many Investors happy.

Enhanced Breach Coverage for Lenders

One model now being developed creates a modified form of Breach Coverage for Lenders to projects where the Project Company depends on a stream of payments from a Host Government party. This new form of Breach Coverage (referred to in this paper as "Enhanced Breach Coverage") stitches together pieces from other coverages, including standard coverage for commercial bank Lenders; procedures for making a claim on a Host Government guarantee; underwriting techniques such as waiting periods and exclusions; the concept of provisional payments; traditional Disputes Coverage; and some fancy arithmetic to reconcile everything.

Lenders' Cover

To begin with, Enhanced Breach Coverage is structured as a type of Lenders' political risk insurance. Many of the elements that make it a workable cover for Lenders make it unworkable for equity investments.

In essence, it is protection against the Project Company's nonpayment to the Lenders of amounts due on the loan *as a result of* the Offtaker's nonpayment to the Project Company of termination amounts due under the Offtake Contract. (As always with Lenders' coverage, there is a big leap in causation implied by the words "as a result of . . . ," but this may be unavoidable.)

Enhanced Breach Coverage is catastrophe coverage: periodic payments on the Offtake Contract are not covered directly. Instead, it is the lump-sum payment due from the Offtaker upon termination of the Offtake Contract, and the Host Government's guarantee of it, that is covered.

The loan amounts covered include accelerated principal amounts (the "Accelerated Loan Amount"), on the expectation that the Lenders would want a complete take-out of their loans if the Offtake Contract is terminated.

Note that Enhanced Breach Coverage is not structured as a subset of expropriation cover. Compensation is not tied to violation of international law, only to mere breach of the Offtake Contract.

Host Government Guarantee Claim Procedures

Enhanced Breach Coverage requires a fully mature claim for payment on the Host Government Guarantee. That is, all of the elements of the agreed-upon procedures for turning a claim for an Offtake Contract payment into a claim for immediate payment under the Host Government Guarantee must have occurred.

Those elements include the following, though not necessarily in the following order, and each must be continuing through the dates of the claim and the claim payment:

Termination of Offtake Contract. Notice of termination of the Offtake Agreement must have been given (a) by the Project Company with respect to nonpayment by the Offtaker, or (b) by the Project Company or by the Offtaker with respect to *force majeure*;

Offtaker Failure to Pay. The Offtaker must have failed to pay to the Project Company all or any portion of the termination amount required under the Offtake Agreement;

Demand for Payment under Host Government Guarantee. The Project Company must have given notice to the Host Government demanding payment in full under the Host Government Guarantee of the termination amount (this requires that there be no unusual or cumbersome conditions to making a draw on the Host Government Guarantee, and that the Host Government have no defenses to payment);

Host Government Failure to Pay. The Host Government must have failed to pay to the Project Company, pursuant to the Host Government Guarantee, the guaranteed amount in full in U.S. dollars;

Lapse of Host Government Cure Periods. The Host Government's failure must have continued for the cure period specified in the Offtake Agreement; and

Notice of Host Government Failure to Pay. Following the expiration of the cure period, the Lenders must provide to the Insurer written notice of the failure by the Host Government to make the Host Government Guarantee Payment, which starts the clock on the Political Risk Insurer's waiting period.

Waiting Periods and Exclusions

The failure by the Host Government to make the Host Government Guarantee Payment must have continued for a specified period following the date of the notice.

There is an exclusion from Enhanced Breach Coverage if the Lenders and the Project Company have not diligently pursued the Dispute Resolution Procedure and all other remedies available under the Offtake Agreement and the Host Government Guarantee.

Note that there is no exception in Enhanced Breach Coverage for losses caused by commercial events. Because the Project Company typically is not creditworthy once the Offtake Agreement payments have been discontinued, a commercial default exclusion would be an exception that swallows the rule.

Final and Provisional Payments

Compensation under Enhanced Breach Coverage is the lowest, at the time the Lender files a claim, of: (a) the Lender's pro rata share of any unpaid termination amount; (b) the covered amount; and (c) the Accelerated Loan Amount.

For most payments with respect to termination of an Offtake Contract, the parties could reasonably expect some dispute from the Host Government, rather than a prompt wire transfer of the full amount.

If the requirements of a claim are satisfied, the Political Risk Insurer will pay the claim on a provisional or final basis, depending on whether the Host Government or the Offtaker has invoked the Dispute Resolution Procedure.

With respect to any portion of the claim for which the Dispute Resolution Procedure has *not* been initiated (after expiration of any applicable deadline for initiation of the Dispute Resolution Procedure) for a corresponding portion of the Host Government Guarantee Payment in question, the Political Risk Insurer will pay a final claim.

However, with respect to any portion of the claim for which the Dispute Resolution Procedure *has* been initiated for a corresponding portion of the Host Government Guarantee Payment in question, the Political Risk Insurer will pay a claim to the Lenders on a provisional basis (a "Provisional Payment").

The Provisional Payment is not a new concept. Political Risk Insurers have long included clauses in their policies that allow for Provisional Payments, but always at the Political Risk Insurer's option. However, the Provisional Payment option is rarely invoked, and often a precondition for a Political Risk Insurer's Provisional Payment is delivery by the insured of some security for repayment.

Happily, under Enhanced Breach Coverage, because the insureds are Lenders, delivery of security for repayment is unnecessary. However, all of the Lender's rights in the loan, including all of its rights to pursue the Dispute Resolution Procedure, are assigned to the Political Risk Insurer in exchange for its claim payment.

Final Determination Following Provisional Payment

If the Insurer has made a Provisional Payment, that payment in essence is money with a string on it, depending on the outcome of the Dispute Resolution Procedure.

If the Dispute Resolution Procedure yields a result favorable to the Project Company, in an amount at least equal to the Provisional Payment, the Provisional Payment becomes final with respect to such amount.

A "result favorable to the Project Company" under the Dispute Resolution Procedure is defined to include the standard outcomes covered under Disputes Coverage: (a) a Final and Binding Award in favor of the Project Company, including by way of settlement, (b) a final resolution following resort to a preliminary Dispute Resolution Procedure, (c) impossibility of the Dispute Resolution Procedure, or (d) Host Government frustration of the Dispute Resolution Procedure. On the other hand, if the Offtaker or the Host Government prevails in the Dispute Resolution Procedure, so that the Project Company was entitled to an aggregate amount less than the amount of the Provisional Payment, then the Lender must repay that portion of the Provisional Payment to the Insurer, with interest.

Note that the attempt to collect payment of the arbitral award is no longer a precondition to making a claim, since under Enhanced Breach Coverage collection is up to the Insurer in any event.

Conclusion

Enhanced Breach Coverage has some wrinkles remaining. For one thing, the calculation of the portion of the Provisional Payment that must be refunded can be complicated, as it depends on (a) the Lender's pro rata share of any recalculated termination amount (i.e., after giving effect to the results of the Dispute Resolution Procedure); (b) the outstanding Accelerated Loan Amount; and (c) the amount that would otherwise be payable under the Political Risk Insurer's policy, after giving effect to the exclusions and limitations.

Nevertheless, at least for Lenders and for certain types of projects, Enhanced Breach Coverage is one tool to manage and mitigate breach of contract risk.

58-68

022 G22
H54

OPIC Modified Expropriation Coverage Case Study: MidAmerican's Projects in Indonesia—Dieng and Patuha[1]

Julie A. Martin
Vice President for Insurance
Overseas Private Investment Corporation

This paper offers an outline of OPIC's modified expropriation or infrastructure coverage as currently used, as well as provides a case study of the MidAmerican projects in Indonesia, the first OPIC claim settlement based on OPIC's infrastructure coverage.

Modified Expropriation Coverage/Infrastructure Language

Summary

Infrastructure projects in developing countries, such as electricity generation and transmission facilities, telecommunications networks, airports, and railways, have traditionally been undertaken by the host government, financed by bank or other credit, and backed by sovereign guarantees. Over the past decade, however, the trends in international investment have shifted markedly. Faced with acute infrastructure shortages and a lack of fiscal resources, developing countries have increasingly opened their power, telecommunications, water, and transportation sectors to private sector investment, including that from foreign investors. In undertaking these projects, typically structured as build-operate-transfer (BOT) or other similar development schemes, foreign investors have entered into direct and extensive contractual arrangements with host governments and governmental entities. Given these relationships, characterized by ongoing performance and payment obligations of the host government or governmental entity, foreign investors have identified the risks of government default, interference in, or withdrawal from a project as among the most significant risks they face. As such, many foreign investors view breaches of key project agreements as their primary political risk.

Form of Coverage

In an effort to address certain concerns of the foreign investor when investing in infrastructure projects, OPIC has developed a modified form of expropriation coverage, commonly referred to as its "infrastructure language." As OPIC's mandate is to cover political rather than commercial risks, OPIC's standard expropriation language carves out actions taken by the host government in the context of a commercial relationship. Recognizing, however, that in some circumstances the host government's failure to fulfill its commercial obligations can constitute a political event, OPIC's modified expropriation coverage enhances the standard expropriation coverage by compensating the investor, under certain conditions, in the event the *host government* does not perform in accordance with the terms of project agreements with the investor or foreign enterprise.

Key Requirements of Coverage

Key requirements of OPIC's modified expropriation coverage include the following:

Dispute Resolution Mechanism: A cornerstone of OPIC's modified expropriation coverage is that the investor must first seek recourse against the host government through the dispute resolution mechanism applicable to the project agreement that has been breached by the government. The host government must fail to honor a favorable award or judgment obtained by the investor pursuant to this mechanism before the investor can seek compensation from OPIC. OPIC would not accept an arbitral ruling against a parastatal.

Violation of International Law: As with other forms of expropriation coverage, OPIC's modified expropriation coverage requires that there be a violation of international law — either that the government action or breach itself violated international law or that the nonpayment of the arbitral award or judgment violated international law (in which case, the underlying breach of contract giving rise to the award or judgment does not have to be a violation of international law).

Total Expropriation: As is the case with OPIC's standard expropriation coverage, modified expropriation coverage for equity investors requires total expropriation.

Assignment of Shares: Under the terms of OPIC's modified expropriation language, the investor is required, concurrent with payment for expropriation, to transfer to OPIC all its right, title, and interest in and to the investment as of the date the expropriatory effect commenced, including claims arising out of the expropriation; and transfer to OPIC the investor's rights with respect to, and cause the foreign enterprise to transfer to OPIC the foreign enterprise's rights with respect to, all net litigation payments (that is, amounts awarded to the investor or the project in respect of the breach of contract pursuant to the dispute resolution mechanism, net of certain encumbrances on such awards). OPIC requires that the transfer of such interests, claims, and net litigation payment rights be free and clear of, and the investor must agree to indemnify OPIC against, claims, defenses, counterclaims, rights of the setoff, and other encumbrances (except defenses relating to the expropriation).

Case Study: MidAmerican's Projects in Indonesia — Dieng and Patuha

Summary

MidAmerican Energy Holdings Company ("MidAmerican"), formerly CalEnergy Company, Inc. ("CalEnergy"), began development of the Dieng and Patuha projects in 1994. The projects involved the development and operation of a series of geothermal electric power generating units in the "Dieng " area in central Java and the "Patuha" area in west Java and the long-term sale of the electricity generated to P.T. (Persero) Perusahaan Listrik Negara ("PLN"), the state owned Indonesian utility, on a take-or-pay basis. Supporting this project was a letter signed by the Indonesian Ministry of Finance which pledged that it will cause Perusahaan Pertambangan Minyak Dan Gas Bumi Negara ("Pertamina"), the state oil and gas corporation that owns all Indonesian geothermal resources, and PLN to honor and perform their obligations under the project agreements (the "Support Letter").

Project development for both Dieng and Patuha proceeded largely on-track until the onset of the Asian financial crisis in 1997. Confronted with the severe depression of the Indonesian economy and the massive depreciation of the rupiah, Presidential Decree (P.D.) No. 37/1997 was issued in September 1997, postponing or placing under "review" many infrastructure projects in Indonesia. At the time the decree was issued, construction had begun on Units 1 and 2 of Dieng. (Unit 1 was not directly affected by the decree and construction continued.) Construction at the Patuha site had not yet started. Pursuant to this decree, as amended by several subsequent decrees also changing the status of various infrastructure projects, the Dieng project was allowed to continue construction of the generation plants, but the Patuha project was effectively postponed. Although Dieng was allowed to continue the development of the site, PLN did not dispatch Unit 1 when it was completed and failed to make capacity payments for the production capacity at Unit 1 of Dieng.

MidAmerican filed for arbitration against PLN for both the Dieng and Patuha projects in August 1998. On May 4, 1999, an international arbitration tribunal unanimously found that PLN was in breach of contract with respect to both projects and awarded MidAmerican $572.3 million. Following PLN's failure to pay the arbitral awards, MidAmerican moved forward with the arbitration proceedings against the Government of Indonesia ("GOI") under the Support Letter issued by the Ministry of Finance. On October 16, 1999, the second arbitration tribunal entered final awards in favor of MidAmerican in the amount of $575.6 million. Following this award, MidAmerican filed claims with OPIC and the private market insurers pursuant to its political risk insurance contracts and received full payment of the claims under those policies totaling $290 million.

Background

MidAmerican Company Description: In 1971, CalEnergy Company, Inc. was established as a developer of geothermal power production facilities in North America. In the 1980s, CalEnergy focused on geothermal development in the United States and in 1992, new management modified its strategy to include additional energy sources and to encompass the emerging global marketplace. As part of its long-range strategy to position itself for a deregulated world energy market, CalEnergy undertook the development of several projects in Indonesia and the Philippines during the mid-1990s. CalEnergy continued this strategy in 1996 with the acquisition of Northern Electric, a major provider of retail gas and electricity services in the United Kingdom and the acquisition of MidAmerican Energy, a successful regional retail energy provider in the United States in 1998. Reorganized as MidAmerican Energy Holdings Company in January 1999, the company has assets of approximately $13 billion and now owns interests in more than 10,000 net megawatts (MW) of power generation facilities and supplies gas and electricity to more than 3.3 million customers.

Indonesian Power Sector Supply and Demand: The GOI has long considered the supply of affordable and reliable electricity to be a vital ingredient for both economic and social development. Faced with the shortage of electricity in certain regions, in 1993 the GOI undertook a restructuring of the energy sector, inviting participation by independent power producers ("IPPs") in power generation throughout Indonesia. In light of the relatively low level of electricity consumption in Indonesia and the projection of 15 percent average annual growth in electricity sales during the 1990s, combined with average gross domestic product (GDP) growth of 7.3 percent (from 1990 to 1997), several foreign companies pursued power projects in Indonesia. During 1993–1997, PLN entered into approximately 26 Power Purchase Agreements with IPPs, several of which were for projects on the Java-Bali grid. Notwithstanding the projections for ongoing growth in electricity sales, even before the onset of the Asian crisis, PLN faced the prospect of excess generation capacity.

OPIC provided insurance coverage for four separate power projects in Indonesia during this general time frame. In addition to the two MidAmerican projects, Dieng and Patuha, OPIC also provided coverage to Edison Mission Energy for its investment in the Paiton project and to El Paso Energy International for its investment in the Sengkang project. Although among the 26 IPP projects, each of the four projects with OPIC support are unique in several respects—the Paiton project was the first IPP in Indonesia; Dieng and Patuha are geothermal projects that rely on a renewable and indigenous fuel source; and the Sengkang project is part of an integrated project that uses indigenous natural gas and is on a different grid system (South Sulawesi) than the majority of the other IPPs.

OPIC Insurance Coverage: From 1995 to 1997, OPIC Insurance issued four contracts to CalEnergy and its then-affiliate, Kiewit Energy Company, Inc. ("Kiewit"), to insure against the risks of inconvertibility, expropriation, and political violence coverage for the Dieng and Patuha projects. The combined Maximum Insured Amount for the two insureds for each project was $175 million. OPIC's Maximum Contingent Liability for these two projects totaled $350 million.

In October 1997, CalEnergy purchased Kiewit's equity interest in Dieng and Patuha. In January 1998, CalEnergy assumed from Kiewit all the rights, interest, and benefit of the OPIC contracts.

Private Sector Insurers: In 1997, as a cost savings measure, CalEnergy reduced the level of the insured investment with OPIC and insured a portion of its investment in Dieng and Patuha with a consortium of private market insurers. The consortium included a Lloyds' of London syndicate, Unistrat Corporation of America, Ace Global Markets Limited, and Sovereign Risk Insurance Ltd.

Concurrent with the enactment of the private sector insurance, OPIC and the consortium of private market insurers entered into a Claims Cooperation Agreement that outlined the process of seeking recovery between insurers in the event of a claim.

Issues

The MidAmerican claim represents an interesting case study because of the unique circumstances in which it occurred. The claim took place against the backdrop of the Asian financial crisis, which affected not only Indonesia — although perhaps there most severely — but the entire region and included the involvement of various international financial institutions (IFIs) including the IMF, the World Bank, and the Asian Development Bank. This case is also the first test of OPIC's infrastructure coverage and of OPIC's Claims Cooperation Agreement with private market insurers. Moreover, this is the first instance in which control of an operating asset requiring significant ongoing maintenance has been transferred to OPIC. Although OPIC is still in the process of digesting all the lessons to be learned from this case, several aspects of the case are noteworthy.

Role of the IFIs: In the aftermath of the Asian financial crisis and the downturn of the Indonesian economy, the IFIs have played a significant role in helping the GOI set priorities and develop general policies in an effort to rebuild the economy. With regard to the Indonesian power sector specifically, the IFIs have exerted a great degree of influence. Under the direction of the IMF in January 1998, on the heels of the signing of an IMF Letter of Intent, the GOI cancelled 12 projects, including several power projects, whose status had recently been reinstated. In 1998, the Ministry of Mines and Energy, under the auspices of the World Bank, issued a report on the restructuring of the Indonesian power sector, emphasizing the need to transition from the current system of IPP participation to a multiseller-multibuyer, merchant power system. Complementing the World Bank report, in 1999, the Asian Development Bank provided a $400 million loan to assist with the restructuring of the

Indonesian power sector, in addition to the corporate restructuring of PLN.

OPIC's Advocacy Role: OPIC has long played an advocacy role for its insured investors, working with both the investor and host government to resolve a conflict before it is raised to the level of an expropriation. With respect to the problems being faced by U.S. investors in Indonesia, particularly in the power sector, OPIC's advocacy efforts have been quite extensive. Such efforts included conducting a series of discussions with GOI and PLN officials to underscore the importance of honoring contractual obligations, especially with respect to attracting future foreign investment in Indonesia; coordinating internal discussions regarding the overall U.S. government message; and conducting discussions with the IFIs. In addition, OPIC has participated in a series of missions to Indonesia, the first of which occurred in July 1999, consisting of a group of six export credit agencies and investment insurers from the United States, Japan, Germany, and Switzerland to engage in direct discussions with PLN and GOI officials, as well as the IFIs. OPIC also assisted in arranging a meeting between PLN and MidAmerican in December 1998 while the arbitration was pending.

International Arbitration: Under the dispute resolution mechanism provisions of the Energy Sales Contract entered into with PLN and the Joint Operating Contract entered into with Pertamina, the state oil and gas corporation, arbitration was to occur under UNCITRAL rules in Jakarta. Although the arbitration proceedings moved forward as envisioned against PLN, following the announcement of the arbitral award in favor of MidAmerican in May 1999, several attempts were made on the part of the GOI (under the previous Habibie administration), PLN, and Pertamina to frustrate the process. These actions include both PLN and Pertamina countersuing MidAmerican in June 1999 and the issuance of an injunction by the Jakarta District Court in July prohibiting MidAmerican from trying to enforce the first arbitral award and enjoining the second arbitration from proceeding under the threat of criminal prosecution. Additional actions taken to frustrate the process included the physical removal of the Indonesian arbitration tribunal member from the second round of arbitration.

While recognizing the potential ramifications for PLN and the GOI should the second arbitration be decided in MidAmerican's favor, actions by PLN and the GOI such as those described were not anticipated and illustrate the need for careful negotiation of the rules that are to govern arbitration proceedings. In particular, had the arbitration clause provided for arbitration outside of Indonesia, the issue of the jurisdiction of an Indonesian court to enjoin the proceedings would not have come up. Notwithstanding the actions of the GOI, also noteworthy is the speed with which the arbitration tribunal was able to decide the second round of arbitration against the GOI. On October 16, 1999, the second arbitration tribunal entered final awards in favor of MidAmerican in the amount of $575.6 million three months after the second arbitration commenced.

Modified Expropriation Coverage: OPIC's infrastructure coverage uses the requirement that the investor go through its remedies as detailed in the project agreements as a means to determine objectively whether the actions taken by a host government fall within the covered category of political risk or should be considered actions taken by the government in a commercial capacity. The MidAmerican claim is the first claim submitted to OPIC under the modified expropriation coverage, and therefore the first opportunity to test how the coverage works in practice. Although attempts were made by PLN and the GOI to thwart the arbitral process, ultimately, the arbitration process was able to proceed in a timely manner and MidAmerican was able to use the nonpayment of the arbitral awards by the GOI as the basis of their claim.

Arbitration Approach vs. Negotiation Approach: In contrast to the arbitration approach taken by MidAmerican, certain other IPPs in Indonesia such as Paiton, Sengkang, Jawa Power, and Unocal, have looked to negotiation with PLN and the GOI to address their difficulties. Although reserving the right to proceed with arbitration should such efforts fail, these IPPs have indicated their preference to enter into restructuring negotiations, given their long-term interest of being involved in the Indonesian power sector. In comparing the different approaches taken by the IPPs, the question that arises is that of moral hazard. In particular, does the existence of OPIC insurance coverage in any way cause investors to act differently than they would have if they had not had OPIC coverage?

Recoveries: OPIC has substantial claims experience and has previously dealt with claims of this size. In the 1970s OPIC made good on claims presented by U.S. investors in Chile that totaled over $315 million. On an inflation-adjusted basis, those Chile claims would be the equivalent of $700 million in today's dollars, well beyond the $217.5 million in claims we have just paid in Indonesia. The Government of Indonesia is currently in negotiations with OPIC officials regarding settlement of the claim. The new Indonesian economic team appears committed to creating a favorable climate for foreign investment and has given positive signs that the new government will take a fresh approach to resolving this matter.

MidAmerican Projects in Indonesia: Chronology of Events

1997

September 23, 1997   Presidential Decree (P.D.) No. 39: As part of the GOI effort to reduce budgetary outlays, the GOI issued P.D. No. 39 which divided all infrastructure projects undertaken by or in conjunction with any state-owned entity into three categories — continued, under review, and postponed.

November 1, 1997   P.D. No. 47: P.D. No. 47 revived 15 infrastructure projects, including MidAmerican's Patuha project.

1998

January 10, 1998   P.D. No. 5: Rescinded P.D. No. 47. Unit 1 of the Patuha project was returned to the list of projects to be reviewed.

July 19–23, 1998   OPIC Advocacy Mission: OPIC team goes to Indonesia to discuss IPP situation with the GOI and PLN and to advocate on behalf of OPIC-supported projects. Meetings also held with the World Bank and the Asian Development Bank (ADB).

August 15, 1998   MidAmerican Files for Arbitration: MidAmerican files for arbitration against PLN for both the Dieng and Patuha projects.

August 25–29, 1998   OPIC Advocacy Mission: OPIC team attends World Bank–sponsored conference on Indonesian power sector restructuring.

September 11–13,1998   Muñoz Visit to Indonesia: OPIC President George Muñoz traveled to Jakarta for discussions with GOI and PLN officials on the IPP situation and to advocate on behalf of OPIC-supported projects.

November 1–5, 1998   OPIC Mission to Indonesia: Ongoing discussions with the GOI and PLN.

1999

February 1999   IPP/PLN Discussions Commence: PLN meetings with the IPPs on a one-to-one basis to discuss interim arrangements commence.

May 4, 1999   MidAmerican Wins Arbitration against PLN: An international arbitration tribunal unanimously found that PLN was in breach of contract and awarded MidAmerican $572.5 million.

June 9, 1999   MidAmerican Sued by PLN and Pertamina: Following the announcement of the arbitral award in MidAmerican's favor, PLN and Pertamina filed papers to countersue MidAmerican.

July 12–15, 1999   Joint ECA Mission: Joint mission of six ECAs: OPIC (U.S.), U.S. Export-Import Bank, Hermes (Germany), ERG (Switzerland), EID/MITI (Japan), and Japanese Bank for International Cooperation hold meetings with the GOI, PLN, World Bank, IMF, and ADB to discuss options for resolving the IPP situation.

July 22, 1999   Injunction against MidAmerican: The Jakarta District Court issued an injunction against MidAmerican that prohibits MidAmerican from trying to enforce the arbitral award against PLN or proceed with the arbitration against the GOI.

September 26, 1999   Interim Agreement: International arbitration tribunal involved in MidAmerican case determines that it continues to have jurisdiction over the proceedings and has the right to switch the venue of the proceedings.

October 11–16, 1999   Joint ECA Mission: Ongoing ECA discussions with the GOI and PLN.

October 16, 1999	MidAmerican Wins Arbitration against GOI: An international arbitration tribunal entered final award in favor of MidAmerican for the amount of $575.6 million.
October 16, 1999	MidAmerican Files Claim with OPIC and Private Market Insurers: MidAmerican submits an application for compensation of $290 million based on the infrastructure coverage language with its political risk insurers.
November 15, 1999	OPIC Pays MidAmerican Claim: OPIC paid compensation to MidAmerican in the amount of $217.5 million for the Dieng and Patuha projects.
December 6–10, 1999	Joint ECA Mission: Meeting of ECAs with the new government to discuss the IPP situation.
2000	
January 12, 2000	President Wahid signs P.D. No. 166: This presidential decree forms the IPP restructuring and rehabilitation committee of the new government. The committee is to be led by Coordinating Minister Kwik.
February 3, 2000	PLN Withdraws Lawsuit against MidAmerican: PLN withdraws its lawsuit contesting MidAmerican's arbitral award.
March 2000	OPIC/GOI Negotiations: OPIC begins negotiations with the GOI regarding the claims settlement.

Note

1. Drafted by Pamela L. Bracey, Senior Investment Insurance Officer.

Comment on Breach of Contract Coverage in Infrastructure Projects

Anne Predieri
Senior Vice President
Banc of America Securities

This topic is particularly interesting to me, and I believe it raises issues with the greatest potential impact for investors in emerging markets. There is no doubt that the risk of unilateral revision of contractual undertakings is one of the most challenging to manage. Most insurers would agree that investors are now much less concerned with traditional expropriation risk. Current expropriation coverage was designed in many ways to deal with issues arising from investor experiences in the 1970s. Inconvertibility coverage addressed the issues of the 1980s. In addition to devaluation, breach of contract is the primary concern arising from the 1990s. Investors are increasingly likely to choose the higher yield associated with an uncovered investment rather than paying political risk insurance premiums when the coverage leaves them exposed to the risks with which they are most concerned.

Rick Jenney has done an excellent job of explaining the facts and the history, and even accurately portraying both the insurers' and the investors' interests. My challenge is to suggest that as the competitive environment in which business decisions are made changes, each of us faces the choice of relying on precedent or evolving our business to meet the requirements of the 21st century.

Rick has outlined a new model for enhanced breach coverage for lenders, which does indeed look promising. I am particularly interested in the note that this coverage is not structured as a form of expropriation coverage and is therefore not tied to a violation of international law. As Ken Hansen pointed out in his earlier paper, the violation of international law test may subject investors to hurdles of unknown height at the time the investment decision is made, which greatly complicates the valuation of the insurance product available. (Some investors conclude that they won't buy anything unless they know what they're getting.) I am grateful to Rick for distinguishing between debt and equity in terms of structuring coverage that may be sensible for insurers to offer. While I agree with the premise that it's not the insurer's job to make a bad deal better (lenders don't like to throw good money after bad money either!), lenders may not have been at the table when the decision to accept imperfect dispute resolution procedures in the off-take contract was made, and may not be willing to make the same affirmative investment decision without coverage.

I would also note that while investors seemed to be willing to simply hope for the best given the arbitration arrangements and contractual arrangements they have accepted in the past, as competitive pressures compress loan margins and returns on investment, and as opportunities for new investment in privatizations and deregulated industries in more developed countries offer higher returns with lower political risks, the decisionmaking criteria have shifted somewhat, making this coverage that much more important. Furthermore, industries such as water will require a new approach to this issue to attract the capital required to develop these sectors in a number of markets. MIGA's developmental interests should provide an incentive to ensure that the "enabling environment," including risk mitigation tools, is appropriate.

In addition to the basic breach of contract risk, Rick articulates quite well the broader issue: the key risk, more than either nonpayment or nonperformance by the host government, is affirmative host government action to interfere with rights previously awarded. This includes regulatory action in a number of projects dependent upon a tariff mechanism to pass through increased costs. The tariff mechanism is a commercial agreement, but the regulator's willingness to implement it in future years remains a political decision in many cases.

The enhanced breach coverage that Rick describes is an improvement, but it is still structured as catastrophic coverage and appears to be designed for cases where the host government has offered a guarantee of termination payments, which is not always an option. Most lenders' policies provide for a certain amount of "creeping expropriation" based on default of one or more scheduled debt service payments "as a result of expropriatory actions." I agree with

Rick, and am indeed painfully aware of the big leap in causation implied by the wording, but I believe there is value in structuring a transaction to facilitate the pro-active engagement of insurers, especially official insurers, while there is still a possibility of resolving the issue, averting the claim, and continuing the business, rather than only having recourse after terminating the project. I would think that development institutions would also have an interest in continuing the underlying investment that originally qualified for their support. I do agree with Rick, of course, that many investors are dissatisfied with arbitration as a solution, so all efforts to address this issue are welcome. The political risk insurance industry offers an exemplary model for rapid evolution in terms of capacity, sources, tenor, and even manuscripted policies. I would submit that the scope of coverage needs to evolve as well, if political risk insurance is to remain relevant to investors going forward. Rick succinctly explains the positions regarding the perfect question, "Can someone help with these risks?": Political risk insurers have long maintained that commercial risk is commercial and political risk is political, and never the twain shall meet. Meanwhile, investors recognize that breach of contract risk is a risk they cannot adequately manage or mitigate, because the reality is that commercial and political risks are increasingly blurred.

PART FOUR

Securitizing Political Risk Insurance: Overview

Theodore H. Moran, Editor

John Finnerty of PricewaterhouseCoopers, LLP, draws lessons from the evolution of the asset-backed securities market to offer suggestions about how political risk insurance might be securitized. The growing interest in the potential to securitize political risk insurance, he observes, derives from the same factors that drove the efforts to securitize property catastrophe insurance: the desire to diversify risk exposure and reallocate risk exposure to those market participants best equipped to handle them, thereby spreading the risks across a broader market and tapping a deeper pool of risk capital.

To make the securitization of political risk insurance feasible, Finnerty argues, several conditions have to be met. As in the case of reinsurance, primary insurers must retain some substantial loss exposure to mitigate problems of adverse selection, asymmetric information, and moral hazard. At the same time, however, the probability of loss and corresponding premiums must be high enough, and the size of the issue large enough, to pay for the transaction costs of the securitization. Finally, the loss trigger must be exogenously determined, out of the control of the insurer, and symmetrically transparent to all participants in the securitization. The market instrument might then be designed like a credit derivative, with a notional principal amount, a strike spread, and an option expiration date.

A key prerequisite for the development of a market to trade political risk exposures is the collection of objective information and the compilation of a political risk index (or indexes for different forms of political risk) that allow purchases of securitization instruments to assess their exposure and determine the rate of return required to compensate them for assuming this exposure. The risk data must be consistently compiled over a period long enough for risk modelers to build statistically meaningful models. The investment vehicles themselves will probably have to cover large pools of individually idiosyncratic risks whose aggregate characteristics can be reliably analyzed, as in the case of securitized mortgage pools.

Drawing on the history of derivative products in other markets, in particular property catastrophe bonds (cat bonds), Finnerty outlines how a political insurance structured note might be priced: it could be designed to pay $1 at maturity at time T provided that no covered political events, as defined in the note agreement, took place during the life of the note. All political risk insurance claims would be aggregated and subtracted from the amount otherwise due the note holders at maturity (net of the insured party's retention). The price of the political risk structured note would then be the present value of the expected maturity payment to note holders, or the face amount of the note minus the expected insurance payout.

Alternatively, the political insurance structure note might be converted into a swap in which the swap writer receives a given payment at time t and agrees to pay out a corresponding amount at time T depending upon the number of covered political events and the amount of the claims that take place during the interval. Finally, in another example, the holder of a political insurance structured note can write a put option, adjusting the strike price to provide whatever level of loss protection is desired at a cost less than full insurance coverage.

Kevin R. Callahan, of Aon Capital Markets, agrees with John Finnerty that capital markets represent a large potential source of capacity for political risk insurance coverage. Most political risk coverage, he argues, is issued on an indemnity basis (dollar for dollar recovery in the event of loss) rather than being hedged through contracts based on changing indices of risk (basis risk).

As in the case of property catastrophe insurance, political risk indemnity capacity is limited in some markets (such as Brazil and Turkey in the political risk market, Florida hurricanes and California earthquakes in the property catastrophe market) where diversification is difficult. The development of derivatives that provide index-based coverage can help in the diversification process, thereby increasing capacity and allowing the market to function more efficiently.

Both technical and cultural barriers have to be overcome, however, to expand the use of securitization to bridge the "disconnect" between those capital market participants who are willing to assume index-based risks and those insurers, lenders, and project sponsors who are searching for sources of potential indemnification.

Neil Doherty of the Wharton Risk Management Center argues that because political risk reinsurance is basically an indemnity contract, it suffers from problems of both adverse selection and moral hazard. Actions by the policyholder that can reduce the potential for loss are not easily monitored, nor, therefore, can the amount of potential damages be well estimated. It is difficult for capital market participants to take a "pure play" on the political risk exposure of the underlying sponsor or lender to a project. The market for political risk is consequently incomplete.

The challenge is to find some index that has a high correlation with a primary insurer's claims for indemnification but over which the primary exercises no significant control.

To satisfy the requirements for securitizing political risk, Doherty asserts, it is indispensable to find a trigger that is objective, transparent, and has low basis risk.

Gerald T. West of MIGA points out, however, that various efforts to measure political risk at the national level have always been considered problematic and the assumptions upon which they have been based are open to serious question (such as the assumption that the political risk component of one prominent index is exactly twice the weight of the financial and economic risk components across all countries and time periods). More broadly, it is important to consider whether political risk is an attribute associated most accurately at the macro level with a country, or, rather, at the micro level with particular sectors or kinds of projects.

Turning to the contention that the trigger for insurance payment must be independent of the control of the insurer, West points out that one of the principal attractions of a public sector insurer like OPIC or MIGA is that the insurer can explicitly play a role in preventing or deterring a loss from occurring (the so-called halo effect). At one point, for example, OPIC estimated that only one in four prospective claims actually resulted in a claim, attributable in large part to the assistance that the insurer could provide behind the scenes in clearing up problems and misunderstandings.

Anthony Faulkner of the Export Credits Guarantee Department of the United Kingdom (ECGD) addresses the specific suggestion that the Berne Union might be able to provide statistics of use for designing a derivatives market for political risk instruments. Faulkner points out that the Berne Union is made up of national export credit agencies and public political risk insurers, with one private underwriter enjoying observer status (AIG). The Berne Union does not have extensive access, therefore, to private sector insurance claims data. Given the role of such official agencies in interceding and even negotiating with host governments on behalf of the insureds, moreover, it is unlikely that the Berne Union could offer any meaningful statistics on how the entire political risk insurance industry performs.

David Bailey of the Export Development Corporation of Canada (EDC) reinforces this point, reporting that EDC, for example, has paid out no more than 12 to 15 investment insurance claims since its inception in 1969. Given the small dimensions of the claims experience on the part of public insurers, as reflected in a recent pooling of information on claims paid and on recovery experience within the Berne Union, Bailey questions whether there will be sufficient data for entities trying to promote the securitization of political risk exposures.

D81 G22

Securitizing Political Risk Investment Insurance: Lessons from Past Securitizations

John D. Finnerty
Partner
PricewaterhouseCoopers, LLP

Financial engineering involves crafting innovative financial instruments to solve financial problems, such as altering an investor's risk exposure.[1] A new financial instrument is truly innovative when it enables market participants to achieve superior risk-return combinations: achieving greater after-tax returns or lower risk or both. The securitization of assets is one of the major contributions of financial engineering and has spawned a host of innovative financial instruments that have achieved more efficient risk allocations.

The securitization of a diverse array of asset cash flow streams has also been one of the main innovative forces shaping the capital markets over the past three decades. Securitization has transformed residential and commercial mortgages and home equity loans into mortgage-backed bonds; automobile, truck, and credit card receivables into asset-backed bonds; and lease payments, franchise fees, music royalties, and a variety of other nontraded cash flow streams into tradable bonds. It can enhance liquidity, permit better portfolio diversification, and facilitate more efficient risk allocations. Investment bankers are continually on the lookout for new assets or liabilities to securitize.

In 1992, securitization spread to property catastrophe insurance as a means of deepening the pool of risk capital available to the property and casualty reinsurance industry. Borden and Sarkar (1996) and Doherty (1997) describe the evolution of property catastrophe securitization instruments, beginning with the property catastrophe options that are currently traded on the Chicago Board

Options Exchange (CBOE), followed by private and public issues of catastrophe bonds (also called act-of-God bonds), followed next by contingent surplus notes, and finally by property catastrophe swaps. The evolution of this class of reinsurance products offers some useful insights for any new risk management products that might be developed to securitize other forms of insurance.

While the asset-backed securities markets were developing, investment bankers were introducing a variety of new currency, interest rate, commodity, equity, credit, weather, energy, and other derivative instruments. The array of new derivatives included property catastrophe options and swaps. Additional classes of derivatives are undoubtedly under development. For example, political insurance derivatives could be developed to change the way political risk exposure is managed. Such instruments have the potential to alter fundamentally how such risk is priced; they would permit investors to diversify their political risk exposure; and they would enable the capital and insurance markets to reallocate political risk exposures to those market participants who are best equipped to handle them.

There appears to be growing interest in the potential for securitizing political risk insurance.[2] This interest is due at least in part to the dramatic rise in foreign direct investment in developing countries in the 1990s coupled with the 1997–98 Asian financial crises and the 1998 Russian debt moratorium, which heightened investor sensitivity to emerging market political risk (see West, 2000). As the emerging markets continue to attract new overseas investment, foreign suppliers of capital are naturally concerned about hedging their exposure to the political risks inherent in such investing.[3]

The factors that are driving the efforts to securitize political risk insurance are similar to those that propelled the desire to securitize property catastrophe insurance, namely, the twin desires to tap a deeper pool of risk capital and to spread the risks of reinsurance across a broader spectrum of market participants. The capital market's experience in securitizing mortgages, credit risk, and property catastrophe reinsurance can provide useful insights into how to go about securitizing political risk insurance.

This chapter is organized as follows. Section I addresses the question: Why securitize political risk investment insurance? Section II discusses how to define and measure political risk for securitization purposes. Section III identifies the factors that are needed to promote the securitization of political risk insurance, while Section IV highlights some barriers to securitization. Section V explains how existing credit derivatives can be used to hedge political risk, albeit with substantial basis risk. Section VI, Section VII, and Section VIII explain the useful lessons for securitizing political risk insurance that can be gleaned from the securitization of mortgages, property catastrophe reinsurance, and credit risk, respectively. Section IX develops a set of contingent-claims models for pricing the new political risk insurance instruments developed in Sections VI–VIII in order to show that existing valuation technology can handle them. Section X discusses some important legal, regulatory, and marketing issues. Section XI offers some conclusions.

I. Why Securitize Political Risk Investment Insurance?

Doherty (2000) identifies three potential benefits of political risk securitization. First, it can lower the contracting cost involved in hedging political risk exposure. It can achieve this cost reduction by ameliorating the adverse selection and moral hazard problems inherent in traditional political risk investment insurance. As discussed further in this chapter, whether a particular event is covered under the policy is often subject to dispute. Also, the amount of damages the policy-holder has suffered due to political events (as opposed to commercial causes) may be difficult to calculate and hence also subject to dispute. Actions that the policy-holder can undertake to mitigate damages are difficult to monitor. These factors make the moral hazard problem a serious concern to a reinsurer.

There are various devices for controlling the adverse selection and moral hazard problems. Chief among these is establishing a long-term relationship between the insurer and the reinsurer; the insurer's need for continuing reinsurance protection holds the adverse selection and moral hazard problems in check. They could also be controlled by inserting appropriate provisions in the reinsurance contract, but that approach requires very careful contract drafting. A better approach may be to use objective payoff triggers that are beyond the primary insurer's control but correlate closely with the primary insurer's losses, if such loss triggers are feasible. This is the approach employed in property catastrophe insurance securitization, which I discuss later in the chapter. The basic idea here is to achieve the optimal tradeoff between basis risk and moral hazard/adverse selection risk. This has worked in the case of property catastrophe insurance; to work in political risk insurance, an objective measure of political-risk-event losses will have to be found (or created if one does not already exist) that is transparent and has low basis risk.

A second benefit from the securitization of political risk insurance is the potential for reducing credit risk. As discussed later in the paper, there are property casualty insurance securitization structures that insulate the insurer from exposure to reinsurer credit risk, put simply, the risk that the reinsurer lacks sufficient funds to pay off on a claim. Removing credit risk eliminates the possibility that the insurer might discover ex post that it has not reduced its overall risk exposure, but rather has only transformed it from property casualty risk to credit risk exposure.

The third benefit cited by Doherty (2000) is the increase in the insurer's risk management opportunity set. A new political risk securitization vehicle can give rise to valuable management options that did not previously exist.

II. Defining and Measuring Political Risk

The term "political risk" has a wide range of definitions in practice. As West (1996) has noted, the term is often used in a general fashion, with the result that it is not always clear exactly what risk elements are included (or excluded). In practice, commercial and political risks are often difficult to distinguish, as for example when the host government has guaranteed payments for electricity under an off-take contract and refuses to make payments because it alleges that the power company breached the contract. Is this risk political, or is it really commercial?

Political risk is best thought of as the corporate exposure to the risk of a political event that diminishes the value of an asset. Political risks should be distinguished from commercial and economic risks. West (1996) distinguishes political risks as those risks relating either to a specific government action, such as a law or regulation, or to instability in a jurisdiction's political or social system, such as a war or an abrupt change in government. He defines political risk as the "probability of the occurrence of some political event that will change the prospects for the profitability of a given investment" (West, 1996, page 6).

Political risk can be measured at either the macro level or the micro level. At the macro level, political risk is assessed on a countrywide basis; it is not specific to any single project within the country. At the micro level, political event risk is specific to a particular project. Most political risk assessment services evaluate risk at the macro level, whereas most parties who desire political risk cover purchase it at the micro level through the conventional political risk insurance market.

Insuring an investment against political risk requires a precise specification in the insurance contract of the political risk events that are covered under the insurance policy. The insurance policy must clearly spell out the covered events in sufficient detail to enable the parties to the insurance contract to agree on whether a covered event has occurred, and if so, to determine whether it occurred during the period when insurance coverage was in force and the amount of the insurance recovery to which the insured is entitled.

There exist derivative financial instruments, called credit derivatives, that can be used to hedge country political risk. They provide imperfect coverage against project political event risk, however, because they generally cover political risk in the macro sense. This paper describes how securities and derivatives, including credit derivatives, can be crafted to provide the sort of micro political event risk coverage currently available through conventional political risk insurance.

A. Types of Political Risk

This paper is concerned with the political riskiness of capital investment projects, which are long-term assets whose political risk exposure is consequently long-term in nature (i.e., more than one year). International trade also involves political risk, but these transactions are short-term in nature and their risks are consequently short-term. The interest in securitizing political risk insurance pertains to long-term insurance contracts of the type used by project sponsors to insure their investments against political risks that jeopardize asset values.

The political risks associated with investments can be classified into four distinct types of risk events.[4]

A.1 Currency Transfer Restrictions

These events involve losses arising from an insured party's inability to convert local currency (received in the form of interest, principal, dividends, royalties, or other remittances) into foreign exchange for transfer outside the host country. The coverage insures against excessive delays in acquiring foreign currency that might result from host government action or failure to act, by unfavorable changes in exchange control laws or regulations, or by deterioration in conditions governing the conversion and transfer of local currency. Currency devaluation is not normally covered under political risk insurance policies.

A.2 Expropriation of Property

This class includes the risk of loss of an investment as a result of acts by the host government that might reduce or eliminate ownership of, control over, or other rights to the insured investment. In the extreme, outright nationalization or confiscation might occur. However, "creeping" expropriation — a series of acts that, over time, effectively expropriate the owner's property — can also occur.

Coverage is often available on a limited basis for partial expropriation, such as confiscation of funds or specified tangible assets. Nondiscriminatory measures taken by the host government in the exercise of its legitimate regulatory authority are not covered.

For total expropriation of equity investments, the insurer usually pays the net book value of the insured investment. For expropriation of funds, the insurer pays the insured portion of the blocked funds. For loans and loan guarantees, the insurance covers the outstanding principal and any accrued and unpaid interest. Compensation is usually paid upon assignment of the insured party's interest in the expropriated investment to the insurer (e.g., equity ownership interest or interest in the loan).

A.3 Breach of Contract

These events entail losses resulting from the host government's breach or repudiation of a contract with the insured party for political (as distinct from commercial) reasons. In the event of an alleged breach or repudiation, the insurance policy usually requires the insured party to invoke a dispute resolution mechanism, such as arbitration (which, of course, must be provided for in the underlying contract) and obtain an award for damages. If, after a specified period of time, the insured party has not received payment or if the dispute resolution mechanism fails to function because of actions taken by the host government, the insurer pays the compensation called for in the insurance policy.

Unfortunately, there is not a bright line between political risk and commercial risk. Some insureds think that political risk insurance covers all wrongful acts by the host government that impair the value of the covered asset. However, most political risk insurance policies distinguish between actions taken by the host government in its governmental role (which may be covered if, for example, they meet the test for expropriation) and actions taken by it as a commercial party (which are generally not covered). To continue an earlier example, suppose a host government refuses to honor its payment obligations under a power purchase off-take agreement. Expropriation policies would normally *not* cover such a situation because the host government might have a legitimate issue concerning the project company's failure to perform. (See Jenney, 2000.) Breach of contract policies *might* cover it; however, the policy's requirements concerning exhaustion of remedies are crucial. In general, disputes coverage will not pay off until all available remedies are exhausted (such as the requirement to achieve an arbitration award and evidence that the host government has failed to comply with the award or else has taken steps to prevent the arbitration process from working).[5] In contrast, breach coverage furnishes greater protection because it pays off when the host government in the example refuses to make the payment that the off-take contract requires.

Since the exhaustion of remedies can take 18 months or longer (see Jenney, 2000), investors would prefer breach coverage over disputes coverage. Jenney describes a modified form of breach coverage, called enhanced breach coverage, which would improve the quality of breach of contract coverage available to lenders. The essential element is coverage of the lump-sum payment due from the off-taker upon termination of the off-take contract and the host government's guarantee of this payment. Such coverage is distinct from expropriation cover because it is linked to the breach of the off-take contract and is *not* tied to a violation of international law.

A.4 War and Civil Disturbance

This class of events involves the risk of loss from damage to, destruction of, or the disappearance of, tangible assets caused by politically motivated acts of war or civil disturbance in the host country. Covered events typically include revolution, insurrection, coups d'état, sabotage, and terrorism.

For equity investments, the insurer usually pays the insured party's share of the least of (a) the book value of the assets, (b) their replacement cost, or (c) the cost of repairing the damaged assets. For loans and loan guarantees, the insurer generally pays the insured portion of the principal and interest payments that are in default as a direct result of the damages to the specified assets that were caused by war or civil disturbance.

War and civil disturbance coverage may also extend to events that, for a period of at least one year, result in an interruption of project operations essential to overall financial viability. This type of business interruption coverage is effective when the investment is considered a total loss; at that point, the insurer pays the book value of the total insured equity investment. For loans and loan guarantees, the insurer generally pays the insured portion of the principal and interest payments that are in default as a result of the business interruption caused by covered events.

B. Macro Measures of Political Risk

The PRS Group's *International Country Risk Guide* (ICRG) provides four different measures of "country risk": (a) political risk, (b) financial risk, (c) economic risk, and (d) a composite-risk index that combines all three risk measures into a single measure. (See Political Risk Services, 1999a.) Investors and sponsors of projects in developing economies generally refer to country risk as "emerging market risk." For the purpose of this paper, I will treat emerging market risk as synonymous with country risk when the latter term applies to a developing economy.

It is important to appreciate that political risk is *not* limited to the emerging markets. For example, many project finance professionals would argue that natural resource projects in the United States are exposed to political risk because of the proclivity within the United States to change the environmental laws and apply the new laws retroactively. However, in this paper I am going to construe the term political risk more narrowly to coincide with the set of political event risks generally covered by political risk insurance contracts provided by the Multilateral Investment Guarantee Agency (MIGA), the Overseas Private Investment Corporation (OPIC), and the various private sector insurers who provide political risk insurance coverage.

The ICRG has been published regularly since 1980. The PRS Group gathers monthly data for a variety of political, financial, and economic risk factors and calculates the three separate risk indices and the composite-risk index just mentioned. Political risk scores are based on subjective staff analysis of available information. Economic risk scores are based upon objective analysis of quantitative data, and financial risk scores are based upon analysis of a mix of quantitative and qualitative information. The subjectivity of the political risk index would be a concern to investors in financial instruments based on it because this subjectivity would suggest some imprecision, which in turn would complicate any analysis of the index's historical experience.

Calculation of the three individual risk indices is simply a matter of summing up the point scores for the factors within each risk category. The composite rating is a linear combination of the three individual index scores with the political risk measure being given twice the weight of the financial and economic risk measures. The PRS Group thinks of country risk as being composed of two primary components: (a) ability to pay and (b) willingness to pay. It associates financial and economic risk with an ability to pay and political risk with a willingness to pay.

Erb, Harvey, and Viskanta (1996) find that significant information is contained in the ICRG composite, financial, and economic ratings. For example, when they formed portfolios based on changes in the risk ratings, they found risk-adjusted abnormal returns in the range of 1,000 basis points (bps) per year. However, they found that trading on the political risk measure did not produce abnormal returns. In contrast, Diamonte, Liew, and Stevens (1996) found that this index did convey information that is useful to investors. At a minimum, the mixed results would suggest the need for further research concerning the usefulness to investors of the information contained in macro political risk measures.

The ICRG definition of political risk encompasses the risk of property expropriation, currency inconvertibility, war and insurrection, and abrogation of commercial contracts on a country-by-country basis. This definition reflects the moral hazard risk that foreign investors generally face when they commit funds to a project in a particular country. However, this macro measure of political risk may not adequately fit the political event risk to which the equity investors in or lenders to a particular project are exposed. In particular, discriminatory actions that a host government might direct against a particular project sponsor are not necessarily directly reflected in the ICRG measure. Nevertheless, the ICRG political risk index does reflect the risk of such actions being taken to the extent it embodies the PRS Group's assessment of the overall risk that any foreign investor or any lender faces that the host government might take such discriminatory actions against them.

Unfortunately, "country risk ratings" are of limited usefulness in political risk investment insurance. They are ex ante macro measures of risk, which may be useful in pricing political risk insurance. However, they cannot be determinative in pricing project-specific risk. Moreover, they are useless in determining the appropriate payoffs within a political risk insurance securitization structure, both because they are ex ante measures and also because they are subjective assessments of risk exposure.

C. *Micro Measures of Political Risk*

The political risk cover that project sponsors are currently able to purchase provides insurance coverage for specific projects (or companies) in which the insured parties have invested equity or to which they have lent money. The insurance policy provides risk cover for political risk events that would impair the value of equity investments in or loans to the covered investment. It is a form of property catastrophe insurance in which the catastrophe is the result of a political event rather than a natural peril, such as a hurricane or a flood. The insurer is exposed to countrywide political risk insofar as a political risk event might affect specific investments in the host country that are covered under one of the political risk insurance policies it has written.

When a host government is involved with a project financially, the nature and degree of political risk tend to become more complicated. For example, the host government may have loaned funds or guaranteed some project debt. Properly structured, such financial commitments can substantially reduce the likelihood of a catastrophic political event that would impair the value of the project. As a second example, suppose that in return for equity in the project, the host government agreed to special currency conversion arrangements that significantly reduce the risk of currency inconvertibility. Such arrangements can often be negotiated when a project generates substantial foreign currency. In that case, mechanisms can be put in place, such as offshore bank accounts out of which loan payments are disbursed, that ameliorate the risk of currency inconvertibility. However, the host government's financial involvement in the project may increase the likelihood that disputes with the government will adversely affect the project, particularly if it tries to use the project to pursue its political agenda and its political goals conflict with the economic interests of the project's other equity investors.

In practice and in comparison to the catastrophic risks covered by property catastrophe insurance for natural perils, political risk cover is more likely to be idiosyncratic with respect to specific projects. The typical political risk insurer tends to be better diversified geographically than most property insurers, who tend to concentrate their business in a specific region to take advantage of economies of scale. Political risk cover is usually arranged in connection with large discrete projects for which foreign providers of capital are willing to bear business, economic, and financial risks but not political or other nonbusiness risks. The idiosyncratic nature of project-based political risks simplifies the pricing of political risk insurance financial instruments backed by a diversified portfolio because the risk-free interest rate can be used to discount the expected future cash flows.

III. Factors That Will Promote Securitization of Political Risk Insurance

Securitizing risk insurance involves balancing basis risk, credit risk, and the incentive conflicts inherent in reinsurance (see Doherty, 1997). At least five factors will promote the securitization of political risk insurance. Froot (1998) discusses these conditions as they apply to the securitization of property catastrophe insurance.

A. *The Insurer's Loss Retention Should Be Substantial*

The market for bonds is broadest when bond investors are exposed to no more than a minimal likelihood of loss of principal. Substantial loss retentions by the insurer mean that the reinsurer's loss exposure is relatively low. This is accomplished by having the insurer (or some other creditworthy party) bear responsibility for the lower loss layers.

Like traditional reinsurance, political insurance securitization vehicles could cut possible losses into multiple layers. Each layer would have a maximum possible loss. Low layers of risk are frequently affected, whereas higher layers are affected relatively infrequently. Froot (1998) points out that most of the cat bond issues to date have had a low probability of loss, reflecting a relatively high reinsurance layer.[6] Several factors are responsible for this loss structure. First, many institutional fixed-income investors are restricted to bonds that are rated investment-grade.[7] The demand for investment-grade bonds is greater than for "junk" debt, which is rated speculative-grade. In assigning a rating for bonds, the credit-rating agencies examine the probability of loss of some portion of principal or interest. A bond with an actuarial risk of loss of about 2 percent or greater is likely to generate a rating below investment-grade, which greatly reduces the number of investors who can buy it.

Second, lower layers of risk are not usually transferred through cat bonds because insurers, reinsurers, and capital market investors do not like to bear the first dollar of loss from a risk. Most insurance contracts stipulate a deductible, or retention. This feature controls moral hazard and mitigates the problems of adverse selection and asymmetric information. (See Niehaus and Mann, 1992, for a discussion of moral hazard and adverse selection incentive conflicts that arise with reinsurance.) If a loss occurs, the insurer pays the first dollars. This encourages responsible insurer behavior, including effective risk mitigation, better loss-evaluation monitoring, and so forth. It also protects reinsurers and investors against private information the insurer has concerning the risk it is transferring. In general, insurers who privately know that the risk of loss is severe are the ones who have the strongest incentive to seek a low deductible.

The issues of moral hazard and adverse selection are particularly important for all forms of reinsurance bonds because the capital markets are at arm's length from the insurer. The traditional reinsurance market brings the coverage seller and the coverage purchaser much closer together because they typically do repeat business and the final recovery is often based on the reinsurer's ultimate net loss experience with the insurer. Thus, there is an ongoing flow of information conveyed by brokers, and there is greater oversight and control over the reinsurer's risk-assumption process. Techniques for managing moral hazard and adverse selection are crucial to insurance securitization, particularly if coverage for lower risk layers is to be provided.

Third, reinsurance pricing has generally favored the securitization of higher risk layers and, thus, larger retentions by insurers. Froot (1998) reports that the pricing in the reinsurance market has been the most attractive in the highest risk layers. The larger cat risks are potentially the most destructive to reinsurers, and they create a substantial need for additional capital. The rates of return for providing this additional capital are thus the highest relative to the amount of risk transferred. Consequently, cat bonds have been designed to securitize the upper reinsurance layers. I believe that the securitization of political risk insurance is more likely to be successful if it is designed for the upper reinsurance layers.

B. The Layer of Protection Should Not Be So High That Securitization Is Uneconomical

A high level of protection entails a very low probability of a loss. But a very low loss probability means that the benefit the insurer will realize through securitization of the reinsurance may not be large enough to justify the expense involved in securitization. At higher risk layers, risk transfer becomes less and less economical. At higher layers, there is a lower probability of loss, and the insurance premium can become very small. In the extreme, the small premium may be insufficient to cover the transaction costs involved in securitization. In addition, the risks embedded in each securities issue, no matter how small, are still unique. This forces investors to expend effort assessing each securities issue's riskiness. Very low-risk reinsurance bonds simply are not economical.

For example, Froot (1998) estimates that the various costs of a cat bond issue can exceed 150 basis points for a $100 million issue. With a 1 percent risk of loss, the actuarially fair insurance premium on such a bond would be 100 basis points. Even if investors were willing to buy bonds that paid only actuarially fair rates of return, the bare minimum charge would be 250 basis points, 2.5 times the minimum return that investors are willing to accept. At higher layers, the probabilities of loss fall. For example, at a layer so high that the actuarial risk is 10 basis points, the minimum charge would be 160 basis points more than 16 times as large! Unless the demand for reinsurance protection is extremely price inelastic, there is too little protection to justify the premium.

C. The Dollar Amount of Risk Transfer Should Be Significant

Because a large portion of the costs of securitization are fixed, these costs need to be spread over a large base. In the preceding example, the 150-basis-point threshold grows as the limit shrinks. A $50 million issue might involve more than 200 basis points in cost. For example, Froot (1998) estimates that two Residential Re cat bond issues sold by USAA ($400 million combined face amount) probably cost about 100 basis points. Either the issuer must pay these costs in addition to the premium or else these costs will reduce the investors' returns. As a result, small issues are likely to be uneconomical.

Standardization can ameliorate the fixed-cost problem. Issuance costs can also be reduced through competition among investment bankers. However, new issue volume for reinsurance securitization must grow substantially beyond current new issue volumes to bring about very low issuance expenses.

D. The Loss Trigger Must Be Determined Independently of the Insured

Insurer control of the loss trigger would give rise to potentially severe moral hazard. Such a situation would almost assuredly inhibit the development of a viable reinsurance securitization market from developing. No one would be willing to trade when the other party can unilaterally determine the economic outcome. In many cases in the insurance market, however, the insured does exercise some influence over the risk, although the degree of influence is usually minor in such cases (e.g., errors and omissions). In such circumstances, moral hazard does not preclude a transaction, but the disadvantaged side of the transaction must be compensated adequately. The greater the moral hazard, the higher the insurance premium the insured must pay.

Moral hazard is potentially very troublesome in connection with political risk investment reinsurance. The covered events are not always clearly defined; what may appear to be a political risk event (such as the host government's refusal to honor a contractual guarantee) may in reality be a commercial dispute that normally would not be covered under the policy. Would securitization diminish the insurer's efforts to limit payoffs to political risk events by refusing to pay a claim when the dispute is commercial? Second, the measurement of damages resulting from political acts is inherently more difficult than, say, measuring the damages from a hurricane. Would securitization reduce the insurer's incentive to minimize insurance payouts? Third, political risk insurance policies typically transfer title to the asset to the insurer when the policy pays off. Recovery of asset value is an important component of the insurer's pricing decisions. Would securitization reduce the insurer's efforts to maximize asset recoveries?

Cat event risks provide relatively limited scope for moral hazard. Cat event risks are highly exogenous. The same cannot be said for political risks because these risks grow out of the potential for disputes between a project sponsor and the host government. To date natural perils have been among the easiest insurance risks to securitize because of their exogenous nature. Nevertheless, even in the case of natural perils, the insured may exert some degree of influence over its losses. For example, the benefits of aggressive mitigation measures and claims management may not inure to the insured's benefit once event risk has been transferred. As a result, moral hazard arises because the insured may expend less effort, resulting in greater potential losses for the reinsurer and investors. Superior securitization structures provide incentives and restrictions to control this moral hazard problem.

Moral hazard can be contained by using an industrywide index of losses to trigger the reinsurance payments. Alternatively, dual triggers can reduce moral hazard. For example, many cat bond triggers are linked, first, to an individual insurer's ultimate net loss and, second, to a cat event as defined by Property Claims Service (PCS).[8] In other cases, the second trigger adds a severity condition to the simple event trigger, such as requiring that a qualifying event must be a hurricane of class three or above, or an earthquake of magnitude 5.5 or greater.[9]

A third way to reduce moral hazard is to base protection on the size of industry losses associated with an event. One company cannot influence industry cat losses as much as it can its own cat losses, so moral hazard is reduced. However, in general, it is not easy to measure industry losses. Collecting data on losses that are directly related to a particular cat event can be difficult. This effort requires sophisticated information technology to classify claims (and paid losses) as specifically associated with a particular loss event. Consolidating information across companies is difficult because companies collect and maintain information differently. As a result, existing loss indexes do not directly measure total industrywide cat event losses, although in the case of natural perils, they appear to provide reliable estimates. This problem is likely to be even more difficult in the case of political catastrophes because of the greater ambiguity in how they are defined.

Industrywide indexes also help standardize the measurement of event risks. This feature helps investors by eliminating the need to analyze separately the properties of each company's individual event risks. Standardization also ameliorates the moral hazard and adverse selection incentive conflicts. These features should, in principle, make industry-index-linked protection cheaper (for the insured) than providing indemnification through an ultimate-net-loss trigger. However, based on evidence from the cat bond market, it is not clear that indexes are cheaper. Nevertheless, if the number of reinsurance securitizations increases and investors more readily come to accept insurance loss indexes as benchmarks, a cost differential might emerge.

Industrywide indexes have a significant drawback for the insurer who reinsures, however. They expose the insurer to basis risk. The cash flows from the reinsurance vehicle do not offset exactly the losses the insurer experiences. Traditional reinsurance involves no basis risk; however, tying the insurance recovery to the insurer's actual losses inevitably involves moral hazard and adverse selection problems. Thus, there is an inherent conflict, which affects virtually all catastrophe reinsurance.

E. The Loss Trigger Should Be Symmetrically Transparent to All Parties to the Securitization

The last important potential concern for investors is asymmetric information. The primary insurer usually knows more about the risks being transferred than does the reinsurer. It may be difficult to cede a risk to another party when that party knows that the transferor has superior information. In that case, the transferee may be reluctant to enter into the transaction. Insurers who wish to lower the costs of reinsurance protection have an interest in credibly providing information and achieving transparency concerning the risks they are transferring. However, third-party investors would naturally be concerned that some insurers might transfer their poorer risks. They will worry that those insurers who view the cost of reinsurance as cheap are those who know that their risk is worse than recognized in the current pricing. The effect of asymmetric information becomes more severe as the cost of protection increases. Thus, the greater the information asymmetry, the greater the risk that adverse selection of transactions will work against the investor.

Using industrywide indexes as loss triggers can help reduce informational asymmetries in much the same way that using them reduces moral hazard. Investors can learn as much about index losses as any particular company would know. In addition, an insurer with risks that are worse than generally believed by investors does not have an incentive to link its protection to an industrywide index because if that insurer loses more than the indexed amount, *it* will suffer, not investors.

Adverse selection depends on the degree of asymmetry in buyer-versus-seller information, not on the overall level of available information. For example, it may be impossible for anyone to know how future courts will handle disputes involving contract breaches covered by political risk insurance. But as long as insurers know as little about such risks as investors do, insurance cover can be obtained, even if very little is known in an absolute sense about the nature of these risks. Indeed, earthquakes and hurricanes have this feature; we know very little about when and where the next big event will occur. But there is no serious information asymmetry. Political risks may be somewhat less problematical because political crises tend to develop over longer periods than natural perils. However, not all political risk events are easy to foresee, as evidenced by the hostilities in Kuwait in 1991. Yet, so long as the ignorance is symmetrical with respect to buyers and sellers, protection for such events can be arranged.

IV. Barriers to the Securitization of Political Risk Insurance

At least five significant barriers must be overcome to securitize political risk insurance.

A. *Lack of Objective Information*

Risk sharing cannot be accomplished unless the purchasers of the securitization instruments can assess their risk exposure and determine the rate of return they require to compensate them for bearing this risk exposure. Information regarding political risk events tends to be fragmented. Gathering this information and doing the computer modeling necessary to assess these risk exposures are likely to be expensive. In contrast to natural perils, for which there are generally accepted central sources of information (e.g., PCS and Guy Carpenter Catastrophe Index (GCCI)), there are no central sources of information for political perils.

The Berne Union, in view of its members' long-standing position as writers of political risk insurance, is presumably well positioned to furnish such information to the market.[10] However, what form this information should take must be addressed before it can be usefully disseminated. To be useful to investors, such information should be classified in a manner that will facilitate securitization. At the very least, it should be country by country and risk class by risk class. At a minimum, information concerning the following events should be provided: (a) currency transfer restrictions, (b) expropriations, (c) breaches of contract, and (d) wars and civil disturbances.

Risk measurement is complicated due to the deterrence efforts of the national and multilateral insurers. The rate at which political risk events occur appears to be far greater than the rate at which political risk investment insurance claims are filed. Nevertheless, the rate at which political risk events occur determines the value of the insurance. Since political risk events that are quietly resolved may never generate any publicity—indeed both parties usually have an incentive to keep the existence of a dispute confidential (see West, 1996)—published statistics will tend to understate the severity of the risk. Moreover, even if this information were publicly available, it seems unlikely that every dispute with political overtones would result in a claim and that at least some of those that do result in a claim would eventually be determined to be commercial disputes not covered by political risk insurance.

The risk data should cover a period long enough that risk modelers can build statistically meaningful analytical models. The criteria for selecting events must be objectively determined and the data must be compiled consistently. The data must be updated regularly, which requires a commitment from a financially capable entity. The Berne Union would seem to be uniquely positioned to fill this role.

B. *High Cost of Assessing Risk Exposure*

In view of the heterogeneous nature of the mix of risks that comprise political risk and the idiosyncratic nature of such risk, assessing political risk exposure is likely to be an expensive process for investors. Investors will not want to undertake the task of analyzing project-specific political risk exposure; it would be too expensive, and they are probably not presently qualified to do it. These costs can be reduced by designing investment vehicles that diversify political risk exposure across a pool of underlying political risk insurance policies. If such pools can be designed and representative historical data can be compiled, these costs might become manageable.

The securitization of mortgages was facilitated by combining large numbers of mortgages into pools that were sufficiently homogeneous that their prepayment characteristics could be analyzed meaningfully on a poolwide basis. Pool characteristics can vary, causing prepayment behavior to vary from pool to pool, but sufficient data are available to build specific prepayment models that project future prepayment rates based on these pool characteristics.

C. *Need for a Compelling Case for Securitizing Political Risk Investment Insurance*

The market for political risk investment insurance is incomplete. This incompleteness at least suggests the opportunity to create new financial instruments that investors and insurers will find mutually beneficial from a risk-return perspective. The new instruments will have to be designed and priced in such a way that both sets of parties can benefit. Measuring political risk exposure is a necessary first step; however, this is difficult for the reasons already noted. Even if all the measurement issues can be addressed satisfactorily, there remains the more vexing question concerning whether securitization can be expected to enhance the risk-return opportunity set for both insurers and investors.[11]

D. Lack of Adequate Pricing Models

Pricing within the political risk insurance market is not actuarially based. In particular, country loss analysis is not yet sufficiently sophisticated to permit insurers to predict loss frequency or severity actuarially. Pricing is not scientific, but rather is based at least partly on subjective factors requiring experience and judgment. Investors who would be offered the securitization vehicles do not have any such experience to draw on, and so their pricing uncertainty will interfere with the market's development.

Pricing is also sensitive to the availability of underwriting capacity. As of this writing, political risk insurance industry capacity appears ample. At least one market participant has expressed the view that the current pricing of political risk insurance is too low to permit the returns that outside investors are likely to require in order to be willing to purchase political risk securities or derivatives. (See Riordan, 2000.)

E. Required Investment in Infrastructure

The securities and underlying risk pools should be designed so that securities dealers can apply existing asset-backed analytical technology and modeling capability to design and price the securitization instruments. A high front-end cost will discourage securities dealers from undertaking the investment necessary to develop the securitization infrastructure. Similarly, when objective information is lacking and costly to assemble, a greater initial investment is required to establish the securities underwriting capability. Securities dealers will not make these investments unless they expect to realize acceptable returns. Keeping down the front-end cost is likely to be crucial if political risk insurance is to be securitized.

V. Using Credit Derivatives to Hedge Political Risk Exposure

Emerging market debt makes up more than half the assets underlying credit swaps (see Finnerty, 1998). Credit derivatives can be useful in arranging debt financing for a project that will be located in an emerging market. Project location can make it difficult to finance such a project. Many potential lenders and equity investors will be uncomfortable lending to or investing in a project just because of its location. These investors can enter into credit derivative transactions to hedge specific political risk exposures, such as the risk of currency inconvertibility.

A. Emerging Market Political Risk

Emerging market risk is the risk that an investment in a project located in an emerging market might lose value because of political or economic events specific to the country in which the project is located. The term emerging (or developing) market refers to economies that are developing and are not yet fully industrialized. Political risk is a large component of emerging market risk. Political events can affect a country's credit standing. Some of these events, such as the risk of expropriation, can be insured against separately. Other risks, which are political in nature but not specific to the project, may not be separately insurable other than through credit derivatives.

Deterioration of the country's credit standing can impair the credit standing of a stand-alone project, causing the project's debt obligations to lose value. Debt obligations can also lose value because of a devaluation, which can trigger an economic crisis. An economic crisis in one emerging country can cause declining prices for the debt of other emerging countries. Such a situation occurred immediately following the sharp devaluation of the Mexican peso in 1995. Credit derivatives are really designed to enable investors to hedge these economic and financial risks, with the result that using credit derivatives to hedge political risk may entail a high degree of basis risk.

Political risk and other forms of emerging market risk are often perceived as significant when a project is located in a developing economy. In addition, certain events can transform a project's economic risk into political risk. For example, suppose a project sponsor is granted a concession to build, own, and operate an electric generating plant, which will be located in an emerging market. The project power company is authorized to charge the government-owned local electric utility an electricity tariff that is payable in the local currency but that is indexed to changes in the local currency/ U.S. dollar exchange rate. This tariff adjustment mechanism is specified in a formula contained in a take-or-pay electric power purchase agreement between the project power company and the utility, which was approved by the government. If the local currency devalues, electricity charges will rise. If the utility absorbs the increases, its financial condition could deteriorate. If it passes them through to its customers, there could be political repercussions. The possible actions of the local government are a concern. If the local currency depreciates sharply in value, it might refuse to allow the electricity tariff to rise by the full amount. Economic risk (and specifically, currency risk) has thus become an added element of political risk to project lenders and equity investors.

Suppose further that the take-or-pay power purchase agreement covers the generating facility's entire electricity output. If the demand for electricity fails to grow as initially anticipated by both parties to the contract, perhaps because the government-owned utility failed to expand its distribution system rapidly enough, there is a risk that the government might breach its take-or-pay obligation by refusing to take all the power it contracted to purchase, or to pay for the shortfall, as the take-or-pay provision requires.

Suppose a prospective equity investor is comfortable with the economics of the project but is uncomfortable with the political risk. For example, if debt issued by the government suffers a reduction in credit standing, the utility's purchase obligation weakens in credit quality, and the project's equity becomes less valuable. Government-issued debt could diminish in credit quality for any of several reasons. Investors (or banks) might perceive greater risk because of a change in the political situation within the country; one of the major rating agencies might have reduced the government's debt rating; the government might have defaulted on a debt-payment obligation; or the government might have taken some policy action that has impaired its ability to pay. The prospective equity investor would want to hedge its political risk exposure.

B. The Sovereign Credit Spread as a Proxy for Political Risk

Designing a mechanism for transferring political risk requires, among other things, a proxy for such risk that is quantifiable. The proxy enables market participants to specify the payoff function and determine an appropriate payment to make to the party who bears that risk. One proxy currently in use is the credit spread on government-issued debt for governments that have debt outstanding that is publicly traded. The government's credit spread is the difference between the yield to maturity on a designated government bond issue and the yield to maturity on a designated benchmark bond denominated in the same currency. Another possible proxy is the value of bank loans to the government, if the government has such debt and it is traded. The credit spread in that case is the risk premium over the London Interbank Offered Rate (LIBOR) that is implicit in the price at which the government debt is trading. A third proxy is the debt rating, if the government's debt is rated by one of the major rating agencies.

C. Using Credit Derivatives to Hedge Political Risk

A credit swap could be used to hedge an institutional lender's exposure to emerging market political risk; however, such a hedging strategy involves a high degree of basis risk unless it is structured properly.[12] The swap would specify a set of credit events. A credit event could be defined as (a) a default by the government on a significant debt obligation, (b) a downgrade of its debt rating, (c) a decline in excess of some specified amount in the price of a designated government debt issue, (d) the government's imposition of foreign exchange controls, or (e) some other political risk event. Specifying only political events would transform the credit swap into a political risk swap. The agreement would also specify the amount of the default payment and the amount of the option premium.

Alternatively, the hedger could use a credit-spread-put, although such a hedging strategy is likely to involve greater basis risk than a swap because the payoff is tied to the credit spread on sovereign debt, rather than to triggering political events. A credit spread put enables a lender to hedge its exposure to adverse developments in the country where a project is located but on a countrywide basis. Thus, a credit spread put is likely to be most appropriate when the hedger desires protection on a countrywide basis, rather than with respect to a particular project and specific events.

A project lender purchases a credit spread put from a financial institution or some other creditworthy counterparty. If the country where the project is located has traded debt outstanding, the credit spread put can specify a traded government debt issue, a notional principal amount, a strike spread, and an option expiration date. The initial redemption date for the specified debt issue should occur no sooner than the option expiration date. If the actual credit spread on the exercise date is above the strike spread, the option writer pays the project lender. The payment, the option payoff, would consist of the difference in bond value calculated based on the difference between the actual credit spread and the strike spread.

Credit forwards are a third hedging alternative from among existing instruments. A protection buyer can sell a credit forward written on a reference bond issued by, or a syndicated loan to, the country where the project is located. The buyer of the credit forward bears the emerging market risk. However, it would also realize the benefit resulting from an improvement in the country's credit standing.[13] As with a credit spread put, the protection is provided on a countrywide basis because the payoff is tied to the change in price of an underlying sovereign debt issue.

All of these strategies would involve a high degree of basis risk. In Section VIII, I discuss how to reengineer credit swaps to reduce their basis risk in hedging political risk exposure.

VI. Lessons from the Asset-Backed Securities Market

The securitization of a new asset class is more likely to proceed smoothly if it utilizes securitization structures with which investors are already familiar.

A. Evolution of the Asset-Backed Securities Market

Residential mortgage loans were the first class of assets to be securitized. The initial securitization model was a pass-through structure. Then investment bankers developed a simple sequential-pay structure. After investors became comfortable with the sequential-pay structure, investment bankers developed more complex structures that were designed to reallocate risk, especially mortgage prepayment risk, more efficiently.

A.1 Mortgage Pass-Through Securities

The asset-backed securities market began in the United States in 1970 when the Government National Mortgage Association (GNMA) issued the first mortgage pass-through securities (see Hayre and Mohebbi, 1989). A mortgage pass-through security simply passes through to each investor that investor's pro rata share of the payments of interest and principal received from a specified pool of mortgages. Prior to the development of mortgage pass-through securities, there was a secondary market for whole mortgage loans. However, trading was cumbersome because of the paperwork involved. As a result, the market for whole loans had little liquidity. Holders of whole loans who wished to sell quickly faced the risk of potentially large losses. The introduction of mortgage pass-through securities created a means of effectively buying and selling mortgages actually, buying and selling undivided joint interests in pools of mortgages that was more convenient and certainly cheaper than transacting in the whole loan market. Most of the mortgage pass-through securities have been created and sold by the Federal Home Loan Mortgage Corporation (FHLMC), the Federal National Mortgage Association (FNMA), and the Government National Mortgage Association (GNMA), the three agencies that were created by the U.S. Congress to provide liquidity in the secondary mortgage market in the United States. This feature of the market is important because these federal agencies shield investors from default risk.

Mortgage pass-through securities also pass through all principal prepayments, exposing investors to mortgage prepayment risk. Life insurance companies and pension funds limited their investments in mortgage pass-through securities because of their aversion to prepayment risk. The collateralized mortgage obligation (CMO) was developed in 1983 in response to this concern.

A.2   CMOs

The earliest CMO, issued by FHLMC, had three classes that receive principal payments sequentially: class A-1 got all the principal payments from mortgages in the underlying portfolio until it was fully retired; then class A-2 began receiving principal payments and got all the principal payments until it was retired; and then class A-3 got all the remaining principal payments. This securitization structure effectively recharacterized the underlying mortgage pool into three classes of securities, one short-term (A-1), one intermediate-term (A-2), and one long-term (A-3). Since the first CMO was developed, the mortgage-backed securities market has experienced a whole host of more complex structures, all designed to reallocate prepayment risk in ways better suited to certain investors' preferences (see Spratlin, Vianna, and Guterman, 1989). Such a reallocation is beneficial when it results in risk-return profiles that better suit investors' risk-return preferences.

A.3   PACs and TACs

Planned amortization class (PAC) bonds and targeted amortization class (TAC) bonds further reallocate the investor's exposure to prepayment risk (see Perlman, 1989). PAC bonds are designed to make principal payments according to a specified schedule so long as prepayments on the underlying mortgage pool remain within a specified range. A PAC class thus gives investors a relatively stable cash flow over a wide range of interest-rate scenarios. TAC bonds evolved from PAC bonds. TACs are "targeted" to a narrower range of prepayment rates. Thus, TACs and PACs represent alternative mechanisms for allocating prepayment risk.

A.4 IOs and POs

As another example of risk reallocation in the mortgage-backed securities market, Interest Only (IO) and Principal Only (PO) CMO classes, called IO STRIPS and PO STRIPS, respectively, are created by dividing the cash flows from a pool of mortgages (or mortgage-backed securities) into two (or in some cases more than two) securities: The IO STRIPS get all the interest and the PO STRIPS get all the principal. (See Waldman, Gordon, and Person, 1989.)

IO STRIPS and PO STRIPS have differing exposures to prepayment risk as well as to interest-rate risk. When prepayments accelerate, PO STRIPS, which have large positive durations, increase in value because principal is received sooner. IO STRIPS, which have large negative durations, decrease in value because the faster repayment of mortgage principal means that the aggregate flow of interest payments is reduced. Both types of instruments exhibit great price volatility.[14]

IO/PO STRIPS are ideal securities for investors who wish to make a bet on prepayment rates (speculate) or institutions who wish to transfer prepayment risk to others (hedge). (See Carlson, 1989.) For example, a financial institution that is concerned that a slowing of prepayment rates (say, due to an increase in interest rates) will reduce the value of its mortgage portfolio can hedge that risk by buying IO STRIPS. A financial institution that wishes to protect a portfolio of high-coupon mortgages against rising prepayments (say, because of a decrease in interest rates) can purchase high-coupon PO STRIPS. If prepayments do accelerate, the increase in the value of the PO STRIPS will at least partially offset the loss on the mortgage portfolio. IO/PO STRIPS can also be combined with other types of mortgage-backed securities to alter the prepayment rate (and interest rate) sensitivities of mortgage portfolios. IO/PO STRIPS add value by altering mortgage portfolio risk-return characteristics in ways that investors find valuable.

Efforts to fine-tune the risk-return characteristics of CMO classes have resulted in compound structures simultaneously incorporating multiple PAC/TAC classes, floating-rate classes, IO/PO classes, accrual classes, and residual classes (see Perlman, 1989; Roberts, Wolf, and Wilt, 1989; and Finnerty, 1993). In each case, securities dealers engineer the CMO so as to achieve risk-return combinations that investors will find acceptable.

B. Structures for Reducing or Reallocating Default Risk

Asset-backed securities are backed by a diversified portfolio of assets. This diversification reduces investors' exposure to default risk. Large institutions might be able to accomplish much of this risk reduction on their own, but achieving similar diversification could be expensive for smaller institutions or for individuals.

In addition to reallocating prepayment risk, the mortgage-backed securities issued by FHLMC, FNMA, and GNMA carry certain payment guarantees, which transfer much of the default risk on the underlying mortgages to the agencies. FHLMC and FNMA guarantee the timely payment of interest and principal on the mortgage-backed securities they issue. The mortgages underlying GNMA securities are either insured by the Federal Housing Administration (FHA) or guaranteed by the U.S. Department of Veterans Affairs (VA). In addition, GNMA, whose guarantee carries the full faith and credit of the U.S. government, guarantees the timely payment of principal and interest on GNMA certificates. Agency guarantees eliminate entirely the investor's exposure to default risk when the agency guarantees the timely payment of principal and interest.

C. Senior/Subordinated Asset-Backed Securities

FHLMC and FNMA are restricted by law to the purchase of mortgage loans whose balance is no greater than a stated maximum and that satisfy certain other requirements. Similarly, there are legal restrictions on the size of mortgage that the FHA can insure or the VA can guarantee. Loans that do not meet these tests are called nonconforming loans. Reducing the investors' exposure to default risk associated with nonconforming loans requires non-U.S. agency entities to assume the unwanted default risk. The earliest mortgage pass-through securities backed by nonconforming loans relied on mortgage pool insurance for credit enhancement. The uncertainty regarding the availability of satisfactory mortgage pool insurance and the high cost of such enhancements led to the development of a senior/subordinated structure to eliminate the need for pool or hazard insurance (see Bhattacharya and Cannon, 1989). Similar structures have also been used to reallocate default risk when securitizing automobile receivables, credit card receivables, and many other classes of assets. The senior/subordinated structure might be used to securitize political risk insurance.

C.1 Basic Structure for Amortizing Loans

Figure 1 illustrates the senior/subordinated structure developed for securitizing loans that amortize, such as residential mortgage loans and automobile installment loans. A pool of amortizing loans is formed and contributed to a grantor trust. Alternatively, in the case of mortgages, the loans can be contributed to a corporation or partnership.[15] The financing entity then issues two (or in some cases more) classes of securities. In the typical case, one class (designated the "senior class") represents a 90 to 95 percent interest in the trust and receives a prior claim on cash payments by the trust. The other class (designated the "subordinated class") represents the remaining interest and provides credit support for the senior class because of its subordinated position. The size of the subordinated class depends on the type of collateral, the extent of the diversification of the collateral, and the experience and capabilities of the servicer.

FIGURE 1   SENIOR/SUBORDINATED STRUCTURE FOR AMORTIZING LOANS

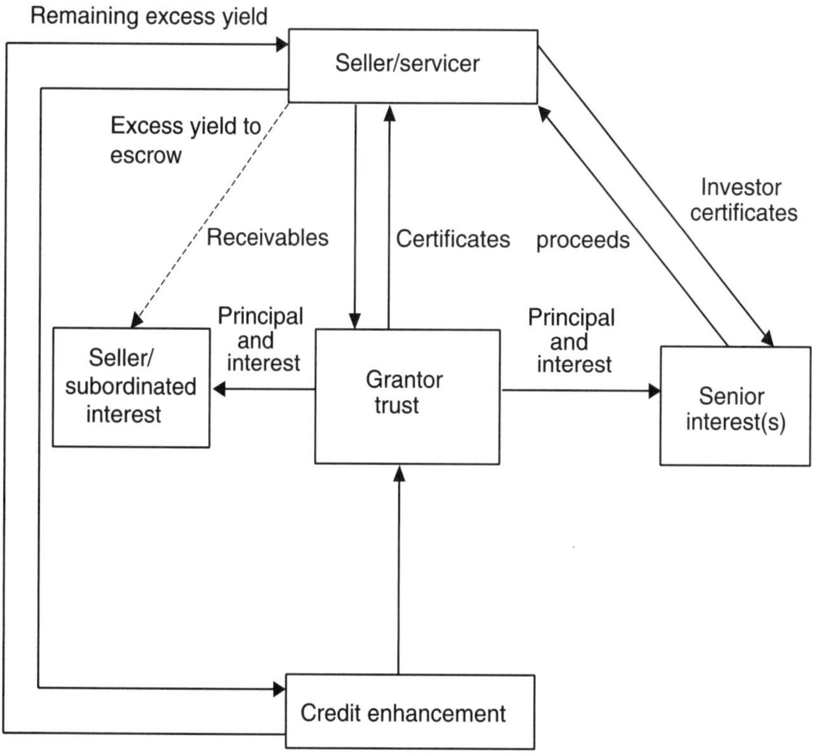

The subordinated class is normally retained by the financial institution that formed the trust (much like an insurance retention), but some institutions have sold the subordinated classes.

Senior/subordinated mortgage-backed securities are generally structured in either of two ways: a reserve fund structure or a shifting interest structure (see Bhattacharya and Cannon, 1989).

C.2 Reserve Fund Structure

The subordinated class is supplemented by a reserve fund to ensure the timely payment of principal and interest to senior certificate holders. The reserve fund is tapped to the extent that cash flow due the subordinated certificate holders is inadequate to cover senior certificate payment shortfalls. The cash for the reserve fund is obtained initially from the cash proceeds of the debt issue.

C.3 Shifting Interest Structure

The ownership percentages of the senior and subordinated certificate holders shift in a way that will compensate senior certificate holders for any payment shortfalls they suffer. The senior certificates have first claim to the trust's cash receipts, and payment shortfalls on the senior certificates are deducted from the subordinated certificate ownership percentage and added to the senior certificate ownership percentage.

D. Application to the Securitization of Political Risk Insurance

A senior/subordinated structure in which the primary insurer holds subordinated notes and outside investors hold senior notes can be useful in controlling the outside investors' exposure to the problems of moral hazard, adverse selection, and asymmetric information. Figure 2 illustrates one possible structure.

The primary political risk insurer (the Primary Insurer), MIGA for example, would establish a special-purpose insurance vehicle (SPIV) to write the political risk cover and issue the notes. The SPIV would write the reinsurance policy, and it would be subject to insurance regulation (something to which outside investors would not wish to be subjected). The Primary Insurer would receive and retain a residual interest certificate (the Residual Interest Certificate), which would entitle it to receive any cash remaining in the SPIV after the reinsurance policy had expired and the SPIV had

FIGURE 2   SENIOR/SUBORDINATED STRUCTURE FOR SECURITIZING POLITICAL
RISK INSURANCE

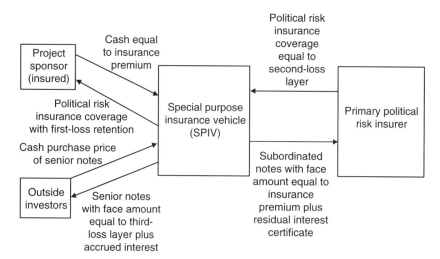

settled all its insurance claims (or fully reserved for them) and repaid all its debt obligations.

The SPIV would issue senior notes (the Senior Notes) to outside
investors. The Senior Notes would have a face amount equal to the
amount of political risk cover in the third-loss layer plus interest
that would accrue during the life of the Senior Notes. The Senior
Notes would be scheduled to mature six months following the expiration of the insurance policy to allow sufficient time for the Insured
to file claims. The yield on the Senior Notes would be determined in
the capital market. The face amount of the Senior Notes would be
set so that the sale of the Senior Notes produces cash equal to the full
amount of third-loss cover as of the Senior Note issue date.

The third-loss layer should be large enough that the overall cost
of the securitization structure is economically beneficial to all the
parties to the transaction. The relative sizes of the second-loss and
third-loss layers will require careful financial engineering to optimize the overall cost.

The SPIV would sell political risk cover to the Insured, which
would provide for an appropriate level of loss retention by the Insured. MIGA and OPIC political risk cover usually require a 10 percent loss retention by the insured party. The first-loss retention helps
control for moral hazard and asymmetric information. The Insured
would pay an insurance premium in cash, which would be pooled
with the cash the SPIV receives from the sale of the Senior Notes.

The SPIV would purchase political risk cover from the Primary Insurer in an amount equal to the second-loss layer. The Primary Insurer would receive subordinated notes (Subordinated Notes) in lieu of receiving the cash insurance premium. The Subordinated Notes would be scheduled to mature one day after the Senior Notes. They would be paid out of the cash remaining in the SPIV after the Senior Notes had been paid in full. The Subordinated Notes together with the Residual Interest Certificate would distribute to the Primary Insurer all the cash that remains in the SPIV after the Senior Notes have been paid in full.

The securitization structure illustrated in Figure 2 is designed to afford a reasonable degree of protection to the outside investors. Since the second-loss layer, written by the Primary Insurer, will be utilized ahead of the third-loss layer, funded by the Senior Notes, the outside investors can rely upon the Primary Insurer to control moral hazard and adverse selection and resolve the asymmetric information problems inherent in writing the political risk cover. This reliance is appropriate because the Primary Insurer has extensive underwriting experience whereas the outside investors may have none. It is also appropriate when the project sponsors are repeat purchasers of political risk cover. In that case, they will want to maintain a good relationship with the Primary Insurer.

The pricing of the Senior Notes is problematical. It will depend fundamentally on the outside investors' loss expectations. These loss expectations will in turn depend on the extent and quality of historical loss experience information. Consequently, the pricing of the first few issues of Senior Notes is likely to be relatively favorable to investors (and unfavorable to the Primary Insurer in relation to the pricing of traditional political risk cover) until outside investors become comfortable that they understand the risks they are being asked to bear. In particular, they will require satisfactory loss experience with prior Senior Note investments before they will invest without requiring a yield premium to compensate for the possibility of adverse selection in the underlying risk pool.

The Senior Notes could be structured as contingent-payment zero-coupon bonds in order to avoid any credit risk exposure to the SPIV. The pricing of such securities is discussed later in the paper.

VII. Lessons from the Securitization of
Property Catastrophe Insurance

The securitization of property catastrophe insurance illustrates the feasibility of securitizing insurance contracts. The differences between political risk insurance and property catastrophe insurance, for example, the political risk insurer's ability to influence the severity of the loss, will require at least some financial reengineering to develop a workable product.

A. Cat Bonds

Financial engineers developed cat bonds (also called act-of-God bonds) to securitize the reinsurance of natural perils, such as hurricanes, earthquakes, floods, and other natural disasters (see Borden and Sarkar, 1996; Doherty, 1997; and Froot, 1998). Cat bonds create a direct link between the payments on the bond and the bond issuer's catastrophic losses. The interest payments or the principal repayments, or both, can be reduced in the event a specified catastrophic loss occurs. The amount of any such adjustment is embodied in a formula that is included in the bond contract at the time the cat bonds are issued. By reducing the bond payments, rather than submitting claims for payment and waiting for the cash to arrive, the cat bond protects the insured party against the reinsurer's credit risk. However, linking the reduction in payments to the insured's actual losses exposes the reinsurer to moral hazard and adverse selection risk.

To illustrate how a cat bond works, it is useful to examine the 1997 USAA transaction. (See Figure 3.) The safe account was a trust administered by an offshore special-purpose reinsurer called Residential Re. Residential Re had a single business purpose, to sell a one-year $400 million reinsurance contract to USAA and issue $400 million face amount of risk-transfer securities to collateralize that reinsurance fully. The proceeds of the cat bond issue were deposited in a trust and invested in highly rated, short-term investments, such as commercial paper. In the event of a catastrophe, the trustee was required to sell investments to cover 80 percent of USAA's losses in excess of $1 billion (until the $400 million was exhausted). In return for writing this reinsurance, Residential Re received from USAA a premium of 600 basis points ($24 million). The premium, along with virtually all of the interest on the commercial paper, was paid to investors, regardless of whether or not USAA experienced a loss.

It is possible, with a little financial engineering, to raise the credit rating on relatively low-layer protection. One method is to provide "principal protection," which was used for the USAA Class A-1 notes. With principal protection, some of the money raised from investors is used to purchase long-term zero-coupon U.S. Treasury bonds at a deep discount. Since these securities will repay principal

FIGURE 3   THE USAA CAT BOND STRUCTURE

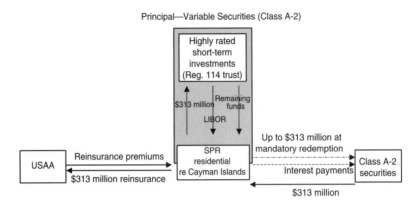

Principal—Variable Securities (Class A-2)

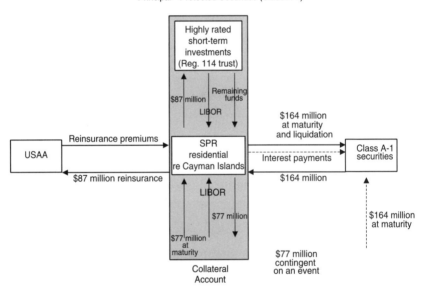

Principal—Protected Securities (Class A-1)

Source: Froot (1998), 21.

with certainty, cat bonds and similar securities can be designed to pay back their principal with certainty. If a cat event occurs, investors lose money because they have to wait a relatively long time to get their principal back; and in the meantime, they receive interest at a below-market rate. Nevertheless, this feature enabled the Residential Re Class A-1 notes to receive the highest rating, AAA.

Naturally there is a cost to this risk-reduction method: it waters down the cat event risk embedded in the bond. Principal protection requires the insurer to raise much more than a dollar of funds for every dollar of risk transfer. The extra money finances the principal protection. For example, Residential Re issued $164 million of Class A-1 notes; $77 million went toward backing USAA's reinsurance, and the rest went toward the purchase of zero-coupon U.S. Treasuries.[16]

To fund the reinsurance, Residential Re issued two types of securities: principal-variable bonds and principal-protected bonds. (See Figure 4.) If there was a loss, principal-variable investors would lose some (or perhaps even all) of their initial investment. These notes paid interest at a rate of LIBOR plus 575 basis points.[17] The principal-protected bonds would have their principal repayment delayed for up to 10 years in the event of a loss, with a reduction in interest along the way. The principal-protected bonds paid LIBOR plus 273 basis points.

Cat bonds are structured so as to reduce the principal repayment obligation in order to eliminate the insured party's credit exposure to the insurer, specifically, the risk that the insurer might default on its insurance payment obligation. Figure 5 provides a list of cat bond issues sold during the period 1995–98. Investors place cash into a trust account from which they receive interest. The trust account pays out to the insured only if a cat event loss occurs. In return for this contingent-payment benefit, the insured pays an insurance premium, which goes into the trust account. If there is no cat event loss, no insurance payouts occur, and the entire trust account is available to pay interest and principal on the cat bonds. Principal is repaid at the end of the designated period. However, if there is a cat event loss, the investors receive only that portion of principal and interest that can be paid after paying the insurer's cat losses. Accordingly, the insured bears no credit risk (unlike traditional reinsurance).

This structure does impose a cost, however. It is costly to set aside in a segregated account sufficient funds to pay the largest possible loss under the reinsurance contract, to always be available no matter how unlikely that loss is. It is clearly inefficient to raise funds to cover the maximum potential loss for each and every risk no matter how remote the likelihood of occurrence. To the extent that risks are uncorrelated, it is more efficient to pool the risks in a fund as traditional reinsurance does.

In summary, cat bonds have certain desirable features, such as the absence of credit risk. They can be designed so as to tie the reduction in payments to an industry loss index in order to ameliorate moral hazard and adverse selection problems. However, that structure entails basis risk for the insurer/hedger. In addition, the

FIGURE 4   SUMMARY OF THE TERMS OF THE USAA CAT BONDS

USAA CAT BOND CONTRACT SPECIFICATIONS			
Issuer:	Residential Reinsurance Limited, a Cayman Island reinsurance company, whose sole purpose is to provide reinsurance for USAA		
Principal Amount:	Class A-1:	$164 million	$87 million principal–variable $77 million principal–protected
	Class A-2:	$313 million	$100% principal–variable
Interest Rate:	Class A 1: LIBOR plus 575 basis points Class A 2: LIBOR plus 273 basis points Interest is paid semiannually.		
Loss Occurrence:	A Category 3, 4, or 5 hurricane		
Reinsurance Agreement:	Residential Reinsurance Limited will enter into a reinsurance agreement with USAA to cover approximately 80% of the $500 million layer of risk in excess of the first $1,000 million of USAA's Ultimate Net Loss		
Ultimate Net Loss:	Ultimate Net Loss = amount calculated in Step 6: Step 1 All losses under existing policies and renewals Step 2 All losses under new policies Step 3 9% of the amount calculated in Step 1 Step 4 Add the amount from Step 1 with the lesser of Step 2 and Step 3 Step 5 Multiply Step 4 by 1.02 for boat and marine policies Step 6 Multiply Step 5 by 1.02 to represent loss adjustments		
Coverage Type:	Single occurrence[a]		
Coverage Period:	June 16, 1997 to June 14, 1998		
Debt Ratings:	Class A-1:	Rated AAAr/Aaa/AAA/AAA By S&P, Moody's, Fitch, and D&P, respectively	
	Class A-2:	Principal variable notes are rated BB/Ba/BB/BB By S&P, Moody's, Fitch, and D&P, respectively	
Covered States:	Alabama, Connecticut, Delaware, District of Columbia, Florida, Georgia, Louisiana, Maine, Maryland, Massachusetts, Mississippi, New Hampshire, New Jersey, New York, North Carolina, Pennsylvania, Rhode Island, South Carolina, Texas, Vermont, and Virginia		

[a] Unlike traditional reinsurance, the form of reinsurance offered by Residential Re was limited to one occurrence. If there was a hurricane that caused $1,300 million of damage, the contract covered 80% of $300 million. If there was another storm that caused USAA losses of more than $1,000 million, USAA would no longer be covered.

Source: Froot (1998), 22.

FIGURE 5   SELECTED MAJOR CATASTROPHE SECURITIZATION ISSUES, 1995–1998

Issuer	Date	Principal amount ($mm)	Maturity	Loss benchmark	Interest rate	Probability of attachment
Normandy Re[a]	Prior to 95	25 +	3 yr	PCS Index	LIBOR+550	1%
ACE Ltd.[a]	1995/96	45	14 mo	PCS Index	UST+450	2%
Cat Ltd.[a]	1995/96	50	5 mo	UNL	LIBOR+1,075	1.1%
CA Earthquake Authority[b]	1995/96	1,000	4 yr	UNL	0	1.27%
AIG (PX Re)	5/96	10	20 mo	Index	6.097%	25%
Georgetown Re (St. Paul Re)	12/96	44.5	11 yr	UNL	14.15%	Various
Georgetown Re (St. Paul Re)[c]	12/96	24	3 yr	UNL	50% profit	Various
Hannover Re II	12/96	100	5 yr	UNL	2.25%[e]	20%
Winterthur	1/97	SF399.5[e]	3 yr	Index	LIBOR+900	20%
SLF Re (Reliance National)	4/97	10	16 mo	Index	LIBOR+273	15%
USAA (Residential Re) A-1	6/97	163.8	12 mo	UNL	LIBOR+576	.7%[g]
USAA (Residential Re) A-2	6/97	313.2	12 mo	UNL	LIBOR+519	.7%[g]
Reinsurer Swap	7/97	35	11 mo	Index	LIBOR+255	.7%[g]
Swiss Re A-1	7/97	42	2 yr	PCS Index	8.645%	.41%[g]
Swiss Re A-2	7/97	20	2 yr	PCS Index	10.493%	.41%[g]
Swiss Re B	7/97	60.3	2 yr	PCS Index	11.952%	.68%[g]
Swiss Re C	7/97	14.7	2 yr	PCS Index	LIBOR+430	Approx. 1%
Parametric Re-Notes	11/97	80	10 yr	Parametric	LIBOR+206	.70%[g]
Parametric Re-Units	11/97	10	10 yr	Parametric	LIBOR+182	.70%[g]
Trinity Re A-1	2/98	22.036	9 mo	UNL	LIBOR+436	.83%[g]
Trinity Re A-2	2/98	61.533	9 mo	UNL	LIBOR+416	.83%[g]
USAA (Residential Re)	6/98	450	11.5 mo	UNL	LIBOR+370[f]	.60%[g]
Yasuda (Pacific Re)	6/98	80	5–7 yr	UNL	LIBOR+925	.94%
Reliance National II	6/98	20	9 mo	Index	LIBOR+820	11.06%[g]
USF&G (Mosaic Re) Tr.1	7/98	21	1 yr	UNL	LIBOR+440	2.75%[g]
USF&G (Mosaic Re) Tr.2[d]	7/98	24	1 yr	UNL	LIBOR+210	.61%[g]

a. Deal not closed—data represent proposed plan.
b. Deal withdrawn and replaced with a traditional reinsurance contract arranged with Berkshire Hathaway.
c. Preferred shares.
d. Includes notes and units.
e. Denominated in Swiss francs.
f. The Pacific Re terms also included a second-event drop-down mechanism which pays LIBOR + 950 bps and has a 5.12% attachment probability.
g. Percentage represents expected loss.

Source: Froot (1998), 12.

cat bonds issued to date have experienced relatively low trading volumes, exposing investors to liquidity risk (see Borden and Sarkar, 1996). The cat bond structure would appear to require some further reengineering.

B. Cat Options

Cat bonds eliminate the insured's exposure to credit risk by providing full collateralization for the insurer's payment obligation. Alternatively, some other creditworthy party could bear this risk. Cat options deal with the credit risk by interposing an options exchange between the insurer and the insured. Exchanges regularly mark option positions to market, impose margin requirements on the (net) obligor, and ultimately guarantee contract performance. With the credit risk problem solved, they also offer the liquidity that results from trading in standardized contracts. In general, the public option markets are designed to promote high-volume, low-cost trading in standardized contracts.

The exchanges achieve standardization of cat-event-linked contracts by structuring cat-event option contracts around aggregate insurance industry measures of catastrophic losses. Consequently, payoffs are tied to industry, rather than individual insurer, losses.

The Chicago Board of Trade (CBOT) trades PCS Catastrophe Insurance Options based on the Property Claims Service (PCS) index,[18] and the Bermuda Commodities Exchange (BCOE) traded contracts linked to the Guy Carpenter Catastrophe Index (GCCI).[19] Figure 6 provides information concerning the CBOT and BCE contracts.

B.1 PCS Options

Introduced in September 1995, PCS Options are European-style.[20] PCS Options are described in Political Risk Services (1999a, 1999b). The option can specify any of nine geographic regions, including five multistate regions, three high-risk states (California, Florida, and Texas), or nationwide. Most PCS indexes have quarterly loss periods; the California and Western indexes have annual loss periods; and the National index has both annual and quarterly loss periods. PCS Options specify a 12-month development period during which PCS refines its estimate of catastrophe losses during the loss period.[21] PCS provides an index for each of the nine geographical regions, which it updates daily. Each PCS loss index represents the sum of insured catastrophic losses in the area and loss period divided by $100 million. There are small cap contracts, which track

FIGURE 6   COMPARISON OF BCOE AND CBOT CAT OPTIONS

	BCOE (Bermuda Commodities Exchange)	CBOT (Chicago Board of Trade)
Contract Specifications		
Index	• GCCI Index	• PCS Index
Reported metric	• 1 unit = .01% of industry loss-to-value ratio[a]	• 1 unit = $100 million of industry losses
Geographic coverage	• 7 geographic areas (U.S. only) available: Northeast, Southeast, Gulf Area, Midwest/West, Florida, Texas (subject to data availability), and National	• 9 geographic areas (U.S. only) available: Northeast, Southeast, East Coast, Midwest, West, California, Florida, Texas, and National
Types of coverage	• Aggregate losses • Single and second loss	• Aggregate losses
Duration of loss periods	• Semi-annual	• Annual/Quarterly[b]
Payoff structure	• Digital/Binary[c]	• Graduated depending on ending value of index
Exchange Operation		
Clearinghouse	• Bermuda Commodities Exchange Clearinghouse	• Board of Trade Clearing Corporation[f]
Clearing member requirements	• No specific restrictions	• $1 million of BOTCC[f] stock • $1.5 million of memberships
Fees	• $20 round trip transaction fee per trade • LIBOR – 100 bp interest on cash margin (after first $250,000) • 200 bp annual utilization fee on securities or letters of credit posted as margin	• Roughly $15 round trip transaction fee per trade[d] • Short-term U.S. Treasury interest rate on cash margin (less ~50 bp)[d] • Zero utilization fee on securities or letters of credit posted as margin
Margin requirements	• 100% posted upfront and held through the term of the contract ($5,000 per contract written) • Variation margin posted only if the market value of margin drops below $5,000	• Approximately 20% posted initially[e] and adjusted daily on a mark-to-market basis • Clearing firms may require members to post additional trading margin
Settlement timeline	• Variable—up to 13 months from the end of the contract	• Last business day of 12th month following end of loss period
Exchange Membership		
Membership requirements	• By application • No specific restrictions	• By application • No specific restrictions

a. For example, if the industry is estimated to have suffered a loss-to-value ratio of 1.5%, the index will be published with a value of 150.
b. California and Western contracts are annual and all others are quarterly, except National contract, which is available in both.
c. Contract pays 100% of value ($5,000) if the ending index value is above the option strike value, and pays zero otherwise.
d. Includes the brokerage fee charged by clearing firms to process members' trades.
e. CBOT cat option participants post margin equal to the greater of the normal margin maintained by other CBOT option traders (and based on a 20% volatility) and 20% of their maximum potential losses.
f. The Board of Trade Clearing Corporation (BOTCC).
Sources: BCOE, CBOT.

aggregate catastrophic losses up to $20 billion, and large cap contracts, which track catastrophic losses between $20 billion and $50 billion. Each index is quoted in points and tenths of a point. Each index point equals $200 cash value.

While PCS Options have a structure that appears to strike a workable balance among basis risk, credit risk, and incentive-conflict problems, trading volumes have been relatively low. (See Borden and Sarkar, 1996.)

B.2 Cat Options

Introduced in 1997, Cat Options were traded on the Bermuda Commodities Exchange until August 1999 when trading was suspended because of low trading volume. Cat Options were based on atmospheric loss events, such as hurricanes, tornadoes, and similar climatic events in five different U.S. regions, Northeast, Southeast, Gulf, Midwest/West, and Florida, plus nationally. (See Bermuda Commodities Exchange, 1998.) The contracts covered losses from either a single event or a second event, or the aggregate loss on covered events, in each case within a designated six-month time period (either January 1 to June 30 or July 1 to December 31). The underlying measure of losses was the GCCI, which measures the insurance industry's loss due to atmospheric events in the form of a loss-to-value ratio (or damage rate).

Cat Options were structured as European binary options. The contract size was $5,000. If a Cat Option was in the money on the settlement date, it would automatically exercise, paying its holder $5,000. Otherwise it would expire worthless.

Even though they were fully collateralized and based on a more detailed index of actual insurance losses than PCS Options, potentially making them more effective for hedging purposes, Cat Options failed to attract sufficient trading volume to maintain a viable market. Discussions with Bermuda Commodities Exchange officials suggested that interest in the market failed to develop, in part, because the insurance industry has experienced several consecutive years with very favorable loss experience, resulting in relatively strong capital positions and relatively weak pricing in the face of weak demand for reinsurance. Interest in Cat Options, PCS Options, and similar products appears very sensitive to where the insurance industry is in the catastrophic loss cycle.

C. Application to Political Risk Insurance

Cat bonds could eventually be used to securitize political risk investment insurance. The critical first step concerns how to design the recovery formula so that it achieves a level of basis risk that is acceptable to the writers of political risk cover while at the same time limiting moral hazard risk, adverse selection risk, and liquidity risk to levels investors will find acceptable.

Structures similar to Cat Options or PCS Options could eventually be used to securitize political risk insurance, although the Cat Option's lack of success to date would indicate that some reengineering may be necessary.[22] The critical first step involves designing one or more suitable indexes of political risk event losses that are immune to potential manipulation.[23] The PCS indexes might provide a useful template. Issues to be addressed include (a) definition of geographical regions, (b) types of political risk cover, (c) time to expiration, (d) length of the development period, and, most important, (e) how the indexes are compiled and who is responsible for updating them.

Tailoring cat bonds or cat options to political risk investment insurance may require substantial financial reengineering, however, because of differences in the nature of the two types of risk. The degree of political risk is not independent of the insured. For example, how effectively the insured manages its relationship with the host government can significantly affect the investment's political risk. Allowing for this dependence in the structuring and pricing of the insurance may be difficult.

Second, as I have noted, deterrence plays a critically important role in political risk insurance. (See West, 1996, 2000.) In contrast to property catastrophe insurance, where the value derives from the insurance payment the insured receives after the damage has occurred, the value of political risk investment insurance derives in large part from the opportunity to avoid a "catastrophe" by using the good offices of the insurer to resolve the dispute before it escalates into a claim. An insurer will try to resolve disputes before they can turn into claims. MIGA, for example, has been so successful that in its first 10 years of operation it had only one insurance claim filed (MIGA, 1999, page 40).[24] The securitization of political risk investment insurance consequently involves the potentially significant moral hazard risk that the insurer might not push its deterrence efforts as aggressively after the insurance has been securitized (and the risk transferred to investors).

Third, post-catastrophe recoveries are an important source of value to the insurer. As noted, the insurer usually takes title to the asset after paying a claim, which permits the insurer to recover value and mitigate its loss. In contrast, there may be nothing left to recover following an earthquake or a hurricane, and policies covering property catastrophes are usually settled in full with the cash payment of the claim. The more complex recovery mechanism in political risk investment insurance policies will have to be linked to a mechanism that will optimize the value of the recoveries and channel this value to security holders.

VIII. Lessons from the Credit Derivatives Market

Derivatives emerged in the 1970s in response to increasingly volatile prices, interest rates, and exchange rates. Recognizing the need for new risk management tools, financial engineers developed a variety of derivative instruments to hedge these risk exposures. This section describes several derivative instruments that could be adapted or designed to securitize political risk investment insurance.

A derivative instrument, or derivative for short, is a financial instrument whose value depends on (or derives from) the value of some underlying asset price, reference rate, or index.[25] There are four basic types of derivatives: forward contracts, futures contracts, options, and swaps. These are the basic derivative building blocks. They are often combined with conventional fixed-rate and floating-rate notes to build more complex derivatives. For example, financial engineers have created structured notes by coupling the basic building blocks with conventional fixed-rate and floating-rate notes.

A. Credit Derivatives

Credit derivatives emerged in 1991 as a useful risk management tool. Total return swaps and credit swaps are the most widely used credit derivatives. (See Finnerty, 1998.) Credit derivatives enable market participants to separate credit risk from the other types of risk and to manage their credit risk exposure by selectively transferring unwanted credit risk to others. This uncoupling of credit risk from other types of risk has created new opportunities for both hedging and investing. The volume of outstanding credit derivatives has grown rapidly and now exceeds $500 billion notional amount by some estimates. Their use continues to expand, and the participants in this market now include banks, industrial corporations, hedge funds, insurance companies, mutual funds, and pension funds. As noted in Section IV, credit swaps can be used to hedge political risk exposure, but basis risk tends to be substantial. It should be possible to reengineer the credit swap structure to securitize political risk insurance with less basis risk.

A credit derivative is different from commodity, interest-rate, currency, and equity derivatives because the underlying investment is not a traded investment. Credit risk is embodied in bonds and bank loans. A bond's value depends on a variety of other factors too, including its coupon, maturity, sinking fund schedule (if there is one), optional redemption features (if the issuer or investors have the right to force early redemption), and credit risk. Credit risk (or default risk) refers to the risk that a security will lose value because of a reduction in the issuer's capacity to make payments of interest and principal.

The value of a credit derivative is linked to the change in credit quality of some underlying fixed-income security, usually a bond, a note, or a bank loan. As credit quality changes, so does the value of a fixed-income security. A deterioration (improvement) in credit quality raises (lowers) the yield investors require and reduces (increases) the price of the bond, other factors remaining the same. A credit derivative can be used to hedge this risk. For example, a bank can use credit derivatives to reduce its exposure to the risk that a loan customer will default. It can transfer this risk to other parties, for a fee, while keeping the loans to this customer on its books. The extent of the protection the hedge affords depends on the nature of the derivative selected.

Credit derivatives are generally short-term in nature, usually having a time to expiration of between one and three years initially. As the credit derivatives market develops, longer-dated instruments may become more readily available. Similar developments have taken place in the interest rate swap and currency swap markets.

A.1 Credit Swaps

The classic credit derivative is the credit swap. A credit swap (or credit default swap) functions like a letter of credit or a surety bond. It enables an investor to insure against an event of default or some other specified credit event. It consists of a single upfront payment, or possibly a series of payments, in exchange for the counterparty's obligation to make a payment that is contingent upon the occurrence of a specified credit event, such as a bond default or a bond rating downgrade. It represents a form of credit insurance, which pays off when the credit event occurs. On the fixed-payment leg of the swap, the buyer of credit event protection (the insured) agrees to make one or more payments, which represent insurance premiums. On the contingent-payment leg of the swap, the seller of credit event protection (the insurer) agrees to make the specified contingent payment. Figure 7 illustrates a credit swap.

The credit event could be a payment default on an agreed-upon public or private debt issue (the reference asset), a filing for bankruptcy, a debt rescheduling, or some other specified event to which the two parties agree. The standard International Swaps and Derivatives Association (ISDA) documentation for credit swaps defines a set of credit events. As a general rule, the credit event must be an objectively measurable event involving real financial distress; technical defaults are usually excluded. The reference credit is usually a corporation, a government, or some other debt issuer or borrower to which the credit protection buyer has some credit exposure.

A credit swap can be viewed as a put option whose payoff is tied to a particular credit event. Indeed, the earliest credit swaps were referred to as default puts for that reason. If a credit event occurs during the term of the swap, the seller/insurer pays the buyer/insured an amount to cover the loss, which is usually par (in the case of a bond) minus the final price of the reference asset, and then the swap terminates. In effect, the buyer/insured puts the reference asset to the seller/insurer at par. The final price is generally determined through a dealer poll.

Credit swaps usually settle in cash, but physical settlement is not uncommon. In that case, the credit protection provider pays the full notional amount (i.e., the par value of the bond) and takes delivery of the bond.

As a third payment alternative, the credit protection provider can be required to pay a specified sum in cash if the specified credit event occurs. This amount could be either a fixed sum or a sum determined according to a formula. The fixed sum or the formula, as the case may be, would be decided at the start of the swap.

FIGURE 7   A CREDIT SWAP

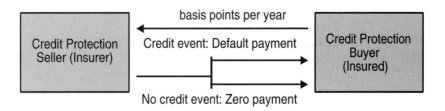

A.2 Basic Credit Swap Structure

Figure 8 illustrates the basic structure of a credit swap. The two parties agree on a notional amount, the term of the swap, the reference asset, the list of credit events, and the payment features. The buyer/insured agrees to make a payment, or a series of fixed payments, and the seller/insurer agrees to make a specified contingent payment if the credit event occurs. If no credit event has occurred by the time the swap matures, then the insurer's contingent obligation expires. Actually, the buyer of credit protection usually has 14 days after the expiration date of the credit swap to determine whether a credit event has occurred, and if so, to document it.

A.3 Credit-Event-Put Trust Structure

A credit-event-put (or event-risk-put) is a variant of the credit swap in which the payoff amount is segregated in a trust. A credit-event put could specify either a fixed or a variable payoff. The credit event may not involve an actual default. For example, it might entail a reduction in debt rating, and the amount of the variable payoff would depend on the extent of the reduction in debt rating. Alternatively, it might simply involve payment of the full principal amount by the seller/insurer in exchange for physical delivery of the reference bonds, that is, a true put. To guarantee the insurer's ability to meet its contingent payment obligation, the payoff can be segregated in a trust. The following example describes a credit-event-put structure employed in connection with an oil and

FIGURE 8   THE BASIC STRUCTURE OF A CREDIT SWAP

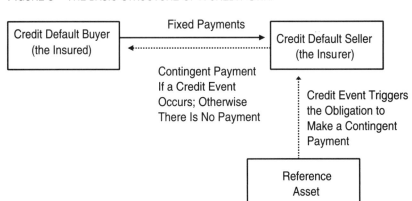

gas financing. A similar structure could be used to hedge political risk.

A BBB-rated oil and gas company purchased a portfolio of producing oil and gas properties. It financed the purchase by borrowing on a nonrecourse basis from a group of institutional investors.[26] The oil and gas company deposited funds into a trust. The terms of the trust provide that if the oil and gas company defaults on any of its outstanding debt, all the funds in the trust will be distributed pro rata among the institutional lenders. Figure 9 illustrates the structure of the oil and gas project credit-event put.

B. Structured Products

A structured note is a package consisting of a conventional fixed-rate or floating-rate note and a derivative instrument embedded in it. Structured products take either of two basic forms. They can be designed around a swap or embedded within a fixed-rate or floating-rate note. The former are called structured swaps and the latter are called structured notes.

Structured swaps have a zero net present value at the time they are entered into.[27] Structured notes, on the other hand, are securities. They are sold in cash transactions. The sale creates an asset for the investor and a liability for the issuer.[28]

B.1 What Structured Products Are Designed to Achieve

Issuers of debt instruments or investors may wish to express a particular view on interest rates or a particular commodity price or ex-

FIGURE 9   THE CREDIT-EVENT-PUT TRUST STRUCTURE

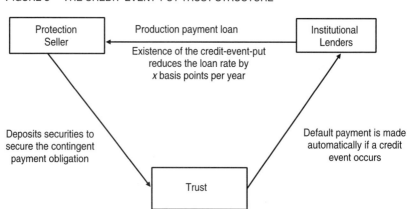

change rate. Structured products permit market participants to act upon a specific view. That view can be tailored in any number of ways, such as whether a stated interest rate will remain within a particular interest rate band, whether the difference between specified short-term and long-term interest rates will change in some specified manner, the direction of interest rates, changes in the shape of the yield curve, shifts in interest rate volatilities, the direction of a particular exchange rate or commodity price, and so on.

B.2 Credit-Linked Notes

A credit-linked note is a form of structured note in which the embedded derivative instrument is a credit derivative, often a credit swap. The credit-linked note typically adjusts the principal repayment to pay off on the derivative instrument embedded within the note, much like a cat bond. For example, suppose an investor purchased a six-month structured note that would repay at maturity $1,000 minus the payoff on an embedded credit put option. The investor has sold the put option to the issuer of the note (and in return gets a higher coupon). If the value of the credit put option is $46.73 on the maturity date, the holder of the structured note would receive $953.27 (= $1,000 – 46.73) per $1,000 face amount. This single payment is equivalent to receiving $1,000 and simultaneously paying off $46.73 on the credit put option.

Credit-linked notes offer a way for institutional investors to participate in the corporate bank loan market. Figure 10 illustrates how a credit-linked note transfers the credit risk on a corporate loan to institutional investors. The bank extends a $50 million corporate loan and issues to insurance companies, money managers, or other institutional investors an equal principal amount of a credit-linked note whose repayment is tied to the value of the loan. If a credit event occurs, the bank's repayment obligation on the note decreases by just enough to offset its loss on the loan. If the credit-linked note pays interest on the same basis as the corporate loan, less a margin to compensate the bank for its cost of originating and servicing the loan, the institutional investors have essentially all the benefit and credit risk of the bank loan without having to take ownership of the loan. Credit-linked notes allow nontraditional bank lenders to participate in the corporate bank loan market indirectly while still investing in securities.

Credit-linked notes were very popular in the early 1990s when the credit derivatives market first began to develop. Their use has

FIGURE 10   A CREDIT-LINKED NOTE

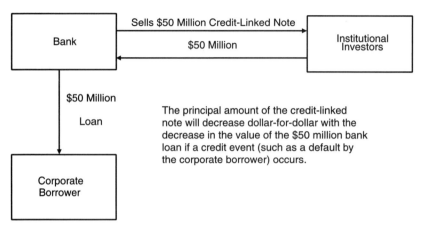

diminished as the swap and option products have grown in importance.

C. Credit Forwards

A forward agreement is a contract that obligates the seller to deliver, and the buyer to purchase, a specified asset on a particular date at a price specified at the time they enter into the forward agreement. A forward agreement for a bond commits the buyer to purchase a specified reference bond at a stated price on a specified future date. A credit forward (or credit spread forward) is a forward agreement that specifies a credit spread and a benchmark bond, rather than a particular price, for the reference bond. Credit forwards were developed in the mid-1990s.

Figure 11 illustrates the pattern of payments for a credit forward. At maturity, the credit forward buyer would make a payment to the credit forward seller equal to $(S_T - S_F) \times$ *Duration $\times$ Amount $\times P_F$* if the actual credit spread for the reference bond when the credit forward matures, S_T, exceeds the credit spread S_F specified in the credit forward. On the other hand, the credit forward seller would make a payment to the credit forward buyer equal to $(S_F - S_T) \times$ *Duration $\times$ Amount $\times P_F$* if the credit spread in the contract, S_F, exceeds the actual credit spread S_T. *Duration* is the modified duration of the reference bond, and *Amount* is the notional amount of the forward contract. P_F is the price of the bond, expressed as a fraction of the bond's face amount, when the credit spread is S_F. The payoff structure for the forward agreement means that the buyer of the credit forward bears the default risk on the reference bond.

FIGURE 11   A CREDIT FORWARD

Pattern of Payments for a Credit Forward

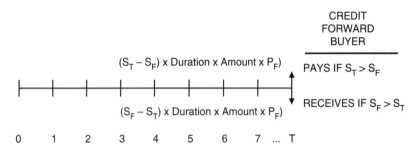

CREDIT
FORWARD
BUYER

$(S_T - S_F) \times$ Duration x Amount x $P_F)$ PAYS IF $S_T > S_F$

$(S_F - S_T) \times$ Duration x Amount x $P_F)$ RECEIVES IF $S_F > S_T$

0   1   2   3   4   5   6   7 ... T

If a credit event occurs, the credit forward transaction is marked to market and terminated. The credit forward buyer pays the seller according to the formula just given.

IX. Contingent-Claims Pricing Models

Since publication of the seminal articles by Black and Scholes (1973) and Merton (1973), contingent-claims analysis has developed into a vitally important tool for valuing complex financial instruments. Contingent-claims analysis has been applied to a broad range of practical valuation problems involving embedded options or securities features that could be modeled as options. This section develops a contingent-claims model for valuing zero-coupon political risk structured notes and derivative instruments based on such securities. It also develops a contingent-claims model for valuing political risk options.

A. Pricing Political Event Risk Securities and Derivatives

Pricing a political event risk instrument requires two critical types of information: (a) the probability that a political risk event will occur and (b) the amount of the net ultimate loss if the covered event occurs. If the event is the expropriation of a specified tangible asset and if, for example, the coverage is written on the book value of the asset plus five years' lost profits in the event the use of the asset is lost for that length of time, then we need to know (a) the probability of expropriation and (b) the amount of the shareholders' recovery if expropriation occurs.

There are two basic approaches to pricing political event risk instruments:

1. Use the historical probabilities of specific political events, such as expropriation, and estimates of likely future recoveries to estimate the future payoffs under the contract. Such data are not readily available, although the writers of political risk cover have accumulated such data. The data detail the events that have occurred and the net ultimate losses that resulted. Whether these data can be used to infer future event probabilities and claims is an empirical issue that requires careful analysis. Such inferences have the obvious limitation that future loss experience may differ significantly from historical experience.

2. Build a mathematical model of the political event risk process. This basic approach is the one most widely used by derivative market participants to price conventional derivative instruments. It is embodied in a variety of proprietary valuation models, some developed by dealers for their own use and others developed by commercial services that furnish valuation estimates for their subscribers. These models generally start by mathematically representing the stochastic process that explains how the value of some critical variable is determined, such as a particular share price, interest rate, commodity price, or credit spread. They use this stochastic process to assess the possible future values of the critical variable. Many of these models are based on the famous Black-Scholes (1973) and Merton (1973) models. This approach also has some important limitations because developing mathematical models that produce workable solutions requires simplifying assumptions, which can impair the model's accuracy.

Pricing political risk derivatives is likely to prove more difficult than pricing most other types of derivative instruments. The challenge is similar to the level of difficulty involved in pricing credit derivatives. Credit derivatives are different from most other derivatives because their "underlying asset" is not priced separately in the capital market. For example, equity derivatives, such as stock options, have common stock as the underlying asset, and common stock is a traded security with a market-determined price, so long as the issuer is a public company. In contrast, credit factors, such as the risk of default, determine the payoff profile of a credit derivative. Credit is not a traded security. Instead, it is an important risk element that affects the value of virtually all debt and equity securities, but to varying degrees. The pricing of credit risk is implicit in the pricing of these securities. But extracting the price of the credit risk involved from the price of the security can be a daunting task. Nevertheless, it must be extracted from securities prices because there is no "credit page" disseminated by any financial data vendor to which a dealer or investor can turn to check on the "price" of the "underlying asset." Similarly, there is no "political risk page" disseminated by any financial data vendor, and using an actuarial approach based on historical data involves similar challenges when using either default data or political event data.

Pricing credit risk is also difficult because prior to default, it is impossible to distinguish unambiguously between firms that will default and those that will not. Similar difficulties arise when trying to predict political events. Discriminant analysis and other statistical techniques are available to try to predict when a political event might occur. But political risk is still a matter of likelihoods; the likelihood that a country's credit standing will deteriorate; the likelihood that it will expropriate property or impose foreign exchange controls; the likelihood that it will breach a commercial contract; and so on. Moreover, such events seem inherently more difficult to predict than economic events, such as default.

To place this challenge in perspective, default is actually a relatively rare event. The typical firm has a probability of only about 2 percent that it will default in any given year. However, the likelihood of default varies considerably between firms. In any particular year, the odds that a triple-A-rated firm will default are only about 2 in 10,000. The odds for a single-A-rated firm are higher, about 10 in 10,000. Toward the bottom end of the credit scale, a triple-C-rated firm has a likelihood of defaulting in any one year of about 4 in 100, and is therefore 200 times as likely to default as a triple-A-rated firm. Complicating these probability assessments is the fact that for any given debt rating, the probability of default can double, or even triple, between the high point and the low point in the credit cycle. Whether political risk ratings, such as ICRG's, are useful in making these probability assessments is an empirical issue. Diamonte, Liew, and Stevens (1996) and Erb, Harvey, and Viskanta (1996) offer mixed results on this point.

As noted earlier in the chapter, there is a second factor in addition to the probability that a political event will occur that fundamentally affects the pricing of political event risk securities. The loss the coverage writer will experience if a covered event occurs may be substantial. The amount of any potential loss is determined not only by the nature of the event but also by the particular terms of the insurance cover and by how much value the insurer can ultimately recover from the host government. Adjusting for these specific factors when pricing the political event risk security will require careful analysis.

A third complicating factor concerns the political risk insurer's ability to influence the severity of the net ultimate loss. For example, MIGA, which began writing political risk cover in 1988, had only one claim filed in its first 10 years of operation and had not paid out on any claim as of April 2000.[29] According to MIGA's 1999 annual report, MIGA was pursuing discussions with the host government and the investor to try to find a satisfactory resolution to the dispute that led to this one claim, which was filed in 1999 (MIGA, 1999). MIGA's Convention directs MIGA to exert its influence to encourage disputants to resolve their differences and avoid having a claim filed.[30] Thus, political risk insurance has a deterrence value, which is likely to be highest when the insurer is a multilateral agency that is affiliated with a lender and can use its influence to drive the settlement negotiations. A private political risk insurer will also try to encourage settlements in order to avoid having to pay a claim but may not have the leverage that a government-sponsored entity has. In any case, the actual history of claims paid will understate the degree of political risk, and the amount of claims paid will understate the cost of political risk events. Any measure of political risk thus needs to take into account the insurer's deterrence capability.[31]

Because of the great variability of political event probabilities and net ultimate losses, historical experience alone cannot provide precise measures of either factor. Unlike credit derivatives, dealers and investors will not be able to extract the capital market's assessments of these probabilities and losses from the prices at which default risky securities are currently trading. In any case, the valuation techniques currently in use all require simplifying assumptions to make them workable. These assumptions can affect the accuracy of the valuations and can lead to a range of estimates for the value, rather than a single value, of a political event risk security or derivative.

The rest of this section illustrates how one might apply the second approach to price political risk insurance securitization instruments.

B. Assumptions

I illustrate the pricing of four classes of political insurance instruments: structured bonds, swaps, bond put options, and call and put index options. I use the Vasicek (1977) model of the interest-rate process as the starting point for my analysis for the first three classes of instruments. Vasicek developed a contingent-claims model for valuing default-risk-free zero-coupon bonds, and Jamshidian (1989) built on Vasicek's work by developing models for valuing European put and call options on such bonds.

I assume that the short-term riskless interest rate r follows a Gaussian diffusion process

$$dr = \kappa(a - r)dt + \sigma dz \tag{1}$$

where κ is the mean-reversion speed, a is the long-run average short-term riskless rate, σ is the volatility of the interest-rate process, z = z(t) is a Wiener process, and κ, a, and σ are constants. In practice, κ, a, and σ can be estimated from historical data (see Lekkos, 1999).

I assume that political risk events occur according to a Poisson process. Political risk events are assumed to be random and independent. They include events that trigger the filing of an insurance claim as well as events that could have triggered a filing but for the insurer's intervention in the dispute to bring about a settlement. The instantaneous probability of a political risk event in a time interval of length dt is λdt, where λ measures the intensity of the political risk event process. The parameter λ also measures the mean number of political risk events per unit of time because the process is Poisson. The instantaneous probability that no political risk event occurs during any interval of length dt is $1 - \lambda dt$ and the probability that more than one political risk event occurs during dt is of an order less than dt. When a political risk event occurs, I assume that the cost, denoted x, is normally distributed with probability density function

$$f(x) = \left(1/\left(\eta\sqrt{2\pi}\right)\right)\exp\left(-(x - \theta)^2 / 2\eta^2\right) \tag{2}$$

with mean θ and variance η^2. This cost consists of the amount of the claim payable to the insured when a claim is paid net of the insurer's ultimate recoveries (expressed on a present-value basis), and the cost to the insurer of resolving the dispute when intervention averts the filing of a claim.

The expected net ultimate loss during a period of length T – t, denoted $\text{Exp}[\tilde{Q}(T - t)]$, is

$$\text{Exp}\left[\tilde{Q}(T-t)\right] = \text{Exp}\left[\sum_{i=1}^{\tilde{n}} x_i\right] = \text{Exp}_n\left[\text{Exp}\left[\sum_{i=1}^{n} x_i \middle| n\right]\right] \tag{3}$$

$$= \text{Exp}_n\left[\text{Exp}\left[nx \middle| n\right]\right] = \sum_{n=1}^{\infty} \frac{e^{-\lambda(T-t)}[\lambda(T-t)]^n (n\theta)}{n!}$$

$$= \theta \sum_{n=1}^{\infty} \frac{e^{-\lambda(T-t)}[\lambda(T-t)]^n}{(n-1)!}$$

$$= \theta\lambda(T-t)\sum_{n=0}^{\infty} \frac{e^{-\lambda(T-t)}[\lambda(T-t)]^n}{n!}$$

$$= \theta\lambda(T-t)$$

where Exp denotes expected value.

C. Price of a Political Insurance Structured Note

Consider a structured note that pays \$1 at maturity at time T provided that no covered political events, as defined in the note agreement, occur during the life of the note. I assume that all insurance claims are aggregated and that the net ultimate loss (i.e., net of the insured party's retention and present-value recoveries) is subtracted from the amount otherwise due the note holders at maturity. As of time t, the net ultimate loss is $Q(t)$, which is based on the actual experience to date and is therefore nonrandom. $Q(0) = 0$. If n covered political events occur during the remaining life of the note, with the net ultimate loss for each distributed in accordance with equation (2), the expected payment to bondholders at maturity is $1 - \theta\lambda(T-t) - Q(t)$. I assume that political event risk is idiosyncratic to the structured note holders; all residual risk can be diversified away. I further assume that dz and $\tilde{Q}$ are independent.

Applying the standard arbitrage arguments, the price $P(r, t, T)$ of the political insurance structured note must satisfy the partial differential equation

$$\frac{1}{2}\sigma^2 P_{rr} + \kappa(a^* - r)P_r + P_t - rP = 0 \tag{4}$$

subject to the boundary condition

$$P(r, T, T) = 1 - \theta\lambda(T-t) - Q(t) \tag{5}$$

where a^* denotes the risk-neutral long-run average short-term riskless rate.

The solution to equations (4) and (5) is

$$P(r,t,T) = [1 - \theta\lambda(T-t) - Q(t)]A(t,T)e^{-B(t,T)r(t)} \tag{6}$$

where

$$A(t,T) = \exp\left[\frac{(B(t,T)-T+t)(\kappa^2 a^* - \sigma^2/2)}{\kappa^2} - \frac{\sigma^2 B(t,T)^2}{4\kappa}\right] \tag{7}$$

$$B(t,T) = \frac{1-e^{-\kappa(T-t)}}{\kappa} \tag{8}$$

where exp[·] denotes the exponential function.

The price of the structured note according to equation (6) is the present value of the expected maturity payment to note holders, which is equal to the face amount of the note ($1) minus the expected insurance payout ($\theta\lambda(T-t) - Q(t)$). The greater the rate at which covered political events occur (λ) and the greater the expected net ultimate loss for each event (θ), the lower the market price of the structured note.

D. Price of a Political Insurance Swap

Equation (6) expresses the price of a political insurance structured note as the present value of the expected maturity payment, which has two components: (a) the present value of $1 minus (b) the present value of the expected loss payment. Thus, the structured note can be viewed as a package consisting of (a) a long position in a default-risk-free zero-coupon bond that promises to pay $1 at T plus (b) a short position in a political insurance swap under which the writer of the swap receives $\theta\lambda TA(t,T)e^{-B(t,T)r(t)}$ at time t and promises to pay $\tilde{Q}(T)$ at time T. In that case, it follows from equation (3) that the expected future swap payment is $\theta\lambda(T-t) + Q(t)$ whose present value equals the initial swap payment. Thus, the swap is initially a zero-net-present-value transaction, as is the case with traditional swaps (see Finnerty, 1999).

Alternatively, the structured note could be arranged as a structured swap in which the swap writer receives P(r, t, T) at time t and agrees to pay out $1 - \tilde{Q}(T)$ at time T, depending on, first, the number of covered political events that occur during [t, T] and, second, the amount of the claims.

E. Price of a Political Insurance Note Put Option

The price of a political insurance structured note will decrease as the number and severity of the covered political events each increase.

The structured note is designed to pay the amount $1 - \tilde{Q}(T)$; it will reduce the principal payment by the amount; of the net ultimate loss for each covered political event that occurs during $[0, T]$ regardless of the severity of the event. Insurance coverages can be designed so as to provide different levels of reinsurance protection, for example, by writing a put option on the structured note and setting the option strike price to provide the desired degree of reinsurance coverage.

I again assume that the structured note has a principal amount of $1. I also assume that the put option is European.[32] Jamshidian (1989) has developed models for valuing European options on default-risk-free zero-coupon bonds using Vasicek's (1977) bond-pricing model. The price of a European put option, $Q(r, t, \tau, T)$, is

$$Q(r,t,\tau,T) = XP(r,t,\tau)N(-h+\sigma_p) - P(r,t,T)N(-h) \qquad (9)$$

where X is the strike price, τ is the expiration date for the put option, T is the maturity date for the bond, $N(\cdot)$ is the standard normal cumulative distribution function (cdf), and

$$h = \frac{1}{\sigma_p}\ln\frac{P(r,t,T)}{P(r,t,\tau)X} + \frac{\sigma_p}{2} \qquad (10)$$

$$\sigma_p = \frac{\sigma}{\kappa}\left[1-e^{-\kappa(T-\tau)}\right]\sqrt{\frac{1-e^{-2\kappa(\tau-t)}}{2\kappa}} \qquad (11)$$

Since the note price P and the cdf are both positive throughout their respective domains, the price of the put option Q varies directly with the strike price X. Lowering X reduces the reinsurance coverage because it increases the number of covered political events that must occur or raises the severity of the covered events before the option comes into the money. Reducing the strike price X raises the payoff threshold and thereby reduces the level and thus the cost of reinsurance coverage. Adjusting the strike price X permits the option purchaser to buy whatever level of loss protection is desired—and at a lower cost than full insurance coverage would require.

F. Political Insurance Index Options

PCS Options illustrate how publicly traded options can be used to hedge catastrophic risk exposure (see PCS, 1995a, 1995b). PCS Options apply to natural perils, but the same structure can be tailored to facilitate hedging political risk. PCS Options are tied to the PCS indexes of insurance industry losses due to natural perils. Tailoring this structure to political risk would require an index of political risk event losses.

F.1 The Index

A political risk index, I, could take either of at least two basic forms. It could take the form of an index of political event losses suffered by a specified set of political risk insurers, such as the Berne Union. Alternatively, it could take the form of an index that measures political risk, perhaps along the lines of the ICRG political risk index.

Whatever index is chosen to serve as the underlying index for the political risk options should be a quantifiable measure. It must be calculated for a specific geographical region; there could be separate geographical indexes, such as for Asia, Latin America, Eastern Europe, and worldwide. The time period must be specified; the PCS options apply to quarterly or annual periods. The value of the index at each point in time should be determined independently of the insurers who are seeking political reinsurance coverage. It should be available on a historical basis for a period long enough to enable market participants to model its behavior and price their option exposure.

F.2 Assumptions

I assume that the index I follows a lognormal jump diffusion process[33]

$$dI / I = (\beta - \lambda k) dt + \sigma_I dz_I + dq \tag{12}$$

where β is the instantaneous expected return on the index, σ_1 is the volatility of the index process, $z_I = z_I(t)$ is a Wiener process,[34] and β and σ_1 are constants. I assume that the value of the index can experience infrequent jumps. The jumps are embodied in dq, where q(t) is an independent Poisson process with a mean number of arrivals λ per unit time. The variable k is defined by k = Exp[Y - 1] where Y - 1 is the random variable percentage change in the index when the Poisson political event occurs and Exp [ ] is the expectation operator over the random variable Y. Y - 1 is a random impulse function that produces a finite jump from I to IY whenever a political event occurs. The resulting path for I(t) is continuous most of the time with finite jumps at discrete points in time. I assume that

dz_1 and dq are independent. When there are no jumps in I, $\lambda = 0$ and dq = 0 and equation (12) simplifies to the Black-Scholes (1973) model.

The probability distribution for Y must be determined empirically. I assume that the Y_j corresponding to successive jumps are independently and identically distributed. If the Y_j are lognormally distributed, then the index I is also lognormally distributed.

F.3 Option Pricing Models

Merton (1976) derives stock option pricing models from a stock price jump process like equation (12). Merton's results lead directly to the following models for pricing political risk index options:

$$C(I,t)=\sum_{n=0}^{\infty}\frac{e^{-\lambda'(T-t)}[\lambda'(T-t)]^{n}}{n!}\,C_{BS}\left(I,E,t,T,r_{n},v_{n}^{2}\right) \tag{13}$$

$$P(I,t)=\sum_{n=0}^{\infty}\frac{e^{-\lambda'(T-t)}[\lambda'(T-t)]^{n}}{n!}\,P_{BS}\left(I,E,t,T,r_{n},v_{n}^{2}\right) \tag{14}$$

where

$$\lambda' \equiv \lambda(1+k) \tag{15}$$

$$r_{n} = r - \lambda k + n\,\ln(1+k)/(T-t) \tag{16}$$

$$v_{n}^{2} = [\sigma^{2} + n\delta^{2}/(T-t)] \tag{17}$$

and where δ^2 is the variance of the natural logarithm of Y, r is the riskless return, t is the time at which the options are priced, and T is the option expiration date. In equation (13), C_{BS} is the Black-Scholes (1973) call option pricing formula

$$C_{BS}\left(I,E,t,T,r_{n},v_{n}^{2}\right)=I\cdot N(d_{1})-E\,e^{-r_{n}(T-t)}N(d_{2}) \tag{18}$$

In equation (14), P_{BS} is the Black-Scholes (1973) put option pricing formula

$$P_{BS}\left(I,E,t,T,r_{n},v_{n}^{2}\right)=E\cdot e^{-r_{n}(T-t)}N(-d_{2})-I\cdot N(-d_{1}). \tag{19}$$

In equations (18) and (19),

$$d_{1} = \left[\ln(I/E)+(r_{n}+v_{n}^{2}/2)(T-t)\right]/v_{n}\sqrt{T-t} \tag{20}$$

$$d_2 = d_1 - v_n \sqrt{T-t} \tag{21}$$

where I is the value of the political risk index at time t, E is the strike price of the option, $N(\cdot)$ is the standard normal cdf, and $\ln(\cdot)$ is the natural logarithm function.

In equation (13), the value of the index call option is the weighted sum of the Black-Scholes option values obtained by conditioning on knowing that exactly n Poisson jumps will occur during the remaining life of the option [t, T] and using the modified riskless rate r_n in place of r and the modified variance v_n^2 in place of σ^2. The value of the index put option in equation (14) is interpreted similarly. The weights in each case are the Poisson probabilities $e^{-\lambda'(T-t)}[\lambda'(T-t)]^n/n!$ where the Poisson process is distributed with parameter $\lambda'(T-t)$.

F.4 Using Option Strategies to Purchase Political Risk Cover

Options, like the PCS Options, can be used to reinsure a layer of loss coverage of the insurer's design. PCS Options pay off an amount that is directly related to the amount of the insurance industry's losses resulting from natural perils within a specified region and a specified time period. The insurer who desires reinsurance coverage can use spread trading—the simultaneous purchase of a call option with strike price E_1 and sale of a call option with the same expiration date and with a higher strike price $E_2 > E_1$—to obtain a layer of reinsurance cover (see PCS, 1995b).[35] In this example, the reinsurance cover corresponds to insurance industry losses in the range from E_1 to E_2. The insurer tailors its reinsurance cover by choosing the type of contract (geographical region and time period) and by selecting E_1 and E_2 appropriately.

Figure 12 illustrates this spread strategy. Buying a call option with strike price E would purchase a layer of coverage corresponding to industry losses in excess of E. Buying a call with strike E_1 and selling a call with strike $E_2 > E_1$ would cap the reinsurance layer at E_2. The insurer's risk cover depends on industry loss experience as proxied by the index I, rather than its own experience. Thus, there is basis risk to the extent that the insurer's loss experience deviates from I.

X. Legal, Regulatory, and Marketing Issues

Innovative financial products often raise new legal and regulatory issues. Political risk insurance instruments are no exception. This section touches on some of the more important of these issues. However, it does not attempt to provide a thorough discussion because that would entail a host of technical issues that are beyond the scope of the chapter.

A. Legal Issues

A.1 Documentation

Derivatives, particularly newer derivatives that may not fit easily within the existing standard documentation, require separate yet effective legal documentation to spell out the rights and obligations of each counterparty to the transaction. The International Swaps and Derivatives Association (ISDA) only recently developed standard documentation for credit swaps. Until it did, the documentation for these transactions varied from dealer to dealer. The absence of standard documentation led to some serious disputes in 1997 and 1998 when emerging market credit problems triggered, or apparently triggered, the default provisions in such swaps. Disputes arose because the definition of a "default" often left room for disagreement. The availability of standard documentation has helped spur the further development of the credit swap market because it has reduced the likelihood of such disagreements and reduced the cost of transacting in credit swaps.

Documenting credit swaps and other innovative derivative transactions has been especially challenging. For example, when the contingent payment depends on the occurrence of a "credit event," what constitutes a credit event has to be defined with sufficient precision that both parties will be able to agree (a) that a credit event has occurred and (b) the date it occurred. Political insurance derivatives, like credit derivatives, are not based on an underlying asset that is publicly quoted or an index that is widely available. Like credit swaps, political risk swaps would be based on the occurrence of a specified event. Just as there is no "credit page" furnished by an information vendor that provides the price of "credit" or that would indicate when a credit event has occurred, there is also no "political event page." Defining a political risk event is a bit tricky, and it will depend on the type of cover desired. For example, currency transfer restrictions can take a variety of forms, some of which are much more onerous than others. Suspending currency convertibility is more serious than restricting access to foreign currency, for example, by requiring all foreign exchange transactions to be approved by the central bank. Some political risk events are relatively easy to document, such as the expropriation of a company's plant when the government seizes it outright. But others are not. A creeping expropriation can be a long, drawn out affair. In addition, political risk cover usually excludes nondiscriminatory measures taken by a host government in the exercise of its legitimate regulatory authority. Whether a particular act falls within this exception is not always free from doubt. Therefore, the definitions must be precise in political risk insurance documentation.

When using a political risk derivative to hedge breach-of-contract political risk exposure under a particular political risk insurance policy, a hedger is really depending on the terms of one legal document—the political risk derivative contract—to protect itself against a breach of the terms of some other document—the commercial contract. Unless the two sets of terms are properly matched, the degree of protection may be imperfect. The hedger in this case is exposed to what might be thought of as "documentary basis risk." Unless the insurance policy's specification of what constitutes a breach is consistent with the commercial contract, the insurer's basis risk may be significant.

Documentary basis risk arises with nonstandard documentation. Prior to the development of standard documentation for political risk swaps, dealers would have to develop their own in-house confirmations for use with the ISDA master agreement. While it has always been contemplated that dealers would adapt the standard documentation to handle new derivative instruments, each set of dealer documentation raises new definitional issues and must be checked separately to avoid documentary basis risk. Fortunately, political risk insurers have increased their cooperation in recent years (and insuring large projects requires cooperation because of the project and country limits individual insurers face), and this improved cooperation has facilitated greater standardization of risk insurance policy provisions and reduced the problem of documentary basis risk.

Potentially more serious is the use of nonderivative contracts to document derivatives transactions. Derivatives have received some negative press in recent years, which has made some companies and investors wary of using derivative instruments. Others have used them but documented them in agreements that avoid using derivative terminology or traditional derivative contract provisions. Financially, the products exhibit the characteristics of derivatives, so the difference is one of form rather than substance. For example, a credit swap may be documented as a "guarantee." However, while it may be convenient for regulatory or other reasons to refer to a credit swap as a guarantee, there may be significant legal differences between the two. Any such differences will depend upon the provisions of state, federal, or foreign law that govern the contract. Thus, the switch in terminology may cause the legal consequences of the "guarantee" to switch also, possibly in ways the counterparties did not intend. Using nonstandard documentation can itself be a legally risky proposition.

A.2 Netting

The ISDA master agreement provides for close-out netting of the counterparties' obligations to one another with respect to all the derivative transactions covered by the agreement when early termination of the master agreement occurs. ISDA has obtained legal opinions in several jurisdictions indicating that the close-out netting provisions are enforceable in those jurisdictions in the event of a counterparty's bankruptcy. In contrast, netting may not be available for nonderivative risk management products.

Netting occurs when there are two or more transactions between two parties. Each party's gains and losses with respect to the other party are offset against one another (i.e., netted) to determine a single consolidated amount that one party owes to the other. Netting is desirable because it reduces each party's credit risk exposure to the other party.

Because political risk derivatives are new, the advantage of being able to net political risk derivative transactions against other derivative transactions may nevertheless not be available in many jurisdictions even under the master agreement. In some jurisdictions, close-out netting in the event bankruptcy occurs is governed by statute, and netting is available only for certain specified types of transactions. To have the netting provisions apply, it is necessary to show that the political risk derivative transaction falls within one of the specified categories. Also, in jurisdictions where the netting legislation predates political risk derivatives, such derivatives will fall outside its ambit unless the legislation can be interpreted broadly enough to include them. Therefore, before entering into a political risk derivative transaction, it would behoove a counterparty to confirm that the netting provisions are enforceable. Otherwise, the political event risk protection might ultimately prove to be illusory.

A.3 Pledge of Shares

A political risk insurer usually succeeds to the claim against the host government when it pays a claim for expropriation. It accomplishes this by requiring the insured equity investor to deliver the shares of stock in the project company as a condition to payment of compensation for expropriation together with an assignment of all rights to compensation from the host government for the expropriation, free and clear of any liens. In effect, the insurer buys the equity investors' ownership interest in the company in exchange for the insurance payment. However, this condition of insurance conflicts with the typical project financing arrangements.

Project lenders usually require a lien on virtually all the assets being financed as well as the shares of the equity investors in the project and a pledge of any rights to compensation for expropriation. Lenders want the pledge of shares because shares are often easier to sell than hard assets, ownership of the shares conveys voting control of the company, and in the event expropriation occurs, the shares offer an additional basis for the lenders' claim against the host government.

The conflicting requirements regarding the pledged shares need to be resolved in order for equity investors to insure their investments. The issue in political risk securitization concerns the need for a mechanism to ensure that the securitization vehicle, acting on behalf of the outside investors, gains title to the assets and succeeds to the claim against the host government when a claim is paid. The securitization vehicle should occupy the same position as the insurer would in a properly designed political risk investment insurance structure.

B. Regulatory Issues

B.1 Insurance Restrictions

If the insurance securitization includes a reinsurance contract (as opposed to an option), then the contract and its writer will have to comply with the applicable insurance regulations. Outside investors will want to avoid becoming regulated, so the financial instruments they purchase will have to qualify as securities. A special-purpose insurer has been used in cat bond transactions to address this issue.

B.2 Investment Restrictions

The Board of Governors of the Federal Reserve System (the Fed) and the Office of the Comptroller of the Currency (OCC) would have to issue guidelines for the regulatory treatment of political risk instruments before banks could purchase them. Similarly, the regulatory treatment under applicable insurance company regulations would have to be determined before insurance companies would invest in these products. Finally, pension funds are restricted by law and policy concerning their investments. Most pension funds make, at most, very limited use of derivatives, and even then, use them exclusively for hedging purposes. And pension funds usually restrict their bond investments to high-grade debt investments, for which there is little or no risk of loss of principal. These investment restrictions would limit their flexibility to invest in political insurance structured notes and political insurance derivatives.

An important consideration in designing political risk instruments is whether they can be engineered to satisfy the investment restrictions that banks, insurance companies, and pension funds face. Whether this can be accomplished will determine whether a viable market for these products can develop.

C. Marketing Issues

The private placement market is initially going to be the more receptive market for bonds designed to securitize political risk investment insurance. A public market might eventually develop, as it has for property catastrophe bonds, but only after the securities structure has been refined and the pricing issues resolved. The private placement market, which consists of sophisticated institutional investors, has usually been the market in which novel securities structures are tested. Private investors are more adept at monitoring the borrower, which will be required in political risk securitizations because of the significant moral hazard and adverse selection problems that characterize political risk insurance.

The initial issue(s) of political risk bonds may need to undergo some reengineering, which is more easily accomplished in private. Pricing may be difficult, and the private placement process affords greater price negotiating flexibility. The issuer and investors directly negotiate the pricing and other terms of the issue, and the transaction does not close until the buyer and seller agree on all the terms. In addition, the private insurers who wish to reinsure may be more willing to share their political-risk-event data with private investors, rather than publishing it in a prospectus filed with the Securities and Exchange Commission, where it is available for public inspection.

XI. Conclusion

As the financial markets have become more volatile, firms have sought better ways to hedge their financial risk exposure, and financial engineers have responded by developing new hedging instruments. Firms have also sought to securitize assets, such as residential mortgages and automobile and credit card loans, to get them off their balance sheets. These past efforts to develop new derivative instruments and securitize assets offer some useful lessons in how the securitization of political risk investment insurance might be accomplished.

Sequential-pay or senior-subordinated structures could be tailored so as to achieve whatever layer of reinsurance coverage is desired. Property catastrophe bonds (cat bonds) could be reengineered to create political catastrophe bonds (political cat bonds), and catastrophe insurance options could be reengineered to create political risk options. Designing a widely accepted set of political event loss or political risk indexes like the PCS property catastrophe indexes would be a precondition for the development of a viable market for such options. Finally, credit swaps, which can be used to hedge political risk — albeit usually with a high degree of basis risk — could be reengineered to create political risk swaps. The credit derivative swap structure, as it already involves a form of insurance, would appear to be the best starting place for developing a political reinsurance security.

Securitizing political risk investment insurance, if it is to be successful, will have to strike a balance among the insurer's exposure to basis risk and the investors' exposures to moral hazard, adverse selection, and liquidity risks. In view of their importance and experience in the political risk cover marketplace, national insurers, multilateral insurers, and the Berne Union can play a critical role in leading these securitization efforts.

References

Bermuda Commodities Exchange, 1998, "Contract Specifications."

Bhattacharya, Anand K., and Peter J. Cannon, 1989, "Senior-Subordinated Mortgage Pass-Throughs," in Frank J. Fabozzi, ed., *Advances & Innovations in the Bond and Mortgage Markets* (Probus, Chicago, IL), 473–483.

Black, Fischer, and Myron Scholes, 1973, "The Pricing of Options and Corporate Liabilities," *Journal of Political Economy* 81 (May–June), 637–654.

Borden, Sara, and Asani Sarkar, 1996, "Securitizing Property Catastrophe Risk," *Federal Reserve Bank of New York Current Issues in Economics and Finance* 2 (August), 1–6.

Carlson, Steven J., 1989, "Hedging Prepayment Risk with Derivative Mortgage Securities," in Frank J. Fabozzi, ed., *Investment Management* (Ballinger, Cambridge, MA), 557–563.

Chan, William, et al., 1997, *Class Notes: A Collection of Articles from Risk* (Canadian Imperial Bank of Commerce, New York).

Cox, Samuel H., Joseph R. Fairchild, and Hal W. Pedersen, 1999, "Actuarial and Economic Aspects of Securitization of Risk," Georgia State University Working Paper (February).

Cox, Samuel H., Joseph R. Fairchild, and Hal W. Pedersen, 1999, "Financial Economics of Securitization and Alternative Risk Transfers," Georgia State University Working Paper (February).

Cox, Samuel H., and Hal W. Pedersen, 1997, "Catastrophe Risk Bonds," Georgia State University Working Paper (October).

Diamonte, Robin, John M. Liew, and Ross L. Stevens, 1996, "Political Risk in Emerging and Developed Markets," *Financial Analysts Journal* 52 (May–June), 71–76.

Doherty, Neil A., 1997, "Financial Innovation in the Management of Catastrophe Risk," *Journal of Applied Corporate Finance* 10 (Fall), 84–95.

Doherty, Neil A., 2000, "Comments on Securitizing Political Risk Investment Insurance: Lessons from Past Securitizations," this book.

Erb, Claude B., Campbell R. Harvey, and Tadas E. Viskanta, 1996, "Political Risk, Economic Risk, and Financial Risk," *Financial Analysts Journal* 52 (November/December), 29–46.

Finnerty, John D., 1988, "Financial Engineering in Corporate Finance: An Overview," *Financial Management* 17 (Winter), 14–33.

Finnerty, John D., 1992, "An Overview of Corporate Securities Innovation," *Continental Bank Journal of Applied Corporate Finance* 4 (Winter), 23–39.

Finnerty, John D., 1993, "Sources of Value Added from Structuring Asset-Backed Securities to Reduce or Reallocate Risk," in Charles Stone, Anne Zissu, and Jess Lederman, eds., *The Global Asset Backed Securities Market* (Probus, Chicago, IL), 27–60.

Finnerty, John D., 1996, "Credit Derivatives, Infrastructure Finance, and Emerging Market Risk," *Financier* 3 (February), 64–75.

Finnerty, John D., 1998, *The PricewaterhouseCoopers Credit Derivatives Primer* (PricewaterhouseCoopers LLP, New York, NY).

Finnerty, John D., 1999, *Structuring Derivative Instruments to Adjust Risk Exposure: The Arithmetic of Financial Instruments* (PricewaterhouseCoopers LLP, New York, NY).

Flesaker, Bjorn, Lane Hughston, and Lawrence Schreiber, 1996, "Credit Derivatives," in John D. Finnerty and Martin S. Fridson, eds., *The Yearbook of Fixed Income Investing 1995* (Irwin, Chicago, IL), 220–232.

Froot, Kenneth, 1998, *The Evolving Market for Catastrophic Event Risk* (Marsh & McLennan Securities, New York, NY).

Ghose, Ronit, 1997, *Credit Derivatives: Key Issues* (British Bankers' Association, London).

Goshay, Robert C., and Richard L. Sandor, 1973, "An Inquiry into the Feasibility of a Reinsurance Futures Market," *Journal of Business Finance* 5 (Summer), 56–66.

Hayre, Lakhbir S., and Cyrus Mohebbi, 1989, "Mortgage Pass-Through Securities," in Frank J. Fabozzi, ed., *Advances & Innovations in the Bond and Mortgage Markets* (Probus, Chicago, IL), 259–304.

Jamshidian, Farshid, 1989, "An Exact Bond Option Pricing Formula," *Journal of Finance* 44 (March), 205–209.

Jarrow, Robert A., and Stuart M. Turnbull, 1995, "The Pricing and Hedging of Options on Financial Securities Subject to Credit Risk," *Journal of Finance* 50 (March), 53–85.

Jarrow, Robert A., and Stuart M. Turnbull, 1996, *Derivative Securities* (South-Western College Publishing, Cincinnati, OH), ch. 18.

Jenney, Frederick E., 2000, "Breach of Contract Coverage in Infrastructure Projects: Can Investors Afford to Wait for Arbitration?" this book.

Lekkos, Ilias, 1999, "Distributional Properties of Spot and Forward Interest Rates: USD, DEM, GBP, and JPY," *Journal of Fixed Income* 8 (March), 35–54.

Marshall, John F., and Vipul K. Bansal, 1992, *Financial Engineering* (Allyn and Bacon, Boston, MA).

Merton, Robert C., 1973, "Theory of Rational Option Pricing," *Bell Journal of Economics and Management Science* 4 (Spring), 141–183.

Merton, Robert C., 1974, "On the Pricing of Corporate Debt: The Risk Structure of Interest Rates," *Journal of Finance* 29 (May), 449–470.

Merton, Robert C., 1976, "Option Pricing When Underlying Stock Returns Are Discontinuous," *Journal of Financial Economics* 3 (January/March), 125–144.

MIGA (Multilateral Investment Guarantee Agency), 1999, *Annual Report 1999* (MIGA, Washington, DC).

Niehaus, Greg, and Steven V. Mann, 1992, "The Trading of Underwriting Risk: An Analysis of Insurance Futures Contracts and Reinsurance," *Journal of Risk and Insurance* 59 (December), 601–627.

OPIC (Overseas Private Investment Corporation), 1999, *Program Handbook: Political Risk Insurance* (OPIC, Washington, DC).

PCS Catastrophe, *PCS Catastrophe Insurance Options: The New Standardized Alternative for Managing Catastrophe Risk* (Chicago Board of Trade, Chicago, IL), 1995a.

_____, *PCS Catastrophe Insurance Options: A User's Guide* (Chicago Board of Trade, Chicago, IL), 1995b.

Perlman, Scot D., 1989, "Collateralized Mortgage Obligations: The Impact of Structure on Value," in Frank J. Fabozzi, ed., *Advances & Innovations in the Bond and Mortgage Markets* (Probus, Chicago, IL), 417–436.

Political Risk Services, 1999a, *International Country Risk Guide* (The PRS Group, LLC, East Syracuse, NY).

Political Risk Services, 1999b, *The Coplin-O'Leary System* (The PRS Group, LLC, East Syracuse, NY).

Riordan, Daniel W., 2000, "International Political Risk Management: Cooperation and Competition in the Political Risk Insurance Marketplace," this book.

Roberts, Blaine, Sarah Keil Wolf, and Nancy Wilt, 1989, "Advances and Innovations in the CMO Market," in Frank J. Fabozzi, ed., *Advances & Innovations in the Bond and Mortgage Markets* (Probus, Chicago, IL), 437–455.

Smithson, Charles W., 1995, "Credit Derivatives," *Risk* (December), 38-39.

Spinner, Karen, 1997, "Building the Credit Derivatives Infrastructure," *Derivatives Strategy* (June), 35-40, 42-43.

Spratlin, Janet, Paul Vianna, and Steven Guterman, 1989, "An Investor's Guide to CMOs," in Frank J. Fabozzi, ed., *Investment Management* (Ballinger, Cambridge, MA), 521–555.

Stone, Charles, Anne Zissu, and Jess Lederman, eds., 1993, *The Global Asset Backed Securities Market* (Probus, Chicago, IL).

Vasicek, Oldrich A., 1977, "An Equilibrium Characterization of the Term Structure," *Journal of Financial Economics* 5 (November), 177–188.

Waldman, Michael, Mark Gordon, and K. Jeanne Person, 1989, "Interest Only and Principal Only STRIPSs," in Frank J. Fabozzi, ed.,

Advances & Innovations in the Bond and Mortgage Markets (Probus, Chicago, IL), 401–416.

Walmsley, Julian, 1988, *The New Financial Instruments* (Wiley, New York).

West, Gerald T., 1996, "Managing Project Political Risk: The Role of Investment Insurance," *Journal of Project Finance* (Winter), 5–11.

West, Gerald T., 2000, "Political Risk Investment Insurance: The Renaissance Revisited," this book.

Notes

1. See Finnerty (1988, 1992), Marshall and Bansal (1992), and Walmsley (1988) for an overview of the process of financial innovation.

2. The U.S. Export-Import Bank recently asked investment banks, commercial banks, insurance companies, and other financial institutions for proposals to help Ex-Im provide loan guarantees and risk insurance for American companies. Political risk insurance is an important part of what Ex-Im Bank offers. See "Ex-Im Bank Seeks Investors for Guarantees," *Wall Street Journal* (February 16, 2000), B13. The concept of publicly traded insurance investments dates back at least 25 years (see Goshay and Sandor, 1973).

3. For example, lenders to projects are generally more willing to purchase project company bonds when they are backed by political risk investment insurance. Credit Suisse First Boston has securitized project debt by pooling senior secured project finance loans, of which up to 20 percent consisted of non-investment-grade bonds backed by political risk insurance. (See West, 2000, and Riordan, 2000.)

4. These four categories coincide with the four basic types of political risk insurance cover written by the Multilateral Investment Guarantee Agency (MIGA) of the World Bank. The Overseas Private Investment Corporation (OPIC) writes coverage for the first three categories of risk and, in addition, provides a variety of special insurance programs. However, OPIC is a national insurer; its cover is generally limited to U.S. citizens or U.S.-owned or U.S.-controlled business entities. See OPIC (1999).

5. Many project lenders and equity investors view disputes coverage as inadequate because the host government's failure to pay might bankrupt the project before the arbitration process reaches a conclusion. The host government therefore often has an incentive to take whatever reasonable steps it can (so as not to be accused of actually impeding the process) to delay the process. The plaintiff may win the arbitration, but it may be a hollow victory if the project has failed in the meantime. On the other hand, the host government must be careful so as not to be seen to be interfering with the arbitration process.

When a host government refuses to honor an arbitral award or refuses to cooperate in the arbitration process to which it had previously expressly agreed contractually, its actions are akin to expropriation without proper compensation.

6. The highest likelihood of loss among all the transactions in Froot's (1998) sample is only 25 percent, and most of these cat bond issues have a probability of loss closer to 1 percent—a one-in-a-hundred likelihood of loss.

7. Bond ratings are published by Moody's, Standard and Poor's, Fitch, Duff and Phelps, and others.

8. The PCS index has potential disadvantages. It is based on surveys rather than hard data. Consequently, it is impossible to verify its accuracy. Manipulation by reporting companies is certainly possible, as are errors. Thus, moral hazard remains a concern with the PCS index. In addition, since large companies sustain a large proportion of losses, estimation errors by larger companies can be important in the overall industry result. Finally, the PCS index is computed on a state-by-state basis. States are large areas in relation to cat event footprints, and insurers' exposures are often unevenly distributed throughout a state. Thus, individual insurer losses may correlate poorly with statewide losses. A reinsurance contract based on the PCS index, therefore, involves significant basis risk; it provides less protection for an insurer than would a contract linked directly to its ultimate net loss.

9. When there is more than one trigger, reinsurance contracts normally require that both conditions are met before the insured is entitled to any insurance recovery.

10. The Berne Union comprises 24 national and multilateral investment insurers, including MIGA, all of whom write political risk investment insurance policies.

11. Doherty (2000) notes that the case for securitizing political risk insurance may be weaker than the case for securitizing property catastrophe insurance. Hurricanes and earthquakes are discrete events, which are more easily modeled than political risk events. Also, natural catastrophes are uncorrelated with financial market returns, and zero-beta investments are attractive to investors for portfolio-diversification purposes. It is unclear how closely correlated political risk events are with financial market returns. This correlation (or lack of it) is really an empirical question that must await the availability of data suitable for measuring it.

12. A credit-event-put trust structure, which is discussed later in the chapter, could be used to eliminate any exposure to counterparty credit risk because it would secure the default payment.

13. A credit forward would provide protection similar to a total return swap. See Finnerty (1998). However, the credit forward is a simpler instrument.

14. PO STRIPS are recognized as "bullish" investments because a decrease in interest rates, which benefits bond prices generally, tends to boost prepayments and hence PO STRIP prices. IO STRIPS are recognized as "bearish" investments because their prices move in the opposite direction. The riskiness of trading and investing in IO/PO STRIPS has been highlighted by some large financial losses securities firms have experienced trading these instruments. See for example, "Anatomy of a Staggering Loss," *New York Times* (May 11, 1987), D1ff, and "J.P. Morgan Had $50 Million in Losses in Trading Mortgage-Backed Securities," *Wall Street Journal* (March 10, 1992), A4.

15. The structure has usually been designed to be tax neutral. If it qualifies as a real estate mortgage investment conduit (REMIC), it will pass the tax attributes of the underlying mortgage loans through to investors. A trust structure can be used for other types of assets. The purpose is to avoid having the securitization vehicle become a taxable entity because creating tax liabilities would raise the cost of securitization.

16. If USAA had set out to protect a lower layer of risk, this ratio would have been worse. The risk transfer set-aside amount would have made up an even smaller fraction of the money raised. Since marketing and other costs of a debt issue depend on the amount raised, the costs of a low-layer cat bond could become prohibitive.

17. This premium represents a reinsurance premium of 600 basis points minus a charge of 25 basis points for transaction costs. LIBOR refers to the London Interbank Offer Rate at which major banks offer funds to one another in the London money market.

18. PCS Catastrophe Insurance Options are the second generation of property catastrophe options traded on the CBOT. The CBOT introduced American options in 1992 based on insurance industry loss ratios provided by Insurance Services Office, Inc. It terminated them in 1995 and introduced European options based on the PCS loss indexes.

19. The Guy Carpenter Catastrophe Index (GCCI) is based on actual data from participating insurers. This feature should eliminate the scope for manipulation. The GCCI also quantifies loss experience at a zip-code level and is a monoline index, which would allow insurers to design a portfolio of zip-code indexes to match their risk portfolio rather than having to rely on a one-size-fits-all statewide index. There are disadvantages to this index, however. Because data collection requires time and considerable aggregation, GCCI results are only available quarterly. Also, not all insurers report their data to Guy Carpenter, so the index is based on a sampling approach. Finally, the GCCI currently reflects only homeowner losses on atmospheric cat events; commercial/industrial losses and other events (such as an earthquake) are not included.

20. European options are only exercisable on their expiration date, whereas American options are exercisable any time on or before their expiration date.

21. The development period immediately follows the loss period. The option contract is settled at the end of the development period.

22. On the other hand, recent trading experience may not be indicative of the product's long-run potential over a full catastrophic loss cycle. PCS Options continue to be available, and how their trading volume reacts when the next wave of catastrophic losses occurs in the United States will furnish a better indication of the product's usefulness.

23. There are several services that measure country risk (see Erb, Harvey, and Viskanta, 1996). Each of these services combines a range of qualitative and quantitative information into a single rating. However, as noted earlier in the chapter, these indexes do not measure actual losses.

24. By way of contrast, MIGA (1999, page 40) reports that at any given time, its legal staff may be working to resolve as many as a dozen investment disputes in different countries. In addition, West (1996) reports that one large (unnamed) national insurer resolved about three-quarters of its potential claims after receiving notification of a potential claim.

25. Derivatives are not really new. Futures contracts on commodities have been traded on organized exchanges since the 1860s. Forward contracts are even older. The Chicago Board of Trade (CBOT) introduced commodity forwards in 1842 and commodity futures in 1865. Compared to commodity forward and futures contracts, financial futures are new. The International Monetary Market of the Chicago Mercantile Exchange (CME) introduced foreign currency futures in 1972 and interest rate futures in 1975.

26. A nonrecourse debt obligation restricts the lenders' ability to seek repayment if there is a default. In the example, the lenders could have the portfolio of producing oil and gas properties liquidated, but because their loans were nonrecourse, they could not seek repayment directly from the oil and gas company.

27. Since no cash changes hands, they were usually off-balance-sheet transactions until the Financial Accounting Standards Board adopted Statement of Financial Accounting Standards No. 133 (FAS 133). Subsequent changes in their value could thus be deferred for financial reporting purposes so long as the swap continued to qualify for hedge accounting treatment.

28. As a result, they were on-balance-sheet. The structured swap form was often preferred because it was easier to keep them off the company's balance sheet. Because the instruments were equivalent financially, the difference in accounting treatment seemed inconsistent. The desire to eliminate such inconsistencies led to the adoption of FAS 133.

29. As a second example of a multilateral insurer's deterrence value, the Russian Directive of August 26, 1998, which severely restricted foreign exchange transactions (such as to pay interest to foreign lenders) expressly excluded projects insured by MIGA.

30. MIGA's 1999 annual report notes that at any given time, MIGA's legal staff may be involved in settling as many as a dozen investment disputes. It described two such disputes that were settled in 1999 (MIGA, 1999, page 40).

31. A similar problem arises in measuring defaults. Often, a debtor can privately negotiate a debt restructuring with its creditors to avert a default. A proper measure of default risk counts such restructurings as "defaults."

32. The publicly traded PCS Options are European, so there may be an advantage to using the same option structure.

33. The model is similar to Merton's (1976) model of share price behavior.

34. The subscript I indicates that the Wiener processes underlying equations (1) and (12) are distinct from one another.

35. Such an option strategy is referred to as a bull spread in the options literature.

Comment on Securitizing Political Risk Insurance

Kevin R. Callahan
Chief Executive Officer
Aon Capital Markets

Dr. Finnerty's paper is a detailed assessment of the issues related to the establishment of a Political Risk Securitization marketplace. The paper adequately reviews most of the conceptual issues related to creating a securitization market, in particular, from the perspective of the investment community. This paper intends to briefly discuss the securitization of political risk from a pragmatic and market perspective.

Defining and Measuring Political Risks

As Dr. Finnerty points out, the risk associated with merging market debt can be bifurcated into two components: (a) political risk and (b) credit risk. To date, capital markets investors have focused primarily on credit risk, although they have taken both risks through their purchase of emerging market debt. Conversely, while insurers and reinsurers have assumed credit risk, their primary area of focus has been the transfer of political risk only. Buyers and sellers in the insurance market have developed fairly standard definitions of political risk, but the market still lacks complete standardization with regard to the terms provided from insurer to insurer, and even transaction to transaction.

A second issue related to the definition of political risk relates to the existing insurance company practice of paying political risk claims. The industry traditionally requires insureds to exhaust all possible legal avenues in recovering assets that have been diminished as a result of "political risk." This process often takes years and can involve significant dispute — this contrasts with the *needs* of the investment market to quickly determine the results of a situation and either utilize or free-up the available capital. Again, Dr. Finnerty points out mechanisms existing in the capital markets to manage this issue. However, there exists a disconnection between the traditional mechanics in the insurance and capital markets.

Buyers of political risk insurance have typically sought coverage on an indemnity basis (dollar for dollar loss recovery), and do not seem to be enthusiastic about "hedging" these risks through contracts based on indices (thereby assuming basis risk). Sellers of political risk insurance do not typically hedge the risk they assume (as typical of insurance companies in other markets) and when they do hedge, it is usually on an indemnity basis. Dr. Finnerty points out the importance of establishing competent indexes in order to attract large amounts of capital to this sector, and the disconnect between investors looking to take index-based risks and insurance companies/insureds looking to manage indemnity risks. This creates a barrier to market development. Many would argue (and Dr. Finnerty alludes to this) that the insurance company, due to its ability to create a diverse portfolio of such risks, is in the best position to manage such basic risk.

Pricing in the insurance market is driven by a number of factors, including supply and demand and the diversification value of adding the risk to the insurer's portfolio. The insurance industry has a limited amount of capital to apply to political risk coverage — that capital is then valued based on the demands placed on it by global insureds. Hedging costs are less of a factor, except in jurisdictions where demand is too large to diversify away the resultant risk (e.g., Brazil, Turkey). In these markets, insurers look to cap their exposure through the purchase of excess of loss reinsurance.

Interestingly, it is this area that points to the enormous opportunity that exists in the area of securitization. The capital markets represent a large potential source of capacity for insurers and large corporations to access protection for aggregation of risk in high demand jurisdictions. The depth of this market can allow for more efficient pricing owing to elimination of the aggregation premium charged by insurers and reinsurers.

The development of a credit derivatives market for the emerging markets is also encouraging for the development of a political risk securitization market. In this market, capital markets investors provide index-based coverage to multinational corporates and holders of sovereign and corporate emerging market debt.

Similarities and Differences with Property Catastrophe Reinsurance

The market for political risk insurance is analogous in many ways to the property catastrophe insurance market. Similarities include the following:

- Both markets are dominated by customized risk transfer on an indemnity basis.
- Both markets have only a modest amount of coverage purchased on an index basis.
- Pricing in both markets is heavily influenced by supply and demand, with pricing currently at the low end of the cycle because of excess insurance industry capital.
- Both markets are challenged by aggregations of risk in high demand jurisdictions — for example, Brazil and Turkey on the political risk front and Florida hurricane and California earthquake in the property catastrophe market.

There are two significant differences:

- Resolution of claims in the property catastrophe market is much quicker because of the binary nature of the risks covered.
- Political risk is much more analogous to the traditional risks assumed by capital markets investors. In fact, as Dr. Finnerty points out, political risk is embedded in many of the emerging market securities currently purchased by capital markets investors.

Pricing/Valuation

Dr. Finnerty proposes a broad array of valuation techniques. Each of these techniques provides a framework for developing an efficient pricing methodology in this potential market. Having said that, the existing markets for political risk (i.e., insurance markets and emerging debt markets) manage to achieve pricing parity on a regular basis. Using one of Dr. Finnerty's frameworks (with dramatic simplification) for assessing "value," we can assess whether political risk insurance is attractive to the investment community.

As Dr. Finnerty points out, the credit risk premium associated with an emerging market country is a function of both (a) ability to pay ("Credit Risk") and (b) willingness to pay ("Political Risk"). By converting emerging market fixed-rate debt into floating-rate debt, the market can determine the premium that exists—that is, the spread over LIBOR being paid on the debt for assuming both the credit risk and the political risk. In the current market, a BB rated nation might pay a premium of 4.0 percent to 5.0 percent over LIBOR on such debt.

Assuming a 4.5 percent premium, we can now determine that the capital markets deem the "political risk" associated with this nation to be less than 4.5 percent. Comparing this to current rates-on-line in the political risk insurance market, we find that political risk coverage in certain capacity-constrained sectors can approach a large percentage of the overall debt spread, while in the majority of markets political risk coverage is a relatively modest component. This inconsistency points to the opportunity for political risk securitization.

Conclusion

The opportunity to securitize political risk is quite significant:
- Capacity in the existing insurance market is limited.
- Pricing in the existing market is relatively attractive.
- Efficiency of the existing market can be improved.

At the same time, as in the property sector, there are some significant technical and (more important) cultural barriers that must be surmounted to achieve success.

Comment on Securitizing Political Risk Insurance

Neil Doherty
**Ronald A. Rosen Professor of Insurance
and Risk Management
Wharton Risk Management Center**

John Finnerty's paper tells us much about the potential securitization of political risk. He sets up design criteria that are needed for a successful securitization. He shows how one might use the models of the credit derivatives market, the mortgage back security market, or the cat bond market to help design a political risk securitization. He shows how formal models of derivative pricing might be used to price such a securitization. Finnerty examines the information available to primary insurers of political risk (and presumably to the investors undertaking projects in emerging markets), and shows how securitization might proceed in the face of such information.

All these points address the question *how*. Hidden in with the answers to *how* are some hints to answer the question *why*.

My comments will address the question *why* securitize political risk insurance. In particular I am interested in whether securitization expands the opportunity set available to insurers who seek to manage their liability portfolio risk and to investors who seek to expand their efficient frontier.

The Market for Political Risk Is Incomplete

A complete market is one in which all parties can write (effectively) unlimited contracts on all possible states of nature. In our context, the market is incomplete if no hedging contracts are available against specific political risks. For example, can a project investor hedge against the specific micro political risk attached to that project (i.e., the expropriation, breach of contract, etc. risk in the country in which the project is located)? The fairly active market for political risk insurance addresses this need.

Second, at a higher level of aggregation, is there a market for macro political risk, that is, at the country level?

This is a little more fuzzy. Certainly there are markets where investors can assume the sovereign credit risk, and presumably this risk can be unbundled from the interest and principal payments to enable an investor or hedger a "pure play" on the country risk. Such an instrument could potentially be of use to a political risk insurer seeking to hedge a subportfolio of policies in the country.

At a still higher level of aggregation, is there a market for the aggregate political risk in part or all of the liability portfolios of insurers?

Well, there is a reinsurance market that addresses this risk so insurers have a hedging instrument.

From the other side, can investors take a speculative position on the bundles of political risk held by insurers?

This is a little more difficult. Certainly they can take an equity investment in an insurer. But this is a residual claim on the insurance entity which bundles political risk together with risk on other insurance lines and investment risk. Under some circumstances, it might be possible for the investor to unbundle this risk. Consider a single line political risk insurer. The value of the insurer, V, will be the sum of the value of assets $V(A)$, plus liabilities, $V(L)$, plus any additional value added (or lost) by virtue intermediation, $V(I)$

$$V = V(A) - V(L) + V(I)$$

If it were not for $V(I)$, the value of liabilities could be backed out as simply the value of the insurer minus the value of assets. Furthermore, if the insurer were publicly traded, and the asset portfolio known and traded, then an investor could replicate the liability portfolio.

$$V(L) \approx V - V(A)$$

Thus, securitizing this risk does not significantly expand the opportunity set for an investor wishing to assume a position in the entire liability portfolio of a political risk insurer. However, suppose an investor wished to assume part of that risk, such as the political risk of a region or country or even a particular project.

Unbundling to this level from the insurer's equity is difficult or impossible for the individual investor.

This seems to be a weaker case for securitization than that for catastrophe risk. Catastrophe risk permitted investors to take a pure play in well-defined and well-modeled events such as hurricanes and earthquakes. Moreover, these events tend to be uncorrelated with financial markets and the estimated zero beta makes them well suited for portfolio diversification. It is unclear whether political risk has the same properties.

Thus on the grounds of market completeness, I think that a compelling case still needs to be made that the securitization of political risk really enhances risk return opportunities for insurers and investors.

Securitization Promises to Lower the Contracting Cost of Political Risk Hedging

The contracting costs of reinsurance include the direct costs of writing a contract and the costs of resolving moral hazard and adverse selection problems. Perhaps the most important *potential* gain for securitizing political risk is a lowering of the adverse selection and moral hazard costs (as I suspect was the case for securitizing catastrophe risk).

The problems of adverse selection and moral hazard arise because the reinsurance is inherently an indemnity contract. Once the reinsurance layer is penetrated, all marginal claim costs are simply passed on to the reinsurer. For political risk insurance, the moral hazard problem in particular can be acute. The event that is insured, and the amount of damages incurred by the policyholder, are not well defined. The actions by the policyholder that can reduce the loss potential are not easily monitored. And the expected loss is difficult to measure. All these characteristics give a high potential for moral hazard and related problems in the relationship between the primary insurer and the policyholder. Moreover, this primary moral hazard can be passed upwards to the insurer-reinsurer interface.

How are such perverse incentives best controlled?

When contracts are not clearly defined and performance can entail a significant probability of dispute, it is often best to control incentive problems by establishing a long-term relationship rather than attempting to find specific contract language. Reinsurance is indeed usually contracted on a relationship basis, and the rights and obligations of the parties are not specified in great detail. The potential for abuse by the primary (selective reinsurance of bad risks, sloppy underwriting, inefficient claim settlement) are held in check by the need to have continuing reinsurance protection. While the value of reputation acts as a control on moral hazard and adverse selection, the control itself is costly. The relationship is brokered, which involves substantial commissions, and the parties are to some extent "locked in" and thereby constrained in exploiting new market opportunities.

Another contractual control that can be used to address moral hazard is to design a hedge product where the payout is correlated with the primary insurer's losses but the primary still bears the full marginal costs of claims. Such objective triggers are used extensively in catastrophe securitization, as discussed by Finnerty.

The idea is to reach a tradeoff between basis risk and moral hazard. Can we find an instrument variable, that is, some index, that has high correlation with the primary insurer's claims but over which the primary exerts little or no control? Some potential candidates are as follows:

- A worldwide index of all the aggregate loss experience of all (or some representative subset of) of primary insurers;
- A weighting of the regional indices of the aggregate loss experience of all (or some representative subset of) primary insurers where the regional weighting reflects the hedging insurer's book of business;
- A weighted average of the changes on the sovereign credit ratings of the countries in which the primary insurer has exposure;
- A weighted average of the ICRG (*International Country Risk Guide*) composite country scores (political + financial + economic risk) in which the primary has exposure; and
- A weighted average of the ICRG political risk scores in which the primary has exposure.

The first two candidates do pick up actual loss experience so the degree of basis risk depends on how the hedging insurer's book is representative of the industry-wide "book of business." The last three are not directly indicative of loss experience but of changes in *ex ante* risk. So one might suppose the basis risk is quite high. However, these are empirical issues.

To make a convincing case for securitizing political risk will, I suspect, require that an appropriate trigger be found that is objective and transparent and has a low basis risk. But even if one can find an index that has an acceptable basis risk, it does not follow that the risk is best securitized.

Any objective trigger that can be adopted in a securitization could also be used in a reinsurance contract. I suspect that a major boost to catastrophe securitization was the inertia of reinsurers in offering such innovations.

Securitization Offers Improved Technology
for Addressing Credit Risk

One of the most compelling cases for securitization of catastrophe risk is that it permitted insurers a hedging alternative with lower credit risk. Catastrophe bonds were, as described by Finnerty, issued by a Special Purpose Vehicle that held the proceeds in trust as collateral for the reinsurance policy sold to the primary insurer. Since the trust holds full collateral for possible claims, there is no credit risk. This contrasts with reinsurance, where the typical surplus to liability ratios are in the order of two or less.

We can now join this point on credit risk with the previous point on moral hazard and basis risk. The following diagram shows credit risk on the vertical axis and basis risk on the lower horizontal axis. Since acceptance of basis risk addresses the problem of moral hazard, then the horizontal axis can also be used to measure (the inverse of) moral hazard. This is shown by the top horizontal, which shows moral hazard decreases from left to right (matching the left to right increase in basis risk). This design space shows how securitization can enhance the risk management frontier for the primary insurer. Reinsurance has credit risk; because it is an indemnity contract it has a low basis risk but high moral hazard. This places it in the top left corner of the diagram. Changing the contract design to include basis risk and changing the collateral makes available the whole design space.

Securitizalion Permits More Flexibility to the Insurer
in Meeting Its Risk Management Objectives

Modern theories of corporate risk management start with an examination of why risk is costly to a firm. Risk creates a set of frictional costs and can promote dysfunctional investment decisions. Moreover, realized losses might deprive the firm of funds for financing new investments. While hedging can address these costs, it is not always the most efficient way. Other approaches, such as using structured debt and contingent equity, can sometimes be cheaper than insurance and more effective in securing the financial resources necessary to undertake new value-enhancing investments.

Consider an example from catastrophe insurance. One reason an insurer might need equity capital after a loss is to continue to sell its current book of business and to take advantage of new investment opportunities. Reinsurance is based on the indemnity concept which is in effect to replace the equity that has been lost. But the amount of equity required to take advantage of postloss opportunities may be determined largely by the impact of the event on the insurer's share price (if the share price is high, a new share issue might be attractive). And after several recent natural catastrophes, insurers' prices actually rose. So an indemnity contract would have provided too much equity. Instruments such as contingent equity, forgivable debt, and convertible debt, permit fine-tuning to the postloss capital needs of the political risk insurer.

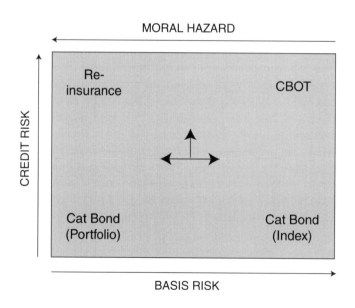

Comment on Securitizing Political Risk Insurance

Gerald T. West
Senior Advisor, Guarantees
Multilateral Investment Guarantee Agency

John Finnerty's paper is clearly an important contribution to the study of securitizing political risks, as the commentaries of Neil Doherty and Kevin Callahan have previously pointed out. It is a significant paper in terms of both its breadth and depth.

Intuitively, it has always seemed that the securitization of political risk would be a very difficult task, but a careful reading of this paper illustrates just how challenging that task is going to be. It is difficult to decide on the proper perspective from which to critique this paper. From an academic perspective, there are many methodological issues that are worth exploring in greater depth. At the same time, from a political science perspective, the assumptions made about political risk forecasting and the use of political risk rankings deserve careful attention. Finally, from the vantage point of an investment insurer, there are a host of practical issues raised by the paper that merit closer examination. My comments will focus on only a few of the rich number of possibilities.

I. Defining and Measuring Political Risk

The second section of the paper deals with defining and measuring political risk. It points out that there is a tremendous micro-macro measurement problem in the field of political risk insurance. At the macro level, it notes that there are many efforts aimed at trying to measure risk at the national level including, for example, the PRS Group's *International Country Risk Guide*. While pointing out a few weaknesses of such ratings, the paper is nonetheless remarkably charitable in its treatment of them. While being concerned with the subjectivity of PRS's political risk index, for example, the paper makes the somewhat facile assumption that the index is, nonetheless, useful and, in any case, that it is among the best of the few indices available.

These macro-measures have always seemed problematic for a number of reasons, not least of which is the many convenient assumptions they make. While one may have a lot of respect for the extensive academic work of William Coplin and Michael O'Leary, the preparation of these indices and the measures that compose them are open to serious question. Moreover, there has always been a serious problem with the assignment of weights. The fact that the political risk component is exactly twice the weight of financial and economic risk components, and that this two-to-one ratio is true across all countries and many decades is very convenient. Aside from its convenience, though, there is not a shred of theoretical justification underpinning that weighting. Similarly, there has been no attempt to provide ex post facto evidence that this two-to-one weighting ratio is accurate. Other systems like PRS could be subjected to similar critiques. Although Finnerty acknowledges some of these shortcomings, his model fundamentally assumes the use of such indices.

As the paper notes, "macro-measure[s] of political risk may not perfectly fit the political risk event to which the equity investors in or lenders to a particular project are exposed." That is absolutely correct—and it is, quite frankly, why sophisticated investors have little or no use for these macro-measures and develop more relevant project-specific or micro-political risk measures for themselves. Among other things, this allows investors to decide whether or not to buy political risk insurance, to bear the risk themselves, or to rely on alternative risk management techniques.

The third section of the paper reviews five factors that are promoting the securitization of political risk insurance. For many of the reasons noted by the other commentators, it is clear that there is much in this section to which we can all agree. More discussion is needed, however, on one point mentioned in the third section: the "insurer control of the loss trigger."

As Finnerty notes briefly, one of the major reasons why investors purchase investment insurance from a public sector provider such as MIGA or OPIC is the hope of obtaining the benefit of some deterrent or halo effect that will help prevent a loss in the first place. While OPIC or MIGA probably would not be able to deter a loss due to war or other political violence, they definitely do have a deterrent effect with respect to the incidence of expropriation and currency transfer loss.

MIGA, for example, has written more than 450 guarantees, and as Mr. Ikawa has mentioned, there has been only one claim. That record might be attributed to brilliant underwriting, luck, some other factor, or a combination of all of the above. There is, however, more to it than this. Some years ago, OPIC estimated that only approximately one in four *prospective* claims actually resulted in a claim. In other words, in three out of four instances, when the investors informed OPIC of problems or potential problems that could lead to a claim, something happened to prevent a claim from actually occurring.

What was it that had happened? Some situations clearly resolved themselves or were disposed of in some way. There is, however, something that might be termed the "conspiracy of silence" that envelops other situations because nobody likes to discuss how these potential claims went away or how some "misunderstanding" between the host government and the investor was suddenly cleared up. It is clear that these potential claims do not just disappear of their own volition. Someone does something to cause these "misunderstandings" to rectify themselves. That someone is often an investment insurer, operating quietly behind the scenes.

To use an analogy, let us suppose for a moment that one wishes to insure the family farm. Property insurance against lightning strikes would be very useful for reimbursing the owners in case of damage. It would be more useful, though, if the property insurer both provides coverage and installs lightning rods on the house. Best of all, however, would be a property insurer who not only provides coverage and installs the lightning rods, but also actively tries to steer storms away from the farm. In essence, much of what goes on very quietly in the public investment insurance business is similar in nature to this analogy.

The problem with this, of course, is that it is very difficult to quantify the "dogs that did not bark," not only because the outside world did not hear about these potential claims that were averted, but also because investment insurers do not generally keep statistics on these matters. Publicizing specific deterrence and advocacy efforts (which are usually done very quietly) would make those efforts more difficult and less likely to bear fruit. In any case, factoring these "near-misses" into mathematical calculations underlying a securitization would be very difficult, if not impossible. Hence, I would suggest that the reality that an investment insurer can have a "finger on the loss trigger" needs to be dealt with more extensively in considering securitization.

II. Securitization and the Need for Objective Information

The fourth section of John Finnerty's paper includes a discussion of five barriers to the securitization of political risks: the lack of objective information; the high cost of assessing risk exposure; the need for a compelling case for securitization; the lack of adequate pricing models; and the required investment in the underlying infrastructure for securitization. These are very real barriers, and the paper correctly notes both the fragmentary nature of information in this field and how good computer modeling requires such information.

It is somewhat surprising that the paper suggests that the Berne Union might play a role in furnishing such data to the risk modelers on a country-by-country basis and on a risk class-by-risk class basis — and that such data be updated regularly. While Anthony Faulkner and David Bailey give their specific comments on this idea below, I would simply note that there are at least four distinct issues that make this an immense and daunting task. First, particularly with the growth of the private market, Berne Union information would represent only a fragmentary, nonrepresentative picture of the overall market. For their part, private insurers are very secretive about these matters. Second, within the Berne Union, there are vast differences in pricing, recovery efforts, and data collection among members. Also, systematic collection of the type of data needed for such models is fairly recent among Berne Union members, and therefore would probably not contain a sufficient number of cases to allow extrapolation (even if the data were comparable across members). Finally, many members might object to the sharing of this data, which many consider sensitive, with those outside the Berne Union.

Beyond these individual barriers and problems related to data-gathering, however, one could have an interesting philosophical discussion about whether or not it is even useful to try to measure risk this way, especially at the country level. In other words, for example, is risk an attribute or property associated with a country or is it in fact better examined as being associated with a particular exposure of assets? While it may be convenient for some purposes to consider certain political risks as a "country property," the reality is that a particular investment's risk of loss attributable to war, expropriation, or currency transfer restrictions is likely to be different from that of another investment in the same country at the same time. Moreover, these "country risk" approaches to measurement are notorious for not distinguishing between short-term and long-term risk. They serve to promote the belief that their country measures equally apply to all sectors and all investors. History, however, suggests that investors are rarely treated the same by the host country. Much depends on the relative size of the investor (or investment), the sector in which it operates, its level of "indigenization," the relations between the investor's home country and the host country, etc. All of these are factors that macro-measures of risk focusing on the country level do not even attempt to cover.

III. Contingent Claims Pricing Models

In another section of the paper, there is an extended discussion of contingent claims pricing models. It is tempting to devote considerable attention to a discussion of some provocative quotes from the paper, for example, that political events "seem inherently more difficult to predict than economic events such as defaults." Given the sorry record of economists in predicting defaults, how much more difficult will it be to deal with political phenomena? The paper also notes or assumes that "political risk events occur according to a Poisson process. Political risk events are assumed to be random and independent." Most political scientists would vigorously criticize, or even dismiss, this assumption. Poisson approaches have been proven to have very limited practical use in political science.

IV. Conclusion

Finally, in the last section, the paper notes the importance of putting together a political risk index. While creating such an index is very important, it is also a very difficult task to complete. The key problem, as noted above, is the validity of the measures used in putting such an index together. Measurement, in many ways, has been and remains a key problem in the whole political risk assessment and management field (and, arguably, throughout the field of political science, given the vagaries of human behavior that underlie political actions). The issue of the index, though, raises an interesting theoretical point: if good measures of political risk existed, would there be a need to securitize? People would probably then have a good basis for making very solid, informed decisions on how to manage those now-predictable political risks.

In conclusion, these comments should not mask the fact that this is truly a pioneering paper. It is an important first step in what will probably be a long process that all those involved in the political risk field will need to consider before trying to securitize political risk. We owe a debt to John Finnerty because his paper gives a much clearer idea of the magnitude and scope of the work that remains to be done.

Comment on Securitizing Political Risk Insurance

Anthony Faulkner
Head of Overseas Investment Insurance
Export Credits Guarantee Department (ECGD)
of the United Kingdom

There are in fact few statistics existing concerning political risk insurance claims. Gerald West of MIGA has raised the question of whether the Berne Union may have a role to play in gathering statistics. The Berne Union is an organization of official export credit agencies and political risk insurers. With the exception of an underwriter with observer status (AIG), all members represent public sector insurers; the split in business between the private and public sector, however, is about 50/50. This would mean that any statistics compiled by the Berne Union would of necessity be incomplete.

Political risk insurers (public and private) make much of their ability to remedy problems without becoming the subject of a claim. These "loss avoidance" situations are very difficult to quantify. How does one determine what was a problem that would have given rise to a claim and which the insurer managed to remedy and a situation that may or may not have resulted in a claim? Much of the value of public sector political risk insurance is seen by the underwriters and their clients as the ability of the underwriter to intercede and negotiate on behalf of the investor with the host government. Statistics on such intervention do not exist and are mainly captured by anecdotal evidence.

I think it very unlikely that there will be any meaningful statistics available which show how the entire political risk insurance industry performs. The industry is made up of various groups of companies and government agencies and, while statistics are available from Berne Union members, few statistics are available from private sector insurers.

Comment on Securitizing Political Risk Insurance

David Bailey
Team Leader
Political Risk Insurance
Export Development Corporation (EDC) of Canada

My observations will reinforce the points made by both Anthony Faulkner and Gerald West. The availability of information on the political risk insurance business, and particularly claims information, has long been an issue in the political risk insurance market.

In the Investment Insurance Committee of the Berne Union (comprised almost exclusively of public insurers), we have for many years been exchanging information regarding insurance business; however, only recently have we started providing detailed information on claims paid. All members have now provided a list of claims paid and recovery experience since the inception of their program. What is interesting is that most members, with the notable exception of OPIC and a few others, do not have extensive claims experience.

EDC, for example, has paid only between 12 and 15 political risk insurance claims since the inception of the program in 1969. This is a reflection of the fact that not many political risk insurance claims have been submitted to the overall market in that period. As most are aware, that trend may be experiencing an interruption.

It is my opinion that this lack of political risk insurance claims experience will be a challenge for entities trying to put together political risk insurance securitization, who typically would seek and rely on considerable historical data to determine likely future trends.

PART FIVE

Cooperation, Competition, and the "Science of Pricing" in the Political Risk Insurance Marketplace: Overview

Theodore H. Moran, Editor

The market for political risk insurance is both growing and evolving very rapidly. This leads to a large number of questions for all participants in the field of political risk management.

With regard to pricing political risk coverage, for example, sponsors and lenders face a growing number of choices for evaluating their options in political risk insurance. How are prices for political risk coverage determined? Is pricing of political risk coverage a science or an art? How much value do various forms of political risk coverage add, and what is the tradeoff between price and value in assessing what coverage to purchase?

With regard to coverage, to what extent do sponsors and lenders face problems in acquiring sufficient coverage for political risk exposure? What is the role of cooperation between private and public underwriters in expanding capacity?

Finally, where is the market going with regard to global versus individual project political risk insurance policies? Can global policies eliminate problems in the patchwork of single project policies, fill gaps, and overcome limitations on coverage? Do individual project policies offer more flexibility and better targeting of coverage?

There is not enough experience or data on loss frequency and/or severity, according to **David James, political risk**

insurance underwriter for the Brockbank syndicate, based in Lloyd's, to say that pricing or rating in the political risk insurance business is actuarially-based. But the judgment that sets pricing or rating can be guided by several factors.

The first factor is the background of the insured: do they tend to behave in a way that can prevent problems from occurring at all? Are they knowledgeable about the cover they are purchasing? Do they have a record that indicates the insurer is not being exposed to adverse selection?

The second factor concerns the legal structures and practical arrangements (use of offshore accounts, debt/equity ratios, payment streams) of the insured project, as they affect recovery potential. Are they tested, or are they untried?

In addition, there is always the question of supply and demand in the market: what are other brokers charging? At the same time, an insurer must consider how the addition of a particular exposure will affect the risk profile of the insurer's portfolio.

Insurers also have to take their own fixed costs into consideration, as well as their reinsurance costs and costs of provisioning. They have to respond to internal pressures for a certain level of performance.

Overall, David James argues that private insurers can generally match or beat the prices of multilateral insurers and export credit agencies, and offer more flexibility in coverage. Global programs can cover multiple types of exposure for a multinational investor across several countries. James does not believe that global programs eliminate gaps in coverage, but he judges that they can add capacity that might not otherwise be available. Brockbank manages its capacity ceilings by nationality of investor, by industry type, by coverage, and by host country, with the last normally becoming the first limitation.

Coinsuring with public sector underwriters does not add capacity in the private market, in the view of David James. Moreover, the presence of export credit agencies does not constitute a significant risk mitigant, he asserts. Even the presence of a World Bank body like MIGA, while more attractive, does not enable the underwriters to ignore the fundamentals of good underwriting.

Charles Berry, Chairman of Berry, Palmer & Lyle Ltd., agrees that political risk assessment is not an actuarial science.

Political risk underwriters do have proprietary information, but as a result of experience rather than research. The identity of the policyholders, the structure of the insured transaction, and the history of recovery all affect premium rates.

The actual price for coverage is determined by supply and demand. As in any market, no single insurer can dictate price, although competitive forces are less strong when risk is high, capacity is short, or demand is extremely large.

With the expansion of private political risk insurance, the market has taken on a life of its own. Public sector players have to accept the fact that the private market is more flexible, quicker to respond, and "fundamentally cheaper," an assertion where Berry and James agree. There is significant potential going forward in developing cooperative arrangements between public and private sector insurers that can deliver greater benefits for policyholders than has been possible in the past.

Finally, concludes Berry, a great new opportunity has arisen in the practice of some developing country governments in partnering with private sector underwriters to provide coverage of political risk in their own countries. Examples include joint ventures between AIG and Uzbekistan, Lloyd's and Bosnia and Herzegovina, private insurers and the COMESA countries of Africa, and AIG and the Corporacion Andina de Fomento (an entity owned by several Latin American governments).

Daniel Riordan of Zurich-U.S. reports that his company uses a five-tiered hazard evaluation measure to establish a base rate for each coverage and country. Zurich then analyzes the customer and the insured risk or project, debiting or crediting the base rate to establish the charged rate. The charged rate is subject to market forces that may influence its final quotation.

Like Brockbank, Zurich relies heavily on the size and experience of the insured, assessing whether the insured has sufficient "clout" and "staying power" to reduce the likelihood of adverse host government actions. Zurich also evaluates the host government's attitude toward private investment as well as the role of opposition groups. It examines the country's history of managing investment disputes and honoring arbitration awards. Finally, Zurich scrutinizes the project itself, including its location, the legal status of its permits and agreements, and its environmental practices.

Riordan offers observations about what buyers should be looking for in an insurer: its reputation for paying claims, financial condition, and underwriting expertise, creativity, and flexibility.

In contrast to David James, Daniel Riordan indicates that Zurich believes that public agencies such as MIGA, OPIC of the U.S., and COFACE of France serve as "significant mitigators" of political risk. Partnering with government insurers enhances the leverage that can be brought to bear on behalf of an insured. In the last two and a half years, Zurich has participated in approximately 40 coinsurance or reinsurance endeavors with public agency providers.

MIGA does not use a country rating system to calculate premium rates, reports **Christophe Bellinger**. Rather, its rates derive from various project and country risk-related questions that underwriters use to propose a premium rate to senior management, following guidelines published by MIGA. While there has been some perception in the market that MIGA is expensive, the agency's ability to manuscript policies, or tailor-make contracts, ensures that an investor or lender pays only for what the buyer wants and needs.

MIGA's purpose is to facilitate foreign investment rather than make a profit, but it must charge premiums sufficient to pay for its own expenses and build adequate reserves to pay potential claims. MIGA cannot insure existing investments and thus has less flexibility than the private market in providing global policies. But by covering a company's new investments and reinsuring old investments (under certain conditions), it can approach the scope of global coverage and discount the premium in recognition of the spread of risks.

MIGA has insured loans in Latin America, with a special purpose vehicle (SPV) as the beneficiary of MIGA coverage that then sold notes to investors in the capital markets. MIGA is currently working with rating agencies to develop a contract that would permit the insured loan to be rated equal to or better than investment grade. This could lead OECD banking supervisory authorities to grant waivers from country risk provisioning.

The proposition that there is sufficient capacity in the political risk insurance market is accurate, according to Bellinger, only for particular kinds of coverage of particular kinds of projects in particular kinds of countries. That is, there may be enough capacity in the market in general, but insurers may not be willing to use it (even at high premium rates) for more difficult countries. For many of the poorest countries, sufficient insurance is not available, and thus MIGA's efforts to cover investments in less popular places (and to entice other insurers to follow MIGA under reinsurance, cooperative or coinsurance agreements) do help build capacity that otherwise would not be there.

Cooperation, Competition, and the "Science of Pricing" in the Political Risk Insurance Marketplace

David James
Brockbank Group, Lloyd's

Introduction

I am an underwriter of Political Risk for the Brockbank syndicate, part of the XL Capital Group, based in Lloyd's. The political risk business we see in Lloyd's is very varied, covering traditional investment protections, war risks on fixed assets and aircraft/marine vessels, as well as contractual and contingency risks for investment and trade.

Being a Lloyd's underwriter gives an insight into a vast amount of the political risk written worldwide. Aside from this, London has a depth of experience in its underwriters, brokers, consultants and lawyers—as such, I hope I am well placed to provide you with an insight into current thinking on pricing-related issues in the private political risk market.

I have been asked to address this conference with a paper on pricing and capacity. The promotional material to this conference raised the value of "global programs," that is, where a buyer seeks to address more than a single investment or loan in one policy, normally covering more than one country. I have tried to give a perspective on the development of this interesting area. I will do my best to advance a basis for discussion, but I would like to start with a few introductory comments.

Pricing of risk cannot be viewed in isolation from other developments in our insurance market. It is not enough to discuss our mar-

170

ket in terms of whether pricing is hardening or softening (i.e., going up or down). With very few exceptions, political risk cannot be considered as a standard commodity. Yet the cost of buying insurance in almost every field has gone down in the last three or so years – at the same time that the market has become oversupplied with capacity. These conditions have increased the profile of political risk underwriting and enabled us as a market to attract increased support from capacity providers. This has combined to produce what I expect to be the high point of the private political risk market in terms of capacity and policy period. The size of the political risk market in terms of premium income and potential liability has focused the attention of capacity providers, regulators, and analysts. As underwriters in the class, we are increasingly being asked to justify our approach and rating. In this paper I would like to try and open the debate on some of the issues surrounding what I have termed "The Science of Pricing," that is, the extent to which there are constant, predictable factors, that ensure a level of predictability in the underwriting of political risk. How much of what we do is "scientific"? How predictable is the pricing of risk and what are the rules or principles that support it? What factors go into the underwriter's assessment of pricing?

What Goes into the Price?

Let's start with an admission. I do not think that any underwriters in our market can say that their pricing, or rating, is actuarially based. That is, country loss analysis is not so advanced as to enable us to predict loss frequency and/or severity accurately. In practice, underwriters have to use their experience and judgment to assess the likelihood of any loss and take a view. As such, we should all be clear that political risk pricing is not a pure science – but, if done properly, it should not be a "punt" or guess either. Hopefully this paper will show the extent to which this is the case.

What the underwriter considers will inevitably be subjective or personal to him or her. I hope that I will be able to give you a flavor of what I look at and speculate on other methods and approaches.

With any inquiry, the starting point is the basic country risk perception – "is this somewhere we want to consider taking risk?" For Brockbank, this rules out North Korea and one or two others. While this list does vary a little from time to time, it is generally very short. Our view is that there are few countries where you simply cannot take risk. Aside from these issues, we also have to consider the ability of our syndicate to take such exposure – does it comply with public international law, notably sanctions? Also, are there implications under the laws of the assured?

Once we have gotten beyond "can we look at this," the next criterion for me is who is the assured. Not all underwriters will agree with this high priority on the "who" question. Some market underwriters will consider that recovery potential is the most important criterion, but I prefer to focus on what my assured can bring to a risk. My reasoning is that if you back the right assured, you can usually keep problems from occurring in the first place – and if they do happen, you have an excellent chance of mitigating your loss. Having a good assured can be viewed in various ways: What is their nationality? Do they understand the social/economic environment in which they are trading or investing? Do they have a record of using the market? This last fact is particularly important, as it counts against fears of anti-selection and should indicate a knowledge of the cover that they are buying. Are we aware of the assured's approach to taking risk? This is particularly relevant to various multinationals and banks that we have assessed and gained comfort from their internal procedures. Understanding our assured is as important to us as understanding country risk.

Recovery potential and security are always an issue in the risk assessment element of pricing. Essentially, if we pay a claim, what chance do we have of getting our money back? Security over an incomplete asset in a country where nobody wants to do business is not worth too much. With this in mind, I feel it is a mistake to place too much emphasis on straightforward asset security – is the title taken effective? Underwriters also have to consider the financial structures and payment streams, the use of offshore accounts, debt to equity gearings and other exposures that the parties may have with each other – secured or otherwise. Ultimately, we will have to be comfortable with the legality of these structures as well as the practical elements: Do they work? Have they been tested?

The current risk perception will also be a significant factor in the initial pricing – in essence, "what is it worth?" This is where market forces come in – particularly in Lloyd's where you quickly become aware of changes in pricing. This brings into play the normal trading issues of other people's expectations and the ability to use them to one's advantage. We may follow the market on some occasions; for example, the price on Turkey has steadily risen even when the analysts' perception is that the risk has dropped. Why?

The largest factor outside of risk perception in pricing is capacity. How much of a given country risk can the underwriter take?

Normally in Lloyd's we aggregate, or total, our risk dollar for dollar, that is, we do not usually weight risk once written. Rather, risk is taken onto our books and applied against our limits for the relevant host country. We also aggregate virtually all types of political risk—confiscation, contract frustration—and credit against our investment and trade country limits. War, terrorism, and aviation repossession are dealt with separately because of the different nature of the risk taken. Our view, although conservative, is that this is the only safe way in which to aggregate. We can foresee scenarios where credit, contract frustration and confiscation are all impacted and losses could result. Other underwriters take the view that book management, that is, insuring a variety of industry and investor nationalities, allows one to gear up reinsurance or capacity. I do not agree with the view that such diversity is ample protection. I am a believer in proper portfolio management as an internal matter of good underwriting practice, but do not consider it sufficient to allow me to overexpose our own capital base.

All insurers have to carry fixed costs: management time, cost of capital, reinsurance costs, administrative and analytical expenses. These have to be considered when underwriters are reviewing their rating levels, capacity, and desired profile. These are day-to-day business considerations for all underwriters, irrespective of class of business. The largest item for a traditional Lloyd's syndicate is likely to be reinsurance. That is, most syndicates purchase protection for their underwriting book from outside entities. This is certainly our practice. The cost and availability of such reinsurance are key to our business plan, although it is reviewed regularly. Rating may vary as a result of reinsurance appetite and costing. This may require time to take effect, as these reinsurance programs will normally be annual or biannual.

The annual cycle can also have impact. This can have an impact on insurers who may wish to satisfy income levels or be under pressure as a result of loss levels. All of these "internal" pressures on an insurer can have an impact.

If the insurer retains more risk, this may have the effect of reducing the impact of reinsurance/renewal cycles but increasing the attention of rating agencies monitoring the impact of emerging market exposure. This is one factor which may yet have an increasing role in our market pricing, particularly for corporate insurers. The view taken by the rating agencies such as Standard & Poor's or AM Best on what monies should be set aside for emerging market risk, that is, the cost of provisioning, is likely to be even more of a factor if the underwriter is using their balance sheet.

It is worth commenting that the private market for political risks operates in partial isolation from the other financial markets for country risk — most notably the banking markets. Our rates, or prices, relate only in very general terms. In part, this is one of the reasons why the banking market feels able to arbitrage on political risk insurance, taking risks in placing some with country risk insurers, and then potentially on-selling the risk or holding the remaining commercial risk. In simple terms, a bank can effectively price for the country risk in the loan at a rate that is higher than the cost of an insurance product, thus increasing the potential return against risk. For example, a bank may seek a margin over borrowing cost at 5 percent, 2 percent attributable to political or country factors, and 3 percent due to commercial risk. If a banker can buy a comprehensive insurance policy at 1.5 percent, he or she has effectively enhanced the return by 0.5 percent relative to the risk taken.

The rating of ECAs and multilaterals makes for an interesting comparison on investment risks. I would expect an ECA and/or MIGA to be cheaper in rating on certain categories such as inconvertibility (due to treaty obligations on a government/institution basis) but not on a package of risk or a multicountry program. Generally, compared to a government underwriter or an ECA, our competitive advantage is not only price but also flexibility of coverage. We can generally match or beat their prices, but we also improve on the ECA coverage due to our ability to include additional risks such as contractual risks and enhanced definitions of net loss, business interruption, license cancellation coverage, and contingency risks. Our primary way of out-pricing an ECA or a multilateral is on a multicountry program, when we attach significant discounts for spread of risk, aggregate limits, and package of risks. Our logic for this is that we are essentially writing catastrophe risk. That is, we consider ourselves exposed to the catastrophe, the exceptional rather than the attritional, or more regularly occurring risks such as pure nonpayment. We may assume our worst case to be a claim in one country in any given program period of, say, five years. If so, why charge the assured a disproportionate cost for insuring the remaining investments during the remaining years? The advantage for us — aside from the commercial — is that this approach guarantees us balance on our book. It ensures that we get a variety of host countries with varying types of investment. A spread of quality investments from multinational clients makes this an attractive option for us. Such clients want the type of enhanced coverage we can offer within a worldwide program at relatively little additional cost.

Finally, I should mention a word about commissions, discounts or brokerage. Certain markets go direct and emphasize their ability to quote "net" rates, that is, rates without brokerage. I am sure all brokers will tell you that they earn their crust, and generally I would endorse this. A broker should add more value than simply a rebating opportunity. But does the net rate practice work? I don't believe so, but I'm probably not the best-placed person to comment. If I am getting value in the presentation of the risk, I hope the assured are likewise receiving the advice and service they require. The brokerage usually also includes a valuable service for all parties — claims adjustment and collection. I would suggest that this alone is worth any differentiation that may arise from including this brokerage, and I have to question the extent to which there is any difference to start with.

Issues

Global Programs

A global program will generally cover a multinational's exposures across a spread of countries. It may cover a combination of debt and equity, including externally held lenders' coverage. The format, rating, and country spread will vary significantly with each program. This is why such programs present a formidable underwriting challenge. The skill is trying to combine a client's individual needs in a way that gives flexibility, encourages future use, and ensures value for money.

Nomally ECAs, multilaterals, and banks will price country risk for each risk taken, giving no discount for volume purchased or spread provided. Lloyd's has excelled in developing an approach which essentially weights the risk taken for the spread provided — a spread discount. This is done at Brockbank using a variable formula that fluctuates according to the number of countries and the difference between the top country value and the overall values exposed.

Often the buyer will also insert an aggregate limit, making the policy "first loss." This limit is usually based on the top country limit. Reinstatements outside the country of loss may also be provided at a cost, incurred either when exercised or in advance. The skill is in assessing capacity, demand, and the client's likely expansion plans. Once the underwriter has information on the values exposed, highlighted the likely coverage required, and addressed the approach to limits, he or she can apply these rates and discounts and calculate a base premium.

At this stage additional factors may be considered — deductibles, industry type, loss history, likely expansion — indeed anything the underwriter thinks will contribute to make a successful program.

Does all this "science" work? Normally, yes. However, the acid test is, does it look right? This is a question of experience. Certain brokers may say that this "science" is all irrelevant — it is only the bottom line that matters. I disagree. While we have to be commercial, we have a responsibility as a market to maintain discipline, and using the "science" of our pricing to ensure an element of predictability remains important.

Properly designed, a global program should be flexible to adapt to different types of investment structures and varying regulatory climates in the host country. I underwrite a program via Marsh & McLennan that takes traditional ECA-style perils together with protection for production sharing contracts, pipeline exposures where the assets are leased — including debt and equity. As such, the program approach demands sophisticated multiline insurers like Brockbank, willing to do a lot of their underwriting in advance. By gaining a high level of comfort on an assured's own risk assessment procedures, attaching new risks is quicker and easier for all parties. This does not reduce the need for proper disclosure, but it ensures that both insurer and insured understand exactly what is needed and come to each other with a high level of understanding of each other's approach.

I do not think global programs eliminate gaps in cover. However, they do make a difference in accessing capacity-driven situations. Another Marsh program I led recently had this issue with a significant amount of new exposure in Brazil at a time when little capacity was available. It was duly bound by the market participants. Underwriters will normally be able to find capacity when they have a loyal client who is committed to using the market, and a global program is an excellent demonstration of this intent.

Value — Which Coverage Is More Effective?

Different coverages are effective in different situations. Finding the right cover for a client's need is the most significant part of the broker's skill. Rather than do a compare and contrast, I would refer you to some information on our paid claims over the last three years.

TABLE 1

PAID CLAIMS	
Coverage	*Sector*
Confiscation	Power, Utilities, Media
War	Extractive Industry
Terrorism/SRCC (strike, riot, civil commotion)	Retail, Leisure, Aviation
Nonhonoring (Arbitration)	Power
Contract Frustration	Trading, Metals, Oil, Sugar
Change of Law	Extractive Industry
Credit	Sugar

Capacity

Capacity is determined at different points and in different ways, depending on the underwriter concerned. At Brockbank, we manage our aggregates by nationality of investor, by industry type, by coverage, and by host country. Normally, country capacity is the first to become an issue. In the past we have had issues with country capacity in Brazil, Turkey, Argentina, China, and Indonesia. Normally, internal limits will feel the pressure first. That is, internally we will have taken a view and have restricted our capacity. When circumstances change, opportunities arise, or key clients ask for assistance, we will review these internal limits. What is more difficult is when our actual country limits are full. These are internally limited by reinsurance. While this is very rare, it can happen, and Brazil is the current difficulty in the market. That said, the following table provides insight as to current estimates of market capacity on any one-risk basis, subject to the country capacity available.

My own view is that this represents the zenith of the market and is only likely to fall from next year. New entrants to our market are often talked about, and they may well happen. My hope is that mature capacity may be attracted; there is enough business to go around provided one is careful and understands the market and how it operates.

Can coinsuring with public sector underwriters assist in getting capacity? The simple answer is no. Having an ECA as part of the structure is not, in my view, a significant risk mitigant. Certainly it is not enough to allow the underwriter to weight their aggregation and thus increase their capacity. MIGA is different for us at

TABLE 2   POLITICAL RISK INSURANCE CAPACITY (IN US$) FROM THE
PRIVATE MARKET PER PROJECT/INVESTMENT

Insurer	Contract frustration		Confiscation	
Lloyd's	250,000,000	(1)	1,000,000,000	
American International Group	50,000,000		150,000,000	
Sovereign Risk Insurance	50,000,000		125,000,000	
Steadfast Insurance Company per				
Zurich U.S. Political Risk	30,000,000		100,000,000	
Exporters Insurance Company				
Limited (2)	65,000,000		65,000,000	
Chubb & Son	25,000,000		50,000,000	
Liberty Mutual	10,000,000	(3)	30,000,000	
Unistrat Assurances S.A.	10,000,000	(4)	10,000,000	(4)
Unity Fire and General per				
Unistrat Corporation of America	10,000,000	(4)	10,000,000	(4)
FCIA/Great American	10,000,000		10,000,000	(5)
Citicorp International Trade Indemnity	14,000,000		30,000,000	
Storebrand Skadeforsikring A/S	−	(1)	25,000,000	(6)
International Insurance Company				
of Hannover	1,125,000		10,000,000	
Trade Underwriters/Reliance National	7,500,000	(7)	−	
HIH Casualty and General Insurance				
Limited per Genesis	5,000,000		10,000,000	
Others	10,000,000		100,000,000	
say ±	500,000,000		1,800,000,000	

Notes:
(1) Additional capacity potentially available for preshipment and bond unfair calling
cover.
(2) Only shareholders in EICL are eligible as policyholders.
(3) Preference given to preshipment and bond unfair calling risks.
(4) Unistrat/UCA capacity cannot be aggregated for the same project investment.
(5) Mobile assets only.
(6) Available only to companies in the oil and energy sector.
(7) Does not underwrite bond unfair calling cover.

Brockbank because of our relationship, and my view is that the presence of a World Bank body adds to the diversity of the portfolio
and can thus be more attractive, but it does not enable one to ignore
the fundamentals of good underwriting.

Conclusion

In conclusion, the private political risk market has come of age. Capacity and line sizes generally are at an all-time high. The depth of

expertise is better than it has ever been in both the underwriting and the brokering sectors. However, we should not be blind to the challenges that remain. Risk modeling is still in its infancy in our area of the insurance market. We have a lot to learn from the other financial markets in risk modeling. The development of our products will also continue. We learn from our claims and from the challenges presented by our clients and their brokers. In my view, the success of the private political risk market in the long term will depend more on our ability to develop and adapt than on traditional limitations such as reinsurance capacity. I hope the market has learned from the boom and bust scenarios of the past, and with the increasing maturity of this market, we will continue to flourish.

To me, the underwriting rules do enable the underwriter to have a degree of predictability. These cannot strictly be considered scientific, but they are not complete "art" either. Long may that continue.

Comment on Cooperation, Competition, and the "Science of Pricing" in the Political Risk Insurance Marketplace

Charles Berry
Chairman
Berry, Palmer & Lyle Ltd., London

David James has produced a valuable account of how Brockbank, as a leading private political risk insurer, addresses underwriting issues, particularly when it comes to prices. The Brockbank approach broadly reflects the approach taken by other political risk insurers in the private market.

It goes almost without saying that private insurers such as Brockbank that take a leadership role are generally well informed on the macro political and economic situation in countries around the world. This information is derived from two main sources: published information and their own experience of writing hundreds, indeed thousands, of risks every year, for different countries, different industries in the same country, and different companies in the same industry.

Private sector political risks underwriters do have proprietary information. However, this proprietary information is not a product of research. Rather, it comes from the unique perspective they get through their spread of underwriting. The cumulative picture they build of what works in a country, and what does not, is far broader than the picture any single corporate entity can have. This breadth of vision provides one of the sources of added value for the clients of the market.

David is right, however, to concentrate on factors other than the analysis of the country's political and economic risks that affect pricing. These other factors play a major part in determining premium rates.

Obviously political risk is not an actuarial science. There is no such thing as abstract political risk in my opinion: political risk very much depends on who you are and what you are doing in a country. The issues that David raises, namely, the identity of the policyholders, the structure of the transaction, recovery potential, etc., all determine the ability of a particular business or transaction to survive a greater or lesser degree of political and economic turmoil, or to salvage a loss after a claim has been paid. These factors rightly affect premium rates in large measure.

However, I would like to emphasize that these rational forms of analysis — and you can debate whether they are a science as David says or simply an art — are not the real determinants of price in the private market.

As with any marketplace, price in the private political risk market is determined by supply and demand.

Supply and Demand and Political Risk Insurance Prices

There is a difference between premium rating and pricing. Underwriters provide premium rates. However, a premium rate is only a price where business is transacted at that rate. Where an underwriter's rate is rejected by the applicant, that rate is not a price, but a rejected offer.

Needless to say there are many more rates in the private insurance marketplace than there are prices. Many applications are rated for premium but never written. Likewise, a bound policy may be premium rated by several competing underwriters: only one of those rates becomes a price.

I make this distinction between rates and prices simply to emphasize that in a competitive market pricing is not dictated by any particular insurer. It is true that certain insurers are more influential than others when it comes to price. It is also true that there is less price competition where the risk is very high, where capacity is short, or where the placement is exceptionally large. Nevertheless, the market sets pricing, not any given individual insurer.

This is true throughout the general insurance market, even in classes of insurance that are capable of actuarial analysis. Actuaries do not set premium rates. They simply tell you whether you are going to make money or not at a given level of market pricing.

It is essential to recognize that the private political risk insurance market is now a true market, beyond the control and influence of any single player. The market has taken on a life of its own, and pricing is fundamentally set by supply and demand.

Furthermore, many of the forces that affect the private political risk insurance market have nothing to do with political risk, foreign investment flows, perception of risk, etc. A major determinant of private market capacity has been and will continue to be the general insurance and reinsurance market cycle, namely, the ebb and flow of capital into the huge property casualty insurance market, in which the political risk insurance market is an almost insignificant part. The property/casualty insurance cycle affects the political risk market, but the political risk market has no material impact on the general insurance industry cycle. A US$70 million loss may be a significant figure in the context of the political risk insurance market, but it is insignificant in the context of the general insurance market as a whole.

The private political risk insurance market is now its own phenomenon. The genie is out of the bottle and cannot be put back. The market has taken on a life of its own, and all of us, underwriters, clients, brokers, ECAs, and indeed governments, can ride the genie, and to a limited extent influence it. However, no one controls the market.

This is a very different environment from the political risk insurance market of old, which consisted mainly of government agencies.

Governments are still involved. But they now sit side by side with a market that is international and ultimately controlled by no individual player. While the individual insurers are all regulated, the market itself is beyond the control of the governments. Like the international capital markets, the private political risk insurance market may influence governments or be influenced by them. But the market has a life beyond governments and ECAs. Some people find this idea disturbing. I find it delightful.

Government and ECA Reaction to the Private Market

Perhaps the interesting question perhaps today is how governments and ECAs should react to this market.

Governments, government investment agencies, and export credit agencies have had four reactions to the phenomenon of the private insurance market. These can be categorized as follows:

Pretend the Market Does Exist

This is the view that for many years prevailed among members of the Berne Union. While this was sustained for a long time by wishful thinking, I really cannot believe that there is anyone left who believes that the private market for political risk insurance is a temporary aberration which will go away. Today, an ECA or government that takes this view is seen as quaintly out of touch.

View the Private Market As a Threat and Seek to Compete with It

This position has been adopted by certain ECAs, and is perhaps understandable from a human point of view. There has been a lot of debate about the rights, and more particularly the wrongs, of such an approach. I would like to emphasize the futility of such an approach. It can only end in frustration for the government or the ECA concerned. Put simply, the private market is more flexible, larger, more nimble, and, as pointed out by David James and for the reasons he explains, fundamentally cheaper than the government investment insurers.

I do not believe that the private market for investment insurance is as yet fully developed. I would like to turn to a more developed market, namely, that for short-term trade credit insurance. Only 15 years ago this market, like that for investment insurance, was dominated by the national export credit agencies that were, in effect, monopolies. Just 15 years later, it is frankly difficult to see how a government export credit agency is going to compete with the private sector in the future. I believe governments simply lack the resources to compete effectively with the global private trade credit insurance market for short-term business.

The political risk insurance market for investments has not yet reached that stage, but is fundamentally heading in the same direction.

Cooperation in Mixed Markets

This is the correct stance for ECAs to take today, and it is indeed the one that is fairly well established among the leading investment insurers around the world. By cooperation I obviously mean structures and solutions for clients that blend the capabilities of a private market with the unique capabilities of organizations such as MIGA,

OPIC, ECGD, and others. A lot has been said on this subject: indeed a great deal more has been said than actually done. Nevertheless, we are clear advocates of this approach wherever it delivers benefits for clients.

Cooperation between government investment insurers and the private market can take essentially two forms:

a. *Risk Syndication*: where government schemes and private insurers each write a portion of the same risk. An early example of this was the three-way syndication we placed in 1990 on Freeport McMoRan's Indonesian mining project involving MIGA, OPIC, and private insurers.

Risk syndication may be initiated by clients working with their advisors, where they see combining government and private insurers as achieving the best insurance solution. Alternatively, syndication may be promoted by an agency, for example, by MIGA under their cooperative underwriting program (CUP).

The CUP has always been a good idea. It can efficiently blend MIGA clout with private market capacity and (lower) rating. Other government investment insurers should produce their own version of MIGA's CUP. However, they should bear in mind that part of the efficiencies inherent in the CUP structure need to be passed back to the policyholder. Unless the CUP produces a better, cheaper insurance product than the policyholder can achieve in the open market, the CUP policy will not be purchased. Investment insurance buyers are not going to take the CUP route simply out of intellectual curiosity.

b. *Reinsurance*: either of government agencies by private insurers or (less commonly) of private insurers by governments. Reinsurance may be arranged on a treaty basis (where the reinsurer agrees to write an agreed portion of the ceding insurers' whole portfolio, for example, ACE's reinsurance of MIGA), or facultatively (namely, on a case-by-case basis). Reflecting the high-value, low-volume nature of investment insurance, facultative reinsurance is becoming quite commonplace.

No matter how cooperation occurs, we believe it is good for policyholders. Many see the benefits of the private market in terms of cost, capacity, flexibility, and speed of response. Yet many also want the benefit of a government scheme "umbrella." Despite the increasing "umbrella" of the private market, as particularly trumpeted by

AIG, and despite disappointments in practice where government schemes have been unable to avoid losses, policyholders still believe that government schemes stand a better chance of using their influence to avoid or minimize losses. We believe the policyholders are right. How are investment insurance buyers to get the best of both worlds? The answer is cooperation between the public and private sectors.

Governments Harnessing the Private Sector and Mitigating Their Own risk

Certain governments have adopted this reaction to the private market, which is very enlightened and is beginning to represent a distinct trend.

This practice enables certain governments in the developing world that do not have conventional ECAs to partner with private sector underwriters to harness the power of the private political risk market in order to mitigate their own political risk. This is done by partnering with private sector underwriters in order to facilitate the provision of political risk insurance on their own political risk. By increasing the availability of political risk insurance in respect of their own country risk, governments are seeking to attract trade and investment flows and improve the market's perception of their own risk.

Examples of this phenomenon are Uzbekistan, with their joint venture with AIG; Bosnia and Herzegovina with their joint venture with Lloyd's; the COMESA countries of Africa that are beginning to work with private insurers in a way that is similar to Bosnia and Herzegovina; and most recently the Latin American Investment Guarantee Company, (LAIGC), a Bermudan-based joint venture between AIG and Corporacion Andina de Fomento, an institution owned by key South American countries. LAIGC is designed to facilitate the provision of political risk insurance in Latin America. The World Bank-supported schemes of this nature in Bosnia, the COMESA countries, and elsewhere are focused primarily on trade rather than equity investment, and thus do not overlap with MIGA's support of investments.

Under these World Bank schemes, countries can borrow International Development Association (IDA) funds and use them to support political risk policies covering their own country risk. Originally the funds may be deposited with an international bank and used to support letters of credit securing each policy. However, from an insurance point of view, the structure is inefficient: each dollar of capital supports a dollar of aggregate policy limit, leading to the development of leveraged schemes with private insurers.

Under the leveraged schemes, the funds are deposited with private insurers. The latter agree to issue political risk policies on behalf of the participating country on pre-agreed terms and conditions and up to an aggregate value that is a multiple of the security funds. For example, under the Leveraged Insurance Facility for Trade (LIFT) scheme, Lloyd's underwriters have agreed with Bosnia and Herzegovina's investment guarantee agency to issue policies with an aggregate value of up to three times the funds provided as security.

I think this phenomenon is sufficiently well developed to call it a trend. Furthermore, I believe it is completely logical. In essence, political risk insurance is a form of bonding: insurers stand surety for the good faith of host governments. It is completely logical that private insurers should seek a direct and close relation with those governments for whom they provide these services. It also makes sense for insurers to seek collateral for at least part of the loss they will suffer if the government in question does what it promised not to do, or fails to do that which it promised to do.

These forms of cooperation between host governments and private insurers are set to grow.

Comment on Cooperation, Competition, and the "Science of Pricing" in the Political Risk Insurance Marketplace

Daniel W. Riordan

Senior Vice President and Managing Director
Zurich U.S. Political Risk

David James has written an excellent paper on the experiences of a Lloyd's underwriter in the current political risk marketplace. I offer the following commentary from the prospective of Zurich Financial Services Group, a global financial services and insurance company, and one of the leading providers of political risk solutions to our target customers: global infrastructure developers and banking customers.

Rating/Pricing

As indicated in David James's paper, political risk insurance ratings are not actuarially based. This fact creates great challenges for underwriters in pricing their products.

Zurich's approach is to use a model for ratings that includes a consistent approach for assessing risk. Our rating model also seeks to provide the best value for our customers while meeting our internal return on equity requirements.

Zurich has developed a rating model that includes a five-tiered hazard level (low to high) for each coverage and country. Our model establishes a base rate. We then analyze the customer and the insured risk or project. Through a series of rating factors involving the insured and the project risk, we debit and credit the base rate to establish the charged rate. The charged rate is subject to market forces, including supply and demand, which can have an impact on the final rate. Most importantly, we believe that it is crucial to apply our rating model in a consistent manner.

Rates are reflective of coverage-specific risk assessments, and adjustments are made according to a comprehensive assessment of underwriting guidelines which typically fall into three main risk categories: the insured, the host country, and the project.

Insured

The insured's size and experience in international markets are also critical factors. Large, experienced companies often provide sufficient "clout" and "staying power" in emerging markets to reduce the potential for adverse host government actions. A strong, influential local joint venture partner with good contacts in the business community and host government is an often overlooked but key element in project risk mitigation.

Host Country

The host government's attitude to the private sector and foreign investors will be an important underwriting and rating issue. Is there a history of nationalization by past or current governments? What is the role of the government's opposition or extremist political parties and how much influence do they have? Does the government have a transparent system for managing investment disputes? Does the government have a history of honoring arbitration awards?

Underwriters typically review the host government's track record of managing its economy and currency. For example, when there is an economic downturn in the country, does the government tighten its belt to strengthen its position in the financial markets? Or, does it print new money and restrict access to foreign currency reserves, creating a potential convertibility crisis?

Project

The project's location, operating agreements, and environmental sensitivity will factor in underwriting and risk rating. Is the project located near a highly populated area or military facility? Does it have proper security protection? Have insurgent groups attacked multinational facilities in the region or country? Are permits and agreements signed with the host government legally binding and transparent in execution? Will the project's environmental controls meet host country and international standards? All of these risk factors, including relevant project documentation, should be evaluated.

I agree with most of David's comments on ratings, but I think one area that is somewhat neglected is recovery. In our view, salvage capabilities following a claim should be a factor in risk assessment, acceptance, and rating.

Another area that is understated is the importance of the insured. Zurich's view is that the insured is the most crucial part of the risk assessment, because it is the experience and capabilities of the insured that will ultimately have the largest impact on the risk in the long term.

Finally, little attention is paid in David James's paper to what the buyer should be looking for in an insurer. In our view, insureds should be evaluating political risk insurers on the following basis: financial condition of the insurer (claims paying ability), underwriting expertise, creativity and flexibility in coverages and policy wording, and the ability to offer new products in response to evolving customer needs. Insureds should also evaluate the insurance company's experience and reputation in the market for paying claims, that is, the insurer's willingness to pay claims.

Distribution

David James's paper touches briefly on the question of distribution channels for political risk insurance, and it is clearly written from the prospective of a Lloyd's underwriter who principally works with Lloyd's brokers. While even some Lloyd's underwriters sometimes work with their customers on a direct basis, it is more typical that they work closely with a Lloyd's broker. In this relationship, the broker rather than the underwriter takes on a substantial role. The role of the broker often includes the drafting of the policy, risk assessment, rating analysis, accounting and collection, claims administration, and loss recovery. In most cases, the broker possesses the underwriting files, including the claims files.

Herein lies an important distinction between the traditional London market and other major market players such as Zurich. Our approach is to invest significantly in human capital, research capabilities, and systems to provide our customers with a one-stop underwriting operation, including policy drafting, structuring and legal advice, accounting/collections, and claims administration.

The question of distribution is a sensitive one, as it involves a number of interests and long-standing relationships. Historically, the point of access to the customer for most insurance products, has been the risk manager, who is the corporate expert and may be the decisionmaker when it comes to property and casualty coverage. However, political risk insurance is quite different, and the key experts and decisionmakers are often financial or treasury managers, or individual transactors involved in structuring an investment or loan.

Zurich's view is that the best interests of the customer will determine distribution. For many political risk insurance customers this will mean working with a specialist broker in London, such as Willis, BPL, JLT, or others. These are brokers who have a deep understanding of this highly specialized business line. For others, it will mean a direct relationship with an underwriter. In some cases, customers may seek to access the market using both direct and brokered channels. Ultimately, the customers have the right to choose based on their own experience, expertise, and needs.

Aggregate Accumulations and Global Policies

Country risk aggregates are a critical portfolio measure that are closely monitored and limited to avoid excessive concentration in a single market. Historically, claims experience has shown that economic and political upheavals resulting in claims are more likely to occur in a single country, but insurers are increasingly reviewing their concentrations across geographic regions.

An area where we have a disagreement with some underwriters is lack of country aggregations on global programs. In our view, no one is served by placing various country exposures in global program "buckets" that do not cross aggregate with other country exposure limits. I believe this is a contradiction in David James's paper as he suggests an approach that "aggregates all risk together without gearing up," but at the same time indicates that Brockbank allows "discounts on pricing accumulations of country risks in global programs". The question raised here is how some underwriters will deal with aggregation under multicountry programs. Is the approach to continue to place these risks in separate, nonaggregating "buckets," or is it better to quantify these risks according to their actual country exposures? We believe the latter model is the prudent one.

David James also describes the arbitrage between covered and uncovered costs. However, this often does not work in practice, especially when dealing with capacity constrained countries (for political risk insurance (PRI)) or where margins have shrunk in the banking market.

Competition

Competition in the political risk insurance market over the last few years has been very good for the customer, providing more choices, new and increasing capacity, and some stabilization of rates.

While we do not see many more new entrants in this business, we expect that most of those in the market, public and private, will be in the business for many years to come. David James suggests in his paper that capacity will fall in the future. We don't see this happening in a significant way, except for some London syndicates who have decided to shift to other business lines or reduce their political risk capacities.

Large capacities will continue to be available in the private market if political risk insurance remains profitable, as we expect that it will. The keys to success will be careful underwriting, consistent approaches to ratings, and prudent portfolio management.

Cooperation

Cooperation is given short shrift in David James's paper. Cooperation among the traditional sources of political risk, the public agencies, and the robust private market is the major positive development in our marketplace, and it deserves more attention.

It is a proven fact that political risk claims can often be averted through coordinated efforts to engage host governments when problems arise. Host governments seeking to attract foreign investors are often willing to discuss and "deal" when confronted with an insurer or group of insurers with meaningful leverage that can be brought to bear on behalf of an expropriated insured. Partnering with government (public) insurers is often advantageous as a means to obtain the necessary claims leverage. In addition, private insurers such as Zurich have their own clout that needs to be considered, measured by financial strength, reputation, and global network.

Zurich believes that the public agencies serve as significant mitigators of risk in emerging markets. OPIC, for example, has had many years of experience in advocating successfully with host governments on behalf of their insureds. OPIC's tremendous recovery record also demonstrates their resourcefulness and perseverance with salvage efforts. Other agencies such as EDC, ECGD, COFACE, and others have long and successful histories in advocacy and recoveries. More recently, MIGA has been "earning its stripes" with successful advocacy efforts.

Most of the public agency providers are prepared to work with private market insurers as demonstrated by their willingness to lead or co-lead a syndicate of insurers for a specific risk and serve as first loss insurers. Private insurers have many opportunities to cooperate with these agencies in terms of both risk mitigation and business identification. In the last two and one-half years, Zurich has participated in close to 40 co-insurance or reinsurance opportunities with public agency providers, such as OPIC, MIGA, EDC of Canada, ECGD of the United Kingdom, EFIC of Australia, and others.

Zurich believes that a good number of the public agency providers of political risk insurance are increasingly seeking expanded cooperation with the private market as a means to better serve their governments and customers. The availability of increased political risk capacity in the private market has led many public agencies to partner with the private market to better leverage their scarce resources and better manage their portfolios and aggregate accumulations.

It is our belief that those public and private market players that embrace the concept of cooperation will flourish in the coming years, and those who do not accept cooperation will see their business slowly decline.

Innovation

Let me expand my commentary from David James's paper to some of the issues in the use of capital markets, including derivatives and bonds, for expansion of political risk capacity. However, the difficulty here is that current pricing of political risk insurance is too low to support much of this potential activity. Larger spreads are required to attract the interests of the capital markets, as only a few capacity-constrained or high hazard markets can support these structures. Perhaps in the future, there will be more opportunities to move further in this direction.

In Zurich's view, there is an immediate opportunity to use political risk insurance to enhance the ratings of corporate or project finance bonds structured as private placements or 144a transactions. This new development is a result of the emerging shift from bank loans to bond issues in developing countries.

Zurich's new coverage for capital market bond issues came about in response to a challenge from one of our customers to think "out of the box" and take our popular lenders coverage wording and adapt it to the needs of institutional bond investors. After working for several months with a number of investment banks and rating agencies, we have now completed three major policies for bond issues in Mexico and Argentina and we are working on a number of others.

In conclusion, the political risk market is at its most exciting period, but many challenges lie ahead. New approaches to political risk and expanded coverages and policy wordings need to be developed. Traditional definitions of political risk may no longer be valid, and underwriters must listen to the needs of their customers and plan accordingly.

Innovation, not capacity, will be the challenge for the political risk market in the future.

Comment on Cooperation, Competition, and the "Science of Pricing" in the Political Risk Insurance Marketplace

Christophe S. Bellinger
Chief Underwriter
Multilateral Investment Guarantee Agency

I believe that the paper by David James accurately reflects where the private market is today. My comments on the subject of pricing, global policies, derivatives, bonds, and capacity are from the point of view of a multilateral insurer that was set up to cooperate with other political risk insurers — private and public — and not compete with them. David provides political risk insurance for both trade and investments. For those of you who don't know MIGA well, MIGA provides long-term insurance for investments only, although clearly the investments that we insure — equity and debt — facilitate cross-border trade. My perspective here, therefore, is limited to that of an investment insurer.

Pricing

Unlike many insurers — private and public — MIGA does not utilize a country rating system to calculate premium rates. Instead, its rates are determined by a set of guidelines identified in the back of MIGA's Operational Regulations. These guidelines contain various project and country risk-related variables that are utilized by underwriters to recommend to MIGA management a premium rate.

MIGA's founders modeled its premium rating system after the one utilized by OPIC, including the use of the concept of "Current Coverage" and "Standby Coverage." The system is based on offering separate coverages for individual types of risks, and by sector, utilizing base rates. These were published in MIGA's information brochures. This approach allowed for more latitude to differentiate rates in accordance with the actual potential for loss. Some export credit agencies have adopted this model in order to work more closely with MIGA. MIGA utilized this approach for almost 10 years.

Experience has shown, however, that the premium rating structure with its "Current" and "Standby" coverages confused many would be users of MIGA. The unfortunate result is that MIGA was viewed as being expensive. What our pricing structure did not reflect is MIGA's flexibility to manuscript policies — that is, to tailor-make contracts. For example, if an investor is only interested in currency transfer coverage, why should it have to buy coverage for all of the other risks that we insure that may not be wanted? While in some cases the scope of the coverage obtained from MIGA may be more narrow than that which would be available from another insurer, the investor paid for what was wanted. Some public insurers are adopting this approach too and now permit investors to purchase single coverages.

About a year ago, MIGA eliminated references in its literature to the base rates. We did this so that potential users of MIGA would contact the Agency to obtain a nonbinding indication, or NBI, for the terms of coverage, including costs. NBIs are common practice in the private sector. We believe that NBIs will help eliminate the misperception that MIGA is expensive.

David remarks that the private sector will charge an extra premium for countries where capacity is scarce. Brazil is a good example of such a country. This may not always be a reflection of the actual risks in the country, but rather a reflection of the market forces of supply and demand at work. Many of you will remember that AIG auctioned capacity in Brazil several years ago. It is understandable why private insurers "charge what they can." As a development institution, however, MIGA cannot, and should not, compete with any other insurer, public or private. MIGA prices its coverages according to risks, which, of course, the private sector also does. After all, MIGA must ensure that its rates are not a deterrent to an investment going forward.

The reason that the private sector exists is to make a profit. MIGA's purpose is to facilitate foreign investment. While MIGA is not profit-oriented, it must still charge adequate premiums to pay for its own expenses and build sufficient reserves from premium income so that it can continue to fulfill its mandate and to pay claims.

Finally, on the matter of competition, MIGA will not lower its prices to "get the deal," or, for that matter "to keep the deal." Once again, it is prepared to manuscript a contract according to the investor's needs. If price is a consideration, then the scope of the coverage may be reduced to bring the costs down.

Global Policies

For an insurer to provide a meaningful global policy, it must be able to insure existing investments, value the exposure simply, and be able to cover OECD risks. For example, the risk manager of a company with investments in 100 countries may not want to be bothered to distinguish between OECD and non-OECD country risks. Most of the investments are likely to be existing. If you ask the risk manager for the value of the shares in each of the company's subsidiaries, you may not get an answer, but ask for the replacement value of the company's assets in, say, France or China, you will, as these are insured annually against property casualty risks under a global policy. Risk managers deal with global policies on a day-to-day basis and want to do so with their political risk coverages too.

While MIGA does not enjoy the same flexibility as the private market to issue global policies, it has done so covering a company's new investments, and, like the private market, discounted the premium accordingly in recognition of the spread of risks.

Unlike the private sector, MIGA cannot insure existing investments. However, MIGA can *reinsure* them under certain conditions. Recently, MIGA explored with the private sector issuing a global policy covering old and new investments. The company decided not to insure its investment with MIGA after all, but the work that we did gave us good experience for the next global policy request.

Derivatives and Contingent Equity

MIGA has no experience with these types of insurance. MIGA would have to learn more about them to see if there are any relevant applications to its business.

Bonds

In 1992, a commercial bank funded its branch bank operations in a Latin American country with a eurobond issue. The loan was insured by MIGA. The bank established a special purpose vehicle (SPV) that was the beneficiary of MIGA's compensation. Three years later, another commercial bank made a loan to a project in another Latin American country; this time the loan was guaranteed by a company. MIGA insured the loan guarantee. The proceeds of

MIGA's compensation were assigned to the commercial bank. MIGA's compensation was further assigned to an SPV that sold bonds to investors in the capital markets. The difference between these transactions and those that we have been hearing about involving Zurich-American and OPIC is that the scope of *their* coverages was discussed with the rating agencies. At the time we issued our coverages, we had no discussion with any rating agency about our involvement in these projects.

The recent publicity surrounding Zurich-American and OPIC's "capital market" transactions has caused some project sponsors to want to have their MIGA-insured loans rated by the rating agencies. As a result, MIGA has been working closely with Moodies and Fitch, two rating agencies, to develop a contract that would permit an insured loan to be rated equal to or better than investment grade. If MIGA is successful in doing so, which we are confident it will be, MIGA's political risk insurance coverage could be utilized as a financial enhancement in the same way that lenders already use the MIGA coverage to benefit from country risk provisioning waivers granted them by some OECD banking supervisors.

In reality, many capital market transactions have yet to close and are expensive to put together. They are not for small and medium sized investments nor for investments in all countries. The marketplace is volatile, as we recently witnessed by the enormous drop in flows into emerging markets. Therefore, it is still too early to tell how successful this product will be in funding projects in the poorest of countries, which are the primary focus of MIGA's activities.

Capacity

Now to capacity. According to David, about $1.8 billion of coverage is available per project for confiscation insurance from the private sector. To this amount, add capacity from the export credit agencies, the multilaterals through their respective partial risk guarantee programs, MIGA, and a multitude of other new public and private players entering the market. One could easily come to the conclusion that there is plenty of insurance capacity. But let us look at this more closely. The capacity is **for confiscation insurance, for the right project,** and **in the right country**. Investors, and more so now, lenders, want more than just confiscation insurance. They also want transfer restriction, breach of contract, and long-term political violence coverages. Let me ask the following question. Are these coverages, and in sufficient quantities, available for a term of 15 years, for a water distribution project involving a subsovereign in a perceived high risk country? The World Bank does not seem to think so as it explores setting up country-specific investment insurance vehicles to support certain sectors. I tend to agree with my World Bank colleagues, although I don't necessarily agree with the solution.

According to official statistics, 12 developing countries receive about 80 percent of all foreign direct investment (FDI) flows. This means that more than 150 developing countries receive less than 20 percent of FDI. Africa alone receives less than 2 percent of foreign direct investment, while in the early 1960s, it received over 30 percent of the flows.

Why is this? There are many reasons. I expect some are due to the high perceived political risks in these countries seen by both investors and insurers — public and private. Here, I think MIGA can play an important role in fulfilling its mission, which is to attract FDI in those 150 countries that receive so little of the investment flows and to do so in cooperation with the private market and the public sector. David talked about the importance of diversification. It is because MIGA had insured investors from 30 countries and investments into 70 countries and is not overly concentrated in any particular sector — and due to its excellent track record, I am sure — that ACE, and later XL, gave MIGA the opening and agreed to follow MIGA's fortunes under reinsurance treaties. In doing so, MIGA has fulfilled another requirement of its convention which is to mobilize private sector capacity. Today ACE and XL are following MIGA into countries and with investors that I expect they would not have pursued on their own. The same can be said for other private insurers participating in projects together with MIGA under its cooperative underwriting program, facultative reinsurance, and coinsurance. MIGA also has been told by some ECAs that they are prepared to follow MIGA into countries that they are not familiar with, especially in Africa.

In summary, the day when there is too much capacity for the poorest of the 150 countries of the world that receive almost no FDI is the day when we can truly say there is plenty of capacity.

I would like to make one final observation. I am pleased to hear that David James does not blindly underwrite on the basis of MIGA's involvement in a project. As your partner in many projects, David, I want to reassure you that MIGA, too, does not blindly underwrite on the basis of its affiliation with the World Bank.

Appendix I

Biographies of Authors

CHRISTOPHE S. BELLINGER

Christophe S. Bellinger joined the Multilateral Investment Guarantee Agency (MIGA), a member of the World Bank Group, in 1988 soon after the Agency was created. He is the Chief Underwriter in charge of worldwide operations. Prior to joining MIGA, Mr. Bellinger was Vice President of Political Risk at AIG (the American International Group) in New York City, one of the largest providers of private political risk insurance. Mr. Bellinger began his career in political risk insurance at the Overseas Private Investment Corporation (OPIC), where he was the Regional Manager for Asia. Before entering the field of political risk insurance, Mr. Bellinger worked for the U.S. State Department and American Hospital Supply Corporation/France.

Mr. Bellinger holds graduate degrees in political science and business from the University of Kansas and the American Graduate School of International Management. He has also studied international law at the Fletcher School of Law and Diplomacy and the Woods Hole Oceanographic Institute.

During Mr. Bellinger's career in political risk insurance, he has been involved in more than 500 investment projects worldwide. The projects have been in the following sectors: power, toll roads, telecommunications, tourism, manufacturing, oil and gas, and services. Mr. Bellinger represents MIGA at the Berne Union and the Association of Export Credit and Investment Insurers.

CHARLES BERRY

Charles Berry has worked as a London-based specialist insurance broker since 1974. He trained at Hogg Robinson before becoming a founding director of Berry, Palmer & Lyle (BPL) in 1983.

BPL is an independent insurance and reinsurance broker specializing in trade credit and political risks.

Mr. Berry was educated at Oxford and Harvard, and is a Fellow of the Chartered Insurance Institute.

KEVIN R. CALLAHAN

Kevin R. Callahan is Chief Executive Officer of Aon Capital Markets, a subsidiary of Aon Group, Inc., which is the commercial brokerage and consulting operation of Aon Corporation. Mr. Callahan is also a Director of Aon Group, Inc.

Aon Group, Inc. is the second largest and fastest growing international brokerage and consulting business in the world.

Prior to joining Aon Corporation in 1996, Mr. Callahan was a Vice President at Goldman, Sachs & Co., where he founded and headed the Insurance Products Group, and was President of GS Risk Advisors, an insurance and reinsurance intermediary. Mr. Callahan spent more than 11 years at Goldman Sachs, specializing in insurance products, the financial services industry, and derivatives business. He is a graduate of the University of Notre Dame, with a B.B.A. in finance and philosophy.

Aon Corporation (AOC) is a holding company made up of a family of insurance brokerage, consulting, and underwriting subsidiaries. Aon is listed on the New York, London, and Chicago Stock Exchanges.

NEIL DOHERTY

Neil Doherty is the Ronald A. Rosenfeld Professor and Professor of Insurance and Risk Management at the Wharton School. A principal area of interest is corporate risk management, focusing on the financial strategies for managing risks that traditionally have been insurable. Such strategies include the use of existing derivatives, the design of new financial products, and the use of capital structure. He has written two books in this area (*Corporate Risk Management: A Financial Exposition* [1985] and *The Financial Theory of Insurance Pricing* [1987] [with S. D'Arcy]) and *Integrated Risk Management, 2000,* as well as several recent papers. Many of the ideas developed in these books (e.g., composites of insurance and debt financing; the use of option models in insurance and reinsurance) are now emerging in the marketplace.

The second of his three major areas of interest is the economics of risk and information, and he has written several papers on the adverse selection, the value of information, and the design of insurance contracts with imperfect information. A third area of interest is the failure of insurance markets and how they might be redesigned. In this area he has written on cyclicality of markets, market crises, and the effect of catastrophes.

ANTHONY FAULKNER

Anthony Faulkner is Head of Overseas Investment Insurance at ECGD. He has worked at ECGD for 25 years. He has spent most of his time in the claims operations of ECGD, including several years as Head of Claims Recoveries. In early 1996, he began work as Head of Overseas Investment Insurance, with a brief to expand the portfolio from the then $300 million portfolio by increasing awareness of the scheme and making it more flexible to the needs of its customers. The portfolio now stands in excess of $1.2 billion and continues to grow to meet the changing needs of equity investors, project sponsors, and lenders.

JOHN D. FINNERTY

John D. Finnerty is a Partner of PricewaterhouseCoopers, LLP. His areas of specialization include the valuation of securities, derivative instruments, and businesses. His derivatives experience includes developing models to value credit derivatives, to value bonds and bond options in the presence of interest-rate-jump risk, and to determine marketability discounts for unregistered common stock.

Dr. Finnerty previously worked for Morgan Stanley and Lazard Frères. As the Chief Financial Officer of College Savings Bank (in the late 1980s), he helped design a structured certificate of deposit that has enabled college savers to hedge tuition inflation risk, and he helped develop a companion strategy that enabled the CD issuer to hedge its tuition inflation exposure. He also obtained four patents on financial products, two while in investment banking and two while with the thrift.

He has also published extensively, including eight books and more than 50 articles and professional papers. His most recent books, *Corporate Financial Management* and *Principles of Financial Management*, were recently published by Prentice Hall.

For the past 10 years, Dr. Finnerty has also served as Professor of Finance at Fordham University, where he was awarded early tenure in 1991. Dr. Finnerty is a former Editor of *Financial Management* and sits on the editorial boards of several other financial publications. Dr. Finnerty received a Ph.D. in operations research from the Naval Postgraduate School, an M.A. in economics from Cambridge University, and a B.A. in mathematics from Williams College.

KENNETH (KEN) HANSEN

Ken Hansen was appointed General Counsel of the Export-Import Bank by President Clinton in 1995. In 1999, he joined Chadbourne & Parke's Project Finance Group as a partner resident in the Washington office. He also spent nine years with OPIC, where he was Associate General Counsel for Investment. Mr. Hansen has taught finance and law at a number of institutions, including Wellesley College, Harvard University, Bryn Mawr College, Haverford College, the Fletcher School of Law and Diplomacy at Tufts University, George Washington University National Law Center, Boston University Law School, and Georgetown University Law Center.

A 1974 graduate of Harvard College and a 1983 graduate of the University of Pennsylvania Law School, he also holds a master's degree in international relations from Yale University and a master's degree in public administration from Harvard.

MOTOMICHI IKAWA

Motomichi Ikawa, a Japanese national, joined MIGA as Executive Vice President in January 1999.

Mr. Ikawa has had a distinguished career in the field of finance, economics, and private investment, including positions at the OECD in Paris and as the Director of the Budget, Personnel, and Management Systems Department at the Asian Development Bank. He has also served with the Japanese government as Assistant Vice Minister for Finance for International Affairs and Director of the Development Policy Division (1992–1993), and as Director of the Coordination Division of the International Finance Bureau (1993–1994). Between 1994 and 1996, Mr. Ikawa was Managing Director of the Coordination Department of the Overseas Economic Cooperation Fund (OECF). During this time he published *The Role of the OECF Toward 2010: The Medium-Term Prospects for OECF Operations.*

His most recent position, prior to joining the World Bank Group, was Senior Deputy Director-General of the International Finance Bureau of the Ministry of Finance in Japan, where he served as the G7's Deputy's Deputy and Financial Sous-Sherpa and was responsible for multilateral and bilateral development finance.

Mr. Ikawa attained his B.A. in economics from the University of Tokyo and was a Ph.D. candidate at the University of California–Berkeley.

DAVID JAMES

David James practiced as a Solicitor with Clifford Chance for five years. During this time, he practiced in the banking and corporate sectors before specialising in insurance law. In 1996, Mr. James joined the Political Risks Team in the Brockbank Group. The Brockbank Group is one of the lead syndicates at Lloyd's of London and is owned ultimately by XL Capital. The Political Risk Team in Brockbank is the largest in Lloyd's with three senior members covering war, investment, trade, and credit business. Two junior members and a dedicated back office team support the underwriters. Mr. James is the class underwriter for Political and War risks specializing in investment business.

FREDERICK E. (RICK) JENNEY

Rick Jenney is a partner in the Washington, D.C., office of Morrison & Foerster and is a member of the firm's global Finance and Investment Group. He specializes in international project finance, political risk insurance, and cross-border investment transactions, with a particular focus on political risk issues. He previously served as Assistant General Counsel of OPIC, where he represented OPIC as political risk insurer in a broad range of project finance, equity fund, and cross-border investment transactions worldwide. Mr. Jenney's political risk insurance experience encompasses both insurance and reinsurance of a broad range of equity and debt investments by developers, commercial banks, and capital markets investors.

Mr. Jenney received his J.D. and M.B.A. from the University of Virginia in 1983. He received his B.A. from Yale University in 1979. He is a member of the New York and District of Columbia bars.

FELTON (MAC) JOHNSTON

Mac Johnston is President of FMJ International Risk Services, LLC, an international investment risk advisor to political risk insurers, investors, governments, and others. The firm has provided underwriting, management, and product development support to major public and private sector political risk insurers. Other areas of specialization are government performance guarantees, guarantee pricing, and political risk management.

Mr. Johnston's career includes 13 years as Vice President for Insurance of OPIC. He was a member of OPIC's senior management committee that considers large proposed financing and insurance proposals. He was OPIC's representative at the Berne Union of export credit and political risk insurers, and twice chaired that organization's Investment Insurance Committee.

Mr. Johnston's experience also includes international banking, independent consulting, and military intelligence. He is a graduate of Colgate University, the Fletcher School of Law and Diplomacy, and Harvard Business School.

SUELLEN LAMBERT LAZARUS

Suellen Lambert Lazarus heads the Syndications and International Securities Group of the International Finance Corporation (IFC). In this capacity she is responsible for mobilizing long-term loan funding from cofinanciers — principally international commercial banks and institutional investors — for IFC projects. The volume of such IFC loan syndications and securities transactions is about $2 billion to $3 billion a year, requiring close relationships between IFC and leading financial institutions throughout the world. The Group also helps structure, underwrite, and place securities offerings with international investors.

Before joining the Syndications and International Securities Group in August 1997, Ms. Lazarus served as Special Assistant to the Executive Vice President of IFC, Mr. Jannik Lindbæk, for three years. Ms. Lazarus joined the World Bank Group in 1983 as Assistant to the United States Executive Director to the World Bank. In 1985, she joined the IFC as an Investment Officer in the East Asia and Pacific Department. In 1992, she transferred to the Chemicals and Petrochemicals Department, where she was promoted to Principal Investment Officer. Before joining the World Bank, Ms. Lazarus worked in the U.S. Department of Treasury in the Office of International Affairs. She received her M.B.A. in finance from the Wharton School, University of Pennsylvania, and her B.S. from the University of Wisconsin.

JULIE A. MARTIN

Julie Martin served as Vice President for Insurance of OPIC from May 1997 to September 2000. In her previous position as Deputy Vice President for Insurance, Ms. Martin acted as chief underwriter for the political risk insurance department, where she took a lead role in the development of new products, establishment of policy, and negotiation of large or sensitive projects. Ms. Martin also served as Managing Director for Latin America and the Caribbean, Regional Manager for South and Southeast Asia and Europe, and an Investment Insurance Officer for a variety of African and Asian countries in OPIC's insurance department. She also served as Director of OPIC's Investment Missions program.

Ms. Martin holds an M.B.A. in finance from George Washington University, an M.S. in foreign service from Georgetown University, and a bachelor's degree from Texas Tech University.

THEODORE H. MORAN

Theodore H. Moran holds the Karl F. Landegger Chair in the School of Foreign Service, where he teaches and conducts research at the intersection of international economics, business, foreign affairs, and public policy. Dr. Moran is founder of the Landegger Program in International Business Diplomacy, and serves as Director in providing courses on international business-government relations and negotiations to some 600 undergraduate and graduate students each year. He is also on the Executive Council of the McDonough School of Business at Georgetown University. His most recent books include *Foreign Investment and Development* (Institute for International Economics, 1998); *Managing International Political Risk: New Tools, Strategies, and Techniques* (Blackwells, under the auspices of the World Bank Group, 1998).

In 1993–94, Dr. Moran served as Senior Advisor for Economics on the Policy Planning Staff of the Department of State, where he had responsibility for trade, finance, technology, energy, and environmental issues. He is consultant to the World Bank Group, the United Nations, diverse governments in Asia and Latin America, and the international business and financial communities. He received his Ph.D. from Harvard in 1971.

ANNE PREDIERI

Anne Predieri joined Banc of America in September 1994 to establish an International Structured Finance office in Washington, D.C. She is currently responsible for arranging political risk insurance and government agency support for Banc of America global project finance transactions.

Ms. Predieri spent 10 years at OPIC in a variety of roles, including Project Finance Officer, Investment Missions Manager, and Deputy Treasurer.

Ms. Predieri has a B.A. with honors from Williams College and an M.A. with distinction in international economics from the Johns Hopkins University School of Advanced International Studies. Ms. Predieri speaks French, Italian, and Spanish.

DANIEL W. RIORDAN

Daniel W. Riordan joined Zurich U.S. in June 1997, to establish and manage Zurich U.S. Political Risk, a global political risk insurance group in Washington, D.C. Zurich U.S. Political Risk delivers world class political risk solutions to leading international investors and financial institutions that operate in emerging markets.

Mr. Riordan was Vice President for Insurance of OPIC from June 1994 to May 1997. He managed OPIC's political risk insurance operations, generating $200 million in premium for investment coverage in 75 countries. Mr. Riordan also served as OPIC's senior interagency policy advisor, and as a member of OPIC's senior management committee, which considers large financing and insurance proposals. He served in several other positions at OPIC, including underwriter, marketing director, chief information officer, and deputy vice president. Mr. Riordan began his career at OPIC in 1982 as an unpaid intern while pursuing his graduate education.

Mr. Riordan is a graduate of the State University of New York College at Oswego and holds an M.A. in international development from the School of International Service at the American University.

GERALD T. WEST

Gerald West is Manager, Operations Evaluation, at MIGA. Prior to joining MIGA in 1991, he served for 10 years as Vice President for Development at OPIC.

Mr. West received his Ph.D. in international politics from the Wharton School of the University of Pennsylvania in 1973. For nine years, he was affiliated with the Foreign Policy Research Institute in Philadelphia and the Wharton School, where he conducted research on a wide range of international political and economic topics.

From 1983 to 1996, Mr. West served as an Adjunct Professor of International Business Diplomacy at Georgetown University, teaching a graduate level course on international political risk assessment and management. Over the last 20 years, Mr. West has consulted and published widely on corporate political risk assessment and management.

Appendix II

(Selected Countries)

Political Risk Investment Insurance: The Renaissance Revisited*

Gerald T. West and Keith Martin

G22

D81

The crises which have occurred in Asia, Latin America, and Eastern Europe in the last four years have served to remind investors that political/economic events do not merely have a *potential* to cause losses, but actually *do*, on occasion, cause losses. The crises themselves, and the fact that they came as a surprise to many forecasters, have caused many investors to pay more careful attention to political risk assessment and management. Project sponsors are finding that to assemble the financing for new ventures, especially for large infrastructure projects, they must now look more closely at political risk management issues.

Following a brief discussion of some macro factors currently affecting the market, there is an extended discussion in this paper of the renaissance in the investment insurance marketplace that has been under way for the last several years. A concluding section discusses trends for the future.

Prospective investors have not previously enjoyed the breadth and depth of choices in the investment insurance market that they have today. Yet it is also clear that project developers have not fully appreciated, at either the strategic or technical level, the alternatives they now have in designing and improving their overall project structures. *new*

---

* This is a revised and updated version of "Political Risk Investment Insurance: A Renaissance," by Gerald T. West (*Journal of Project Finance*, Summer 1999, pp. 27–36).

Macro Trends

Several 1990s trends have had a profound impact on the political risk investment insurance market. Foremost is the dramatic rise of foreign direct investments (FDI) flows into developing countries. Globalization, liberalization, and privatization served to increase FDI flows more than sixfold during the period from 1990 to 1999. FDI flows to developing countries as a percentage of total long-term flows also rose dramatically in this period, from 24 percent in 1990 to 68 percent in 1999. At the same time, official development aid to them fell to 18 percent of overall flows.

As developing and emerging market countries competed to attract FDI and gain investor confidence, losses due to traditional political perils were rare. Investors suffered relatively few expropriation losses; currency transfer losses were equally low as most investment returns were modest and a significant repatriation of profits was not expected to occur until later in the decade. While losses attributable to war increased somewhat over the period as the Cold War–enforced stability eroded and internal conflicts broke out in many countries (especially in Africa), the losses remained fairly small and confined to somewhat predictable places.

For political risk investment insurers, the dramatic increase in FDI flows during the period translated into a growing market with very modest losses (until the onset of claims arising from the Asian

FIGURE 1   INVESTMENT INSURANCE PROVIDED BY BERNE UNION MEMBERS

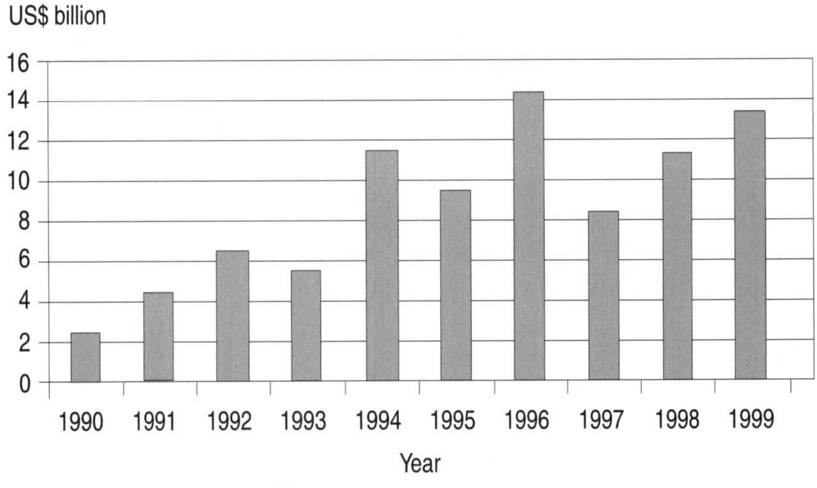

US$ billion

Year

Source: 2000 Annual Report of the Berne Union.

FIGURE 2   RATIO OF FDI COVERED BY BERNE UNION INVESTMENT
INSURERS TO FOREIGN DIRECT INVESTMENT FLOWS TO DEVELOPING
COUNTRIES

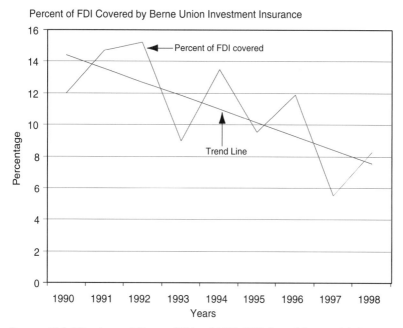

Percent of FDI Covered by Berne Union Investment Insurance

Sources: Global Development Finance 1998 and 1999; 1999 Annual Report of the Berne Union.

crisis). Figure 1 notes the collective coverages written by the 24 investment insurance members of the Berne Union.[1]

It should also be noted, however, that relative to the total flow of
FDI, the percentage of investment covered by the 24-member Berne
Union investment insurers had been on a downward trend until
1998, when there was a slight increase (see Figure 2). While Figure 2
does not include the political risk coverages provided by private
insurers, it is clear that many investors were either bearing the risk
of loss themselves or using other risk mitigation instruments.

The future continues to look auspicious for political risk investment insurers. An anonymous 1999 survey of 152 investors[2] supports the conclusion that many investors are now more concerned
about political risks than before, but do not believe they have adequate coverage for their projects or that current coverage options
are insufficient. According to the survey, half of all investors stated
that political risks were more of a concern for them now than before, while only 12 percent indicated that they were now of less concern. A significant number of investors (about a third) believe that

only a "minority" of their political risks are mitigated by current insurance products, indicating that products currently available are not meeting their expectations. Finally, many investors plan to increase their spending on political risk insurance in the next five years, using a combination of public and private insurers, as well as other instruments (e.g., captive insurers and finite insurance, if available).

One interesting development in the wake of the financial crises has been the divergence between the capital markets and foreign direct investment. While FDI has continued to increase every year — even in 1997 and 1998, the main years of the crisis — reaching an all-time high of US$192 billion in 1999, international capital market flows (including bank lending and bond financing) have largely collapsed. In 1996, those capital market flows peaked at US$151.3 billion, but have since fallen to US$46.7 billion in 1999 (which is less than half of their 1998 levels). The Russian Federation's debt moratorium in October 1998 dramatically reduced investor interest in emerging markets' equity issues; many Russian bonds were downgraded to "junk status." Equity prices in 12 out of the 15 major emerging stock markets plunged (with a range of 21 to 85 percent); some of these markets, with the notable exception of the Russian Federation, have subsequently recovered most or all of those losses. For most middle income developing countries, however, access to the international capital and derivatives markets remains restricted, and maturities are shorter.

While some of this weakness in the capital markets is attributable to the continued strength of the developed economies, and of the United States in particular, the source resides primarily in the continued nervousness of capital markets investors about long-term future political and economic developments in emerging markets. In this context, the political risk insurance coverage for capital markets transactions that is currently being pioneered by OPIC, MIGA, and Zurich-U.S. (see below) may prove to be a small, but important, catalyst to stimulating capital markets financing for projects in developing countries.

As investors assess the array of investment opportunities in developing markets today, they are far more wary than they were in the early 1990s. The previously rosy international investment perspective that drove the demand for capital markets and derivatives products has turned pessimistic, and many prospective investors are sitting on the sidelines, despite promising signs of economic recovery in many of the countries hardest hit by the crisis (e.g., Republic of Korea, Malaysia, and Brazil). This has led to a split between those engaged in direct investment, who continue to actively explore the significant opportunities available in developing countries, and those in the capital markets, who are still focusing on the potential for financial instability in emerging markets.

Clearly, there are countries and sectors which were hard hit by the 1997–1998 crises and have not recovered. Where losses have materialized and a country shows few signs of recovery, disillusionment is evident. Investors have been more attentive to their prospective ability to earn and repatriate profits; the necessary legal and regulatory safeguards required for capital and derivative markets to operate efficiently in many emerging economies are being more carefully assessed; and the effects of the credit crunch on the availability and cost of capital for limited recourse projects are very evident.

Overview of the Investment Insurance Market

While in the 1990s, many political risk insurers were also quietly improving and redesigning their coverages and increasing their capacity. As late as 1997, the three main groups of investment insurers largely served separate markets and had clearly defined roles (see Figure 3). For new investments, national agencies dominated the market because of the length of their tenor, the scope of their coverage, and their available capacity; private insurers served investors whose investments were not eligible for coverage from national providers and those with special needs. Multilateral insurers complemented the capacities of these two groups, especially with respect to investments that would not be eligible for coverage from national agencies, contributing capacity to very large investments and to special projects in transition economies and the poorest countries.

FIGURE 3 POLITICAL RISK INVESTMENT INSURANCE MARKETPLACE: 1997

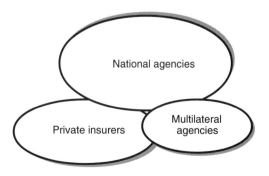

A different market has now emerged (see Figure 4). It is a larger, more complex, and more competitive marketplace. New companies backed by significant capital, such as Sovereign, Chubb & Son, and Zurich-U.S., entered the market. Also, private insurers dramatically improved the quality and tenor of their offerings. Although it seemed in 1998 that the effects of the Asian crisis (and of some of the losses incurred there and in Russia) would curtail the availability and amounts of private insurance capacity that can be accessed by investors, this has not yet happened. Capacity and rates in the private market appear to have remained stable, with only a moderate hardening of the reinsurance market taking place. The strong reinsurance market is, to a significant extent, supporting the long-term political risk coverages underwritten by both private and public providers.

While many private insurers (and some public insurers) are now facing major claims, or have already paid claims, from their existing exposures in Indonesia, Russia, and Pakistan, this does not appear to have deterred the private insurers. Some are even pointing out that the claims payments had served to remind clients both that political risks are real and that insurers do pay valid claims. There is some debate about what the claims have meant for cooperation between public and private sector providers. On the one hand, the claims may underscore the value to private insurers of coinsurance with a public insurer, since there is a better chance that some of the losses will be recouped due to the public insurer's efforts.[3] On the other hand, a few private insurers have complained that public insurers are making claims determinations and recovery efforts subject to political considerations regarding the relationship between the public insurers' home country and the host country that has caused the claim.

FIGURE 4 POLITICAL RISK INVESTMENT INSURANCE MARKETPLACE: 2001

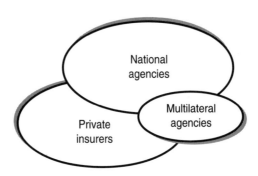

Before describing the new developments in this market in more detail, and venturing some observations about future trends, it is useful to comment briefly on the utility of investment insurance as a risk management instrument.

The Utility of Political Risk Insurance in Risk Management

The intrinsic benefits of purchasing political risk insurance have been detailed elsewhere.[4] However, some benefits are worthy of particular note. Both debt and equity investors obviously recognize the compensatory value of investment insurance, but they often pay inadequate attention to two other important risk mitigation features: *deterrence* and *leverage*. This is especially the case in limited recourse financings.

Deterrence Value

The role of an investment insurer in the *settlement of investment disputes* is rarely discussed, much less analyzed. Political risk insurance, especially from national and multilateral agencies, can act as an effective deterrent against host government interference with insured private investments. Moreover, should an expropriation or currency transfer dispute occur, buyers clearly believe that, *ceteris paribus*, the investor stands a much better chance of successfully resolving the matter if a national or multilateral agency is involved as an insurer. (This thesis is clearly being "empirically tested" in East Asia; the results so far are mixed.)

One can observe both "carrot" and "stick" aspects to this deterrent effect. First, with respect to the "carrot," one must remember that there is often a complex web of political, economic, and commercial relationships between the investor's "home" country and the host developing country. These relationships are endangered by a messy dispute or claim involving their national insurer. Moreover, bilateral trade and investment treaties may be potentially violated; national security arrangements (actual or pending) may be threatened or inhibited; and ongoing trade discussions may be disrupted. All these actions have real and reputational costs to the host country. Moreover, if the host country is undergoing a severe economic downturn, where can this country turn to obtain credits or loans other than the industrialized countries, or to the multilateral development institutions where the industrialized countries have significant influence? Finally, if the host country wishes to attract new foreign investment, it ironically needs these national investment insurers (and the multilateral insurers), who need to be prepared to issue new coverages (which they would obviously not do while dealing with a serious investment dispute or actively seeking compensation from the host government for a loss).

Some components of this deterrent effect also serve as a "stick," to be used against host countries that cause losses to national insurers and do not reimburse them. Some home countries have, by legislation or practice, introduced nearly automatic sanctions against countries that have not effectively compensated their national insurers who have assumed (through subrogation) the rights to an insured investor's assets or shares (in the case of expropriation claim) or to the local currency (in the case of a currency transfer claim). These sanctions can range from temporary suspension of a specific government program to complete cessation of all investment insurance, export credit, and foreign assistance. Moreover, in the case of a dispute or claim with a multilateral insurer or guarantor which is not resolved, there is the risk of a complete suspension of ongoing credit or loan activity (e.g., in the case of MIGA, a member of the World Bank Group, possible suspension of new IDA credits or IBRD loans).

Thus, considering all the "costs" associated with not satisfactorily resolving a dispute with an investor insured by a major national or multilateral insurer, a host country decisionmaker certainly has many incentives (and disincentives) to carefully weigh before taking a prospective action against an insured investor. Indeed, once the full cost of prospective action against an insured investor is realized, these disputes often become "misunderstandings" that are quietly and successfully resolved.

It is difficult to label a specific government action (or inaction) as something that resulted from deterrence when such an action may well also be termed "enlightened self-interest." Such actions can be very narrow and might be attributable to other factors. For example, the Russian Directive of August 26, 1998, which introduced temporary restrictions on residents' operations involving capital movements, caused widespread concern among investors. However, the projects insured by MIGA were excluded from these restrictions by way of Article 8.1 of that Directive. Whatever the government motivation for this action was, the MIGA-insured investors in Russia were pleased with the exemption.

Direct evidence that deterrence has taken place is difficult to verify. In MIGA's case, the issuance of over 475 guarantees in more than 70 countries between 1990 and 2000, and the receipt of just one claim, suggest deterrence was operative in some instances, since good underwriting cannot, by itself, justify such a record.

For many investors, the deterrence value is one of the prime reasons why they purchase insurance from public insurers, or at least insist on their involvement in the project. A further recognition of the value of this deterrence phenomenon is the fact that some project sponsors will deliberately involve multiple public and multilateral insurers and lenders in the same project, even when efficiency would argue for fewer participants.

Leverage Value

The second benefit of investment insurance that is often not acknowledged is leverage. Many lending institutions who underwrite debt in limited recourse project financings are also regular buyers of political risk investment insurance. Many of these OECD commercial bank investors are subject to very strict provisioning requirements with regard to their cross-border exposures.[5] To offset any further squeeze on the projects' economics brought about by these provisioning requirements, lenders often purchase political risk insurance from national or multilateral providers. (Such coverages then allow a lender to either eliminate or significantly reduce country risk provisioning requirements.)

Lenders also value political risk insurance for its ability to improve the overall risk/return profile of the project. Such insurance, often offered at attractive rates and tenors by insurers, allows lenders to extend the terms of their loans and thus improve the project's amortization profile.

These deterrence and leverage effects are added features that make political risk insurance a more attractive risk management mechanism in today's more difficult market for project finance. Figure 5 illustrates these features.

A 1998 survey of all MIGA's clients (conducted on a confidential basis by an independent consultant for MIGA) revealed that they have diverse goals in mind when purchasing MIGA coverage. Some investors clearly value compensation against potential losses as much more important than the benefits of deterrence. Conversely, investors who value investment insurance's deterrent effect tend to minimize the importance of the compensation benefit, although this clearly does not mean that these investors do not expect to be compensated in the event of a loss. Over three-quarters of those respondents who valued the deterrent effect more than the compensation benefit also ranked MIGA's coverage as absolutely critical to their decision to proceed with the investment.

FIGURE 5   PERCEIVED VALUE OF POLITICAL RISK INSURANCE

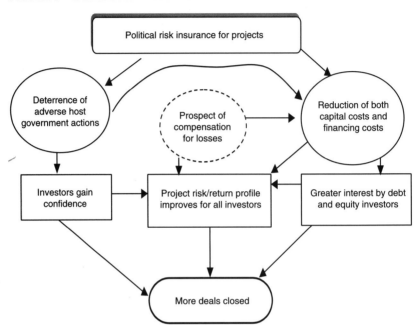

Since MIGA's clients are only a small proportion of all investors using investment insurance, one cannot generalize to the larger universe of all investors. However, the results of the survey provide insight into investors' concerns and how the political risk insurance market can respond to their varying needs. Currently, the market is better able than ever before to provide investors with whatever they require — be it deterrence, greater capacity, long-term coverage, and complementarity with other risk mitigating instruments.

New Developments and Future Challenges

It is useful to separate factors that will affect the political risk investment insurance marketplace into those which primarily impact the future demand for coverage, and those which will impact the future supply of coverage.

Demand Factors

The 1997 East Asian financial crisis and its aftermath have provided investors with a very concrete reminder that political risk is not "dead or irrelevant," as some had confidently announced a few years ago. Political risks have a history of simply "mutating" and presenting different management challenges to investors.

Several factors will fuel the demand for political risk insurance in the medium term. First, while demand for infrastructure financing has temporarily slackened, demand for investment insurance of such financings has increased. For example, MIGA gross issuance of new political risk insurance coverage for infrastructure projects increased from $228.7 million in fiscal 1999 to $748.6 million in fiscal 2000. This also reflects the fact that many large infrastructure projects in emerging countries had not been canceled, but were postponed until the economies began recovering and the cost and availability of capital began to improve. In many emerging markets, however, that recovery has yet to begin, so it is doubtful that demand for coverage of infrastructure projects has peaked already.

Second, while the new project pipeline has contracted in Asia, the demand for corporate restructuring, particularly merger and acquisitions, is expected to push up demand for financing in the region. In the five Asian countries most affected by the crisis, participation by foreign investors in merger and acquisition activities increased from $1.1 billion in 1996 to nearly $6 billion in 1997.[6] By 1999, overall FDI to three of those five countries (Malaysia, Philippines and Thailand) had reached near-record levels. In Korea, FDI reached US$8 billion in 1999, the largest amount ever, and a 250 percent increase over 1997 levels. In all of these cases, mergers and acquisitions accounted for much of the activity.[7]

Interestingly, while public investment insurers were expecting significant amounts of coverage to be written for projects in these East Asian countries, this has, by and large, not materialized. There are several plausible explanations for this. In the case of Malaysia and Korea, the fact that few, if any, political risk insurance losses were suffered during the crisis, coupled with the rapidity and depth of the economic recovery in both countries, appears to have persuaded investors to return to those countries without political risk coverage. In the Philippines, investors—particularly in the power sector—remain nervous about sufficient consumer demand to support the current pipeline of large-scale infrastructure projects. This means that a number of investors have chosen not to go forward with new projects and hence do not require political risk coverage. Only in Thailand have investment insurers seen a certain measure of interest for coverage of new projects.

In Indonesia, both investors and investment insurers are waiting for clarification of the situation. A number of investment insurers, including OPIC and several Lloyd's syndicates, have now paid substantial claims to insured investors whose projects in Indonesia's power sector were adversely impacted by the economic and political turmoil in the country. OPIC's claims payment of US$217.5 million was one of the largest in its history. MIGA paid out its first claim, for $15 million, in June 2000, for a power project in Indonesia.

On the qualitative side, demand for investment insurance will also be driven by the perceived resurgence of classical political risk as a result of the social dislocation and political turmoil brought about by the economic crisis. While no government has engaged in wholesale expropriation for nearly two decades, the possibility of selective expropriations is higher than ever in some countries, due to rising nationalism. Mergers and acquisitions in East Asia have fueled some nationalistic paranoia among both government and business elites, who fear that foreigners are conspiring to buy into local companies at "fire-sale" prices to gain dominance over their economy. Similarly, where privatizations involving heavy foreign participation have resulted in layoffs, increased rates for basic services, or a deterioration in the quality of those services, protests have occurred and can be expected to include calls for nationalization or result in violent attacks on the company's facilities. Finally, expropriation and civil war risks are obviously higher in countries where the government has been weakened and society is divided by differences.

Civil wars and general chaos in several African countries — combined with a desire on the part of some investors to tap into the continent's markets and resources — have fueled demand for investment insurance in Africa. Demand for coverage is highest in those African countries that are emerging from crises but have good business prospects (e.g., Mozambique). While this demand remains very modest when compared to Latin America, it is noteworthy that MIGA was able to substantially increase coverage for projects in Africa in fiscal 2000; they now represent 12 percent of MIGA's entire portfolio. The concern for investment insurers, however, is that the risk of civil strife is probably the highest risk facing their investments in Africa — and it is the one risk for which there is virtually no opportunity for recoveries once a claim has been paid.

In addition to these classical political risks, investors also face more economic uncertainties. Many forecasters and international institutions are predicting that global economic growth will continue at a modest pace for the next few years. This will hamper the efforts of most developing countries to raise capital. Currency exchange volatility will impede the ability of investors to service their foreign currency debts and purchase needed imports. Large-scale movements of currency may also result in some countries' inability to maintain sufficient foreign currency reserves, hence leading to a currency crisis. Many investors will continue to suffer from business volatility arising from erosion of their customer base, vulnerability to regional uncertainties, selective discrimination, cancellation of operating and export licenses, and contract abrogation. Because of the breadth and depth of these kinds of uncertainties, limited recourse investors are likely to be heavy purchasers of political risk investment insurance in the next few years.

Supply Factors

The demand "pull" for investment insurance in the 1990s stimulated competition and innovation and has been paralleled in some respects by a supply "push." Some of this push was fueled by the soft insurance market, as private underwriters sought better margins in market niches where competition has not driven premiums to low levels. In some instances, existing investment insurance providers seem to have dramatically improved their coverage offerings to maintain existing market share and meet increased demand. Some private entrants seem to be entering the political risk market just to keep pace with their competition and be a "full service" insurer to their clients.

It is useful to discuss four aspects of the changing investment insurance market in more detail: capacity, tenor, innovation, and cooperation/collaboration among insurers.

Capacity

During the last two years, private insurers have responded to the increased demand stimulated by recent economic and political uncertainties in developing countries by increasing their classic confiscation, expropriation, nationalization (CEN) capacity per project by an estimated 14 percent (from an estimated $1.4 billion in 1998 to $1.6 billion in 1999).[8] Lloyd's of London still accounts for a large share of this increase; its CEN capacity reached $900 million in 1999, compared to $800 million during the previous year. It should be noted, however, that Lloyd's capacity is notoriously difficult to estimate for several reasons. First, the market measures itself in terms of premium that can be written, not capacity per se. Second, it depends very heavily on the availability and rates for reinsurance. Finally, both reinsurance and primary insurance capacity will often depend on events in totally unrelated lines of the insurance business.

On the last two points, it is worth noting that, historically, the general insurance business has been cyclical, with periods of low losses (and high profits) counterbalanced by times of high insurance losses. When losses occur, capacity may dry up not only in the specific sector affected, but in altogether different lines as well (since reinsurers usually cover a variety of lines of insurance). The private insurance market is currently coming out of one of the longest cycles of low losses in its history, and many have predicted that the end of the cycle (and, hence, higher losses) would result in increased premiums and decreased capacity. At the same time, however, large amounts of capital have flowed into the insurance industry from a variety of sources, resulting in both increased capacity and historically low premium rates. There is, therefore, a significant fear that, at some point, large losses totally unrelated to political risks (e.g., due to a particularly damaging hurricane season), will affect the political risk insurance market and lead to a withdrawal of capacity and/or significantly higher premium rates in the private political risk insurance industry. As a consequence, investors will always have a latent concern about sudden swings in private political risk insurance capacity. In sum, both overall investment insurance capacity and capacity for any given risk in a particular country are volatile for a variety of reasons over which private investment insurers have little control.

Figure 6 gives a more detailed perspective of the available capacity of private insurers per project, showing additional capacity coming from Lloyd's, Zurich-U.S., and a composite group of other private insurers.

Collectively, the national insurers have expanded their issuance of investment insurance significantly in the 1990s. New coverage issued by Berne Union members (which encompasses 24 national investment insurers and MIGA) rose dramatically in the 1990s. Their total portfolio on December 31, 1998, was about US$42 billion, an increase of 62 percent over 1992 levels. Berne Union members' coverage is expected to stay near, or even exceed, these record levels as individual OECD governments announce special initiatives to support various special recovery initiatives and as investors in large, complex projects in the developing world continue to seek the involvement of public insurers. Furthermore, the recent addition of AIG to the Berne Union will automatically increase those figures.

With respect to capacity limits, official agencies have also demonstrated considerable flexibility (see Table 1). Many national agencies are very "elastic" and can supply large amounts of coverage for projects deemed to be in the "national interest" because of procure-

FIGURE 6   CEN PER PROJECT CAPACITY OF SELECTED PRIVATE INSURERS

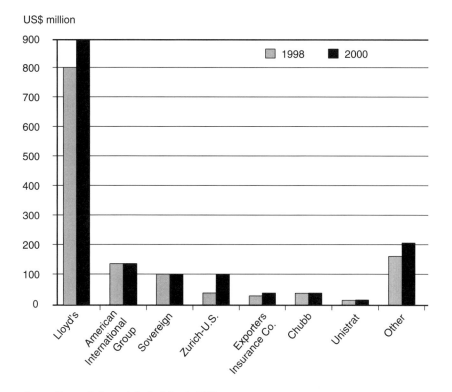

US$ million

Source: Berry, Palmer & Lyle, March 2000.

ment in the home country or for political reasons. (OPIC and MIGA, with their per-project limits of US$200 million, are the exception, although those limits could be revised.)

The supply push has resulted in a situation that makes it theoretically possible for nearly US$2 billion of capacity (from both public and private sources) to be mobilized for a single project. However, with respect to very large projects (more than US$1 billion), or projects considered more "risky," a common situation often arises, namely that the combined capabilities of all interested insurers may well fall short of investors' coverage requirements. From the perspective of the investment insurers, however, the demand seems to have become increasingly "lumpy," with heavy demand for large amounts of coverage in a relatively small number of projects, sectors, and countries. In mid-2000, for example, demand for coverage of infrastructure projects in Brazil clearly exceeded available coverage.

TABLE 1   LIMITS OF SOME PUBLIC AND PRIVATE INVESTMENT INSURERS
(AS OF MARCH 2000)

Investment Insurer	Country limits (in US$ millions)	Project limits (in US$ millions)
AIG	1,000 (higher in certain countries)	150
Sovereign	250	100
Zurich-U.S.	300–1,000	100
Chubb	100	50
OPIC	about 1,800 (15% of insurance outstanding)	200
EDC	Variable	No official limit (but about 100)
MIGA	up to 685	up to 200
ECGD	Variable	Variable

Tenor

While the national agencies have always provided long-term coverage (up to 15–20 years has been the norm), the tenor offered by
private insurers had been essentially limited to one to three years
until 1996. As Figure 7 notes, by mid-2000 this had dramatically
changed and ten-year coverages are now common. Two recent developments suggest that further improvements are likely. First, ACE
Global Markets, one of the largest managing agency groups at
Lloyd's of London, agreed in April 1999 to facultatively reinsure
MIGA for its coverage of a mortgage lending project in Argentina;
the tenor was 15 years. Second, in May 1999, Zurich-U.S. announced
that its maximum tenor had been extended from ten to fifteen years.
Although the amount and availability of coverage for some investments may be limited, these actions suggest that the trend toward
more capacity for longer tenors is likely to continue, barring un-
foreseen losses either in the political risk insurance industry or in
unrelated lines (see above).

   While availability and cost may continue to inhibit utilization of
this extension of tenor, it is clear that project developers may not
yet fully appreciate the added flexibility they now have in designing and improving their overall project structures.

   It is also often overlooked that the longer tenor now offered in
the combined public-private market can also help project sponsors
access the secondary bond market. Securitized project bonds can be
made more attractive to portfolio investors if they are backed by

FIGURE 7   MAXIMUM TENOR OFFERED BY SELECTED PRIVATE INSURERS IN 2000

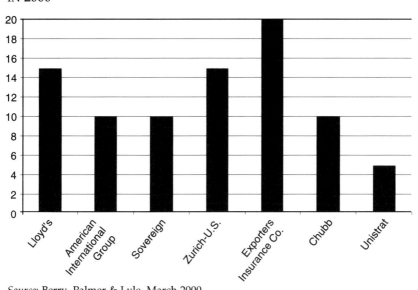

Source: Berry, Palmer & Lyle, March 2000.

political risk insurance. CS First Boston (CSFB), for example, has started pooling senior secured project finance loans, of which 20 percent of the portfolio are rated non-investment grade, but are backed by political risk insurance.[9] Indeed, a number of securitizations in "difficult" markets would not happen without support from the investment insurance market.

Product Innovation

The combination of heightened demand, increased capacity, competition, and longer tenor of coverage has stimulated innovation in the last few years, as has the growing complexity of the investments to be covered. Nearly every month witnesses a new coverage "wrinkle" or combination that has never been previously accomplished. Several recent examples can be noted.

- *BCP/Brazil*: In April 2000, MIGA signed its largest guarantee to date, supporting US$230 million of a $650 million loan from a syndicate of lenders to BCP in Brazil. In taking on the US$230 million coverage against transfer restriction and expropriation, MIGA utilized its Cooperative Underwriting Program (CUP, see below) and brought new partners into the CUP. MIGA is the insurer of record, but is retaining only

US$55 million for its own account, with the remaining US$175 million being covered by a variety of private insurers (Chubb, Unistrat, and seven Lloyd's syndicates). The underlying project involves the establishment and operation of a cellular network in metropolitan São Paulo, providing improved tele-communications infrastructure in Brazil. This project dem-onstrates how effectively private and public insurers can work together to provide needed coverage in a very tight market, leveraging each other's advantages for the ultimate benefit of the investors and the host country's economy.

- *Multicountry Pipelines:* A growing trend, especially in the power sector, is toward integrated multicountry projects which involve hydrocarbon or power production in one coun-try and the transmission thereof to one or more other coun-tries. Such projects are currently under way or in the planning stages in western Africa, Latin America, and the Caspian re-gion. These projects, which are often very large and expen-sive, are posing new challenges to investment insurers, who have traditionally dealt with political risks on a per-country basis. Demand from investors is, however, driving insurers to reassess the situation. In fiscal 1999, for the first time, MIGA insured two gas pipeline projects with multicountry cover-age, that is, coverage against actions by the host government of one country that may affect the assets of the same project located either in the host country or in another country.

  - In the first case, MIGA provided US$14.5 million in in-surance for El Paso Energy International's investment in one of the largest foreign investments in Latin America, the construction of a 3,150-kilometer natural gas pipeline from Santa Cruz (Bolivia) to Porto Alegre (Brazil). The project will have direct economic benefits to the Bolivian economy through increased investment in upstream gas exploration and production activities, boosting the nation's income by an estimated US$400 million per an-num. At the same time, the project will benefit Brazil by diversifying its energy supply and by substituting natu-ral gas for more polluting fuels in the areas served by the pipeline.

  - MIGA also issued US$31.4 million in coverage to EPED Holding Co. for its investment in a natural gas transmis-sion project from Argentina to Chile. The project is part of an integrated energy project and will transmit natural gas from Argentina to Chile through the construction and operation of a 641-kilometer pipeline. The natural gas will replace high-sulfur fuel oil, coal, and firewood, alleviating pollution and deforestation in the areas of Chile using gas from the pipeline.

- *Creeping Expropriation and Breach of Contract Coverage*: In the context of investors' concerns that current coverage available from investment insurers is not adequate to protect them against all the risks they face, considerable attention is now being paid to "stretching" what can be covered under political risks. This is also a reflection of the fact that privatizations, particularly in the infrastructure sector, have resulted in new situations where the line between political and commercial actions is becoming blurred, and where the role of parastatals and subsovereigns has made the accountability of the host country's central government less certain.

  - Of greatest concern to many investors today is "creeping expropriation," that is, where a series of events by a government (or a subsovereign or parastatal entity) result in a deprivation of the investor's rights. While many public investment insurers want to accommodate investors' needs in this area, they often worry about the blurred distinction between commercial and political risks giving rise to claims for which they will find it difficult to recover from the host governments. This is an evolving area where cooperation between investors, private insurers, and public insurers will be critical in developing better coverage that addresses investors' concerns without endangering the sustainability of public insurers and the profitability of private insurers.

  - With increasing numbers of privatizations, BOOT (Build-Own-Operate-Transfer) projects, and off-take agreements, investors and lenders have sought coverage from public insurers against breaches of host government commitments. Traditionally, public insurers have been reluctant to offer such breach of contract coverage, since these commitments often involve a gray area between political and commercial risk. (Private insurers, by contrast, have long offered contract frustration coverage, since they need not be as concerned about the distinction between commercial and political risks.) Over the past few years, however, because their expropriation coverage may, on occasion, have included such coverage, public investment insurers have decided to clarify matters and respond to investor demand by offering more expansive and explicit breach of contract coverage. MIGA, for example, recently provided coverage for a buy-lease-back arrangement and maintenance agreements between a private company and the Lesotho government for some 1,200 vehicles against specified breaches by the host government, a coverage that probably would have been unavailable from MIGA some years ago.

- *Coverage for Capital Markets Transactions*: In January 1999, OPIC announced its decision to provide political risk coverage of up to US$200 million per project of bonds (such as 144A bonds) issued in the U.S. capital markets. This new product should facilitate limited-recourse projects in developing countries obtaining an investment-grade rating that may be higher than the country's sovereign rating and thereby enable them to access badly needed long-term financing. OPIC and Zurich U.S. have since covered several capital markets transactions, albeit for private placements, and MIGA is currently completing its first coverage for a Section 144A issue. It remains to be seen whether the coverage offered by investment insurers (who are only covering explicitly political risks) will be sufficient for investors in public placements, since many are concerned about devaluation risk and other commercial perils and are unaware of the full benefits of investment insurance. Other investors, particularly those who have done traditionally "higher risk" investments in developing markets, are primarily interested in the high yields these transactions offer and are concerned that the premium paid for political risk insurance will reduce the spread too much. In short, the capital markets coverage, while recognized by rating agencies, arrangers, and others as a potentially very important catalyst for tapping the capital markets for developing country projects, is not a product that will meet the needs of all investors.

- *Banco Santander/Brazil*: In May 1999, MIGA issued coverage of $100 million of three-year notes from Banco Santander, S.A., of Spain to its wholly owned Brazilian subsidiary to fund its lending activities. MIGA's contract, totaling $107 million in coverage, was coinsured under the CUP (see below) with Great Northern Insurance Company of the Chubb Group and with five Lloyd's syndicates. The transaction was noteworthy because it was the first issue of this tenor in Brazil since mid-1998.

While most of these innovations have been evolutionary in nature, rather than revolutionary, in the aggregate they have significantly improved the risk management options now available to project financiers.

Cooperation and Collaboration Among Investment Insurers

Perhaps the most important development in the investment insurance marketplace in recent years is the increased cooperation among investment insurers in large projects, especially infrastructure projects. For example, MIGA, which has a mandate to complement other investment insurers in facilitating investment into developing countries, has signed project reinsurance arrangements with British, Canadian, French, Japanese, Norwegian, and U.S. national agencies. MIGA has also participated in coinsurance arrangements with a large number of private and public insurers. Such collaboration among insurers effectively increases the available insurance capacity for project developers and enhances the deterrent benefit for both insurers and insureds.

The long-term reinsurance arrangements which MIGA concluded in February 1999 with two Bermuda-based private insurance companies, ACE Insurance Company Limited (ACE) and XL Capital Limited (XL), show how an insurer can better serve the needs of prospective clients, augment its level of activity, and yet contain its own net exposure. The agreements build on an earlier agreement signed in April 1997 between MIGA and ACE. The key terms of these new reinsurance arrangements are as follows:
- ACE and XL will each assume exposure of up to US$50 million per project and up to US$150 million per country; and
- MIGA will retain complete discretion as to its pricing policy and underwriting decisions.

As a result of these agreements, MIGA's per project and per country limits have increased substantially. With the infusion of US$150 million in capital in April 1998, plus an anticipated US$850 million over the next three years, MIGA's Board of Directors approved in February 1999 an increase in its *net* per project limit from US$50 million to US$110 million and its *net* per country limit from US$250 million to US$350 million. Recently, the Board further increased the *net* per country limit to US$385 millionThe combination of expanded reinsurance and an increase in its per country and per project limits now allows MIGA to offer up to US$200 million of *gross* coverage to a single project, and a total of at least $655 million *gross* in a country. (Additional amounts of coverage can be mobilized through the

CUP, facultative reinsurance with public and private insurers, as well as other forms of coinsurance.)

A recent example of this private-public sector cooperation is the reinsurance agreement that MIGA signed with the ACE Global Markets' Syndicate of Lloyd's of London covering a $50 million loan by Lloyd's Bank of the United Kingdom to its wholly owned subsidiary in Argentina. The loan will be used by the bank to expand its residential mortgage lending operations through Lloyd's Bank's network of 51 offices in the country. The reinsurance agreement, with a maximum tenor of 15 years, allowed MIGA to provide additional coverage for the project, which, in turn, enables Lloyd's Bank to offer longer-term residential mortgages to its clients.

Another MIGA initiative which also reflects how public and private investment insurers may cooperate, is MIGA's Cooperative Underwriting Program (CUP). This mechanism combines coverage from public and private insurers (up to US$300 million per project) in a manner similar to the IFC's A- and B-loan syndications. Under this arrangement, MIGA "fronts" the insurance for the private insurer(s) along with its own coverage, effectively sharing (for a price) its "status" as a multilateral entity and as a member of the World Bank Group.

A byproduct of the increasing cooperation among insurers is a trend toward the standardization of policy wordings. As private insurers cooperate more often with MIGA, EDC, and OPIC, they increasingly become accustomed to, and accept, the policy wordings of these agencies. This trend is likely to continue and become a standard for a number of reasons: buyer acceptance of their wordings; the openness of EDC, OPIC, and MIGA to cooperate with other insurers; and the prominence of these insurers in the marketplace.

Conclusions

Like all markets, the investment insurance market will be subject to many forces that will influence its future evolution. The difficult task is not so much to identify all these factors, but to consider their interactions and to *net* them out to determine the resultant magnitude and direction of the market. In that spirit, the authors offer the following observations:

- Stimulated by losses to uninsured investors, and notwithstanding stagnation in investment flows to developing and emerging markets, the issuance of political risk investment insurance will steadily increase, with specific growth in parts of Asia, the former Soviet Union, and Latin America. Issuance in Africa and the Middle East will also increase, but will remain a relatively small percentage overall.

- Due to increased losses, historically low premium rates in other insurance areas will not be sustainable over the longer term. Increased losses will result in a continued firming of rates. This will have some effect on the political risk investment insurance market as reinsurance capacity becomes more expensive.

- Notwithstanding some insurance losses in the political risk insurance area, capacity should remain fairly steady. Buyers should continue to benefit from competition among insurance providers, and premium rates should remain relatively stable, albeit with an upward bias.

- Events in East Asia, the former Soviet Union, and Latin America will result in sharper differences in the treatment afforded uninsured investments and investments insured by private insurers versus those covered by national or multilateral providers. The value of deterrence should thus become more clearly established.

- Assembly of limited recourse debt financing for mega-infrastructure projects will be very difficult without long-term investment insurance. Fortunately, cooperation and collaboration among insurers should continue to grow, especially with respect to such large projects.

- After the recent and dramatic increases in tenor in the private market (from 1 to 3 years to 10 to 15 years), there will be no further extensions in the near future and there will be greater price variation for tenor.

- As a result of significant losses in 1999 and 2000, insurers and reinsurers may reexamine their rates and their project and country limits. The result should be more variance across insurers, and hence a greater need for buyers to shop their insurance needs.

Notes

1. The Berne Union was founded in 1934 with two main objectives: to promote international acceptance of sound principle in export credit insurance and investment insurance; and the exchange of information relating thereto. The national and multilateral members of the Union's Investment Insurance Committee, currently numbering 24, provide investment insurance coverage against political risks. In 1999, AIG became the first private insurer writing coverage for its own account (not that of

a national government) to join the Berne Union; it currently has Observer status but will be eligible, in 2001, to apply for full membership.

2. Although the survey was sponsored by MIGA, it was undertaken by an outside firm and respondents were unaware of any connection to MIGA.

3. It is worth noting, for example, that OPIC has a record of recovering almost 100 percent of the expropriation claims it has paid out, not including the recent claim paid in Indonesia.

4. Gerald T. West "Managing Political Risk Insurance: The Role of Investment Insurance." *Journal of Project Finance*. Winter 1996, pp. 5–11.

5. See, for example, Robert H. Malleck. "Political Risk Insurance, International Banks, and Other International Lenders" in Theodore H. Moran, ed. *Managing International Political Risk*. Blackwell Business. London. 1998. pp. 173–178.

6. *Global Development Finance 1999*. The World Bank. Washington, D.C., p. 60.

7. *Global Development Finance 2000*. The World Bank. Washington, D.C., p. 43.

8. Source: Presentation by Charles Berry, Chairman of Berry, Palmer & Lyle Limited, on "Political Risk and Trade Credit Insurance From the Private Market," during the 9th Annual Insuring Export Credit and Political Risk Convention, London, February 10–12, 2000.

9. Source: CS First Boston's presentation on Project Finance Loan Securitization, presented during the conference on New Solutions and Opportunities for Developing and Financing Projects. Paris, France, February 17–19, 1999.

Appendix III

Managing International Political Risk

Theodore H. Moran, ed.

published by Blackwell from the first MIGA-Georgetown Symposium, 1998.

This volume can be ordered from Blackwell Publishers
350 Main Street
Malden, MA 02148
Tel. 781-388-0473
800-216-2522
Fax 781-388-8210

Table of Contents

II
LESSONS IN THE MANAGEMENT OF INTERNATIONAL POLITICAL RISK
FROM THE NATURAL RESOURCE AND PRIVATE INFRASTRUCTURE SECTORS

Appendix IV

More about MIGA

----

1. MIGA Member Country List

Member Countries (153)

Industrialized Countries (22)

Australia, Austria, Belgium, Canada, Denmark, Finland, France, Germany, Greece, Iceland, Ireland, Italy, Japan, Luxembourg, Netherlands, Norway, Portugal, Spain, Sweden, Switzerland, United Kingdom, United States

Developing Countries (131)

Africa: Angola, Benin, Botswana, Burkina Faso, Burundi, Cameroon, Cape Verde, Central African Republic, Congo (Democratic Republic of), Congo (Republic of), Côte d'Ivoire, Equatorial Guinea, Ethiopia, Eritrea, The Gambia, Ghana, Guinea, Kenya,

Lesotho, Madagascar, Malawi, Mali, Mauritania, Mauritius, Mozambique, Namibia, Nigeria, Senegal, Sierra Leone, Seychelles, South Africa, Sudan, Swaziland, Tanzania, Togo, Uganda, Zambia, Zimbabwe

Asia/Pacific: Bangladesh, Cambodia, China, Fiji, India, Indonesia, Republic of Korea, Lao People's Democratic Republic, Malaysia, Federated States of Micronesia, Mongolia, Nepal, Pakistan, Palau, Papua New Guinea, Philippines, Samoa, Singapore, Sri Lanka, Thailand, Vanuatu, Vietnam

Middle East/North Africa: Algeria, Bahrain, Arab Republic of Egypt, Israel, Jordan, Kuwait, Lebanon, Libya, Morocco, Oman, Quatar, Saudi Arabia, Tunisia, United Arab Emirates, Republic of Yemen

Europe/Central Asia: Albania, Armenia, Azerbaijan, Belarus, Bosnia and Herzegovina, Bulgaria, Croatia, Cyprus, Czech Republic, Estonia, Georgia, Hungary, Kazakhstan, Kyrgyz Republic, Latvia, Lithuania, Former Yugoslav Republic of Macedonia, Malta, Moldova, Poland, Romania, Russian Federation, Slovak Republic, Slovenia, Turkey, Turkmenistan, Ukraine, Uzbekistan

Latin America/Caribbean: Argentina, the Bahamas, Barbados, Belize, Bolivia, Brazil, Chile, Colombia, Costa Rica, Dominica, Dominican Republic, Ecuador, El Salvador, Grenada, Guatemala, Guyana, Haiti, Honduras, Jamaica, Nicaragua, Paraguay, Panama, Peru, St. Kitts and Nevis, St. Lucia, St. Vincent and the Grenadines, Trinidad and Tobago, Uruguay, Republica Bolivariana de Venezuela

2.   Contacts for the Guarantees Department

Vice President

        Roger Pruneau
        Vice President
        (202) 473-6168
        mail to: Rpruneau@worldbank.org

Louise Davidson
Assistant to the Vice President
(202) 473-5106
Ldavidson@worldbank.org

Chief Underwriter

Christophe S. Bellinger
Chief Underwriter
(202) 473-6163
Cbellinger@worldbank.org

Federica Dal Bono
Business Development Officer
(202) 458-9292
Fdalbono@worldbank.org

Country Development Group

Stine Andresen
Manager
(202) 473-6157
Sandresen@worldbank.org

Finance and Syndications

Peter Jones
Manager
(202) 458-0443
Pjones1@worldbank.org

Infrastructure

Philippe Valahu
Manager
(202) 473-8043
Pvalahu@worldbank.org

Telecom, Oil & Gas, and Mining

>   Patricia Veevers-Carter
>   Manager
>   (202) 473-0600
>   Pveeverscarter@worldbank.org

Agribusiness, Manufacturing, and Services

>   Roland C. J. Pladet
>   Manager
>   (202) 473-2059
>   Rpladet@worldbank.org

Representative Offices

>   Isabella Stoehr
>   Tokyo, Japan
>   813 3597-9100
>   Istoehr@worldbank.org

>   Emily Harwit
>   SARAJEVO, Bosnia
>   387 71 440-293, ext. 3019
>   Eharwit@worldbank.org

>   Carmen Nonay
>   Europe
>   41 31 312-0870
>   Cnonay@worldbank.org

>   Ivan Rossignol
>   HARARE, Zimbabwe
>   263 4 726 246
>   Irossignol@worldbank.org

3.   MIGA Publications

*(All publications can be accessed or ordered via MIGA's website,
www.miga.org)*

- *MIGA ANNUAL REPORT 2000*

- Publication on Developmental Impacts: *MIGA and Foreign Direct Investment: Evaluating Developmental Impacts* (1998) is based on reports made to MIGA's Board of Directors analyzing the developmental impact of a group of 25 MIGA-guaranteed projects. It represents the Agency's first attempt to communicate to the public the developmental impact of MIGA-guaranteed investments. The publication should be particularly useful for readers who want to better understand how private foreign direct investment (FDI) can have positive effects on the development process. It demonstrates how MIGA, through facilitating FDI, has directly contributed to the economic development of its member countries.
  - A *new, expanded report* on the developmental impacts of MIGA-guaranteed projects, covering 52 evaluated projects, will be published in January 2001. Please see MIGA's website for ordering information.
- Cooperative Underwriting Program
- European Union Investment Guarantee Trust Fund for Bosnia and Herzegovina
- Insurance Broker's Guide
- Investment Guarantee Guide
- The IPA*net* Briefing
- *MIGA and the New Africa.* (Also available in French.)
- *MIGA: The First Ten Years*
- *MIGA News.* (A quarterly update on MIGA's activities.)
- MIGA Press Releases
- West Bank and Gaza Investment Guarantee Trust Fund

4. Website

Please also see our award-winning website, *www.miga.org*

Appendix V

Acronyms and Abbreviations

ADB	African Development Bank
AIG	American International Group
BCE	Bermuda Commodities Exchange (also shown as BCOE)
BOOT	Build-Own-Operate-Transfer
BOT	Build-Operate-Transfer
CBOE	Chicago Board Options Exchange
CBOT	Chicago Board of Trade
CEN	Confiscation, Expropriation, Nationalization
CME	Chicago Mercantile Exchange
CMO	Collateralized mortgage obligation
CSFB	Credit Suisse First Boston
CUP	Cooperative Underwriting Program
ECAs	Export Credit Agencies
ECGD	Export Credits Guarantee Department of the United Kingdom
EDC	Export Development Corporation of Canada
EID/MITI	Export, Import & Investment Insurance Department/Ministry of International Trade and Industry
ERG	Geschäftsstella für die Exportrisikogarantie
Ex-Im	U.S. Export-Import Bank
FDI	Foreign direct investment
FHA	Federal Housing Administration

FHLMC	Federal Home Loan Mortgage Corporation
FNMA	Federal National Mortgage Association
GCCI	Guy Carpenter Catastrophe Index
GDP	Gross domestic product
GNMA	Government National Mortgage Association
GOI	Government of Indonesia
IBRD	International Bank for Reconstruction and Development
ICRG	International Country Risk Guide
IDA	International Development Association
IFI	International financial institutions
IMF	International Monetary Fund
IO	Interest only
IPP	Independent power producers
ISDA	International Swaps and Derivatives Association
LAIGC	Latin American Investment Guarantee Company
LIBOR	London Interbank Offer Rate
LIFT	Leveraged Insurance Facility for Trade
MDB	Multilateral development banks
MIGA	Multilateral Investment Guarantee Agency
NBI	Nonbinding indication
NIS	Newly independent states
OCC	Office of the Comptroller of the Currency
OECD	Organization for Economic Co-operation and Development
OECF	Overseas Economic Cooperation Fund
OPIC	U.S. Overseas Private Investment Corporation
PAC bonds	lanned amortization class bonds
PCS	Preferred creditor status
PCS	Property Claims Service
PO	Principal only
PRI	Political Risk Insurance
PRS	Political Risk Service (group)
REMIC	Real estate mortgage investment conduit
SPIV	Special-purpose insurance vehicle
SPV	Special purpose vehicle
SRCC	Strike/Riot/Civil Commotion
TAC bonds	Targeted amortization class bonds
UNCITRAL	U.N. Commission on International Trade Law
USG	U.S. Government
VA	U.S. Department of Veterans Affairs